MORGAN STOCK

Morgan by Morgan

A Member of the Greatest Generation

PARK PLACE PUBLICATIONS
PACIFIC GROVE, CALIFORNIA

Morgan by Morgan
A Member of the Greatest Generation

by Morgan Stock

ISBN 978-1-877809-09-5

Printed in U.S.A.

First U.S. Edition: May 2008

Published by
PARK PLACE PUBLICATIONS
PACIFIC GROVE, CALIFORNIA
www.parkplacepublications.com

ACKNOWLEDGEMENTS

I wish to thank the following people
who helped bring my book to completion:
Kathy Kopp, for selecting, improving and arranging
the pictures, and, of course, proofreading.
Laura Dadiw, for naming and arranging the chapters,
numbering the pages, and more
proofreading to rectify my mistakes.
Mike Snyder, for improving the cover
and making the pictures brighter.
Last, but certainly not least, Jim Nero,
who forcefully told me to name my book
"Morgan by Morgan."
Really last, my wife, June Stock,
for answering questions and encouraging me
to keep writing for the two years
required to complete the book.

DEDICATION

I dedicate this book to my four children:
David, Kevin, Brian and Maggie.

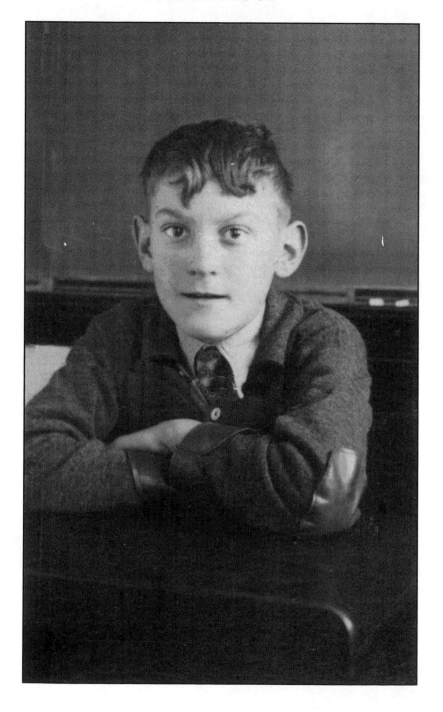

CONTENTS

CHAPTER 1

Newark, Ohio

I WAS BORN IN NEWARK, OHIO, JULY 8, 1919. I'm sure it was a lovely day, for I wouldn't enter into this world on a dark and stormy night. I would just stay inside, as our dog Peggy did, until beautiful weather appeared again. I remember clearly I spoke to Mother by the way of a sturdy kick and she agreed that it was best to come into the world when all is lovely in the garden. Believe me; it has been beautiful ever since, uh, with a few exceptions!

Mother and Father had three children prior to me. Sister Frances was the oldest, and then came brother Clem; I think he was born during a fierce storm, for he was the wild one. Ahead of me by three years was sister Katherine. That's the family: mother and dad and four children.

We lived on a two hundred and fifty acre farm four miles from Newark and three miles from Granville. These towns played a very important part in our lives and are located in the exact center of Ohio about thirty miles east of Columbus. I must tell you when anyone asks where any of the locals come from, they would always reply, "Nerk, UhHiUh" or "Granville, UhHiUh." We never took the time to say New-ark or round the lips to pronounce the O's in Ohio. We had to hurry and get the chores done.

My first recollection was of an incident triggered by brother Clem. He was nine years older than I, so he was twelve or thirteen when I was three or four. He put me on rough Johnny buck sheep. Of course, Johnny tore off with me clinging onto his wool, but when he jumped over the crick (that's the word for creek in Ohio), I was flung off into the water. The crick wasn't deep and I was able to climb out, bawling all the way to the house. Clem at least stood by and would have pulled me out if I couldn't have made it. That's the first of many stories you will hear about Johnny.

Mother's name was Anna Lou Evans; she was born and raised on the Evan's family farm but left the farm when she married Jacob Clemens Stock, and lived in Newark for a time before going to Savannah, Georgia, where father played clarinet in the orchestra at the De Soto Hotel. In fact, brother Jacob Clemons Jr. was born in Savanna. After three years they moved back to Newark.

By this time Mother's bachelor brothers, George and Elias were alone on the farm, and when George died, Elias asked Mother and Dad to come help with the farming. They were happy to oblige, so Uncle Elias was with the family when I was born. I have pleasant memories of Elias. Probably the first thing I remember is sitting at the breakfast table next to Elias; he would help me with my eating by cutting the pancakes into neat squares and tell me they were building blocks and we were building a house in my stomach. I liked that. On Sundays during the summer he would hitch up Dan, a riding horse, to the small buggy and take Katty and me for a ride on the dirt road that ran past our house. In the winter he would take us sleigh riding. He was a typical farmer who loved the animals, the farm fields, and all of our family.

He must have loved us for he put up with a lot from me; I slept with him and I was a bed wetter. Writing about this embarrasses me. It wasn't every night, but probably a couple of times a week. I was eleven or so when I had my last and worst experience with wed bett (I also have trouble with Spoonerisms.) Occasionally, I stayed overnight at Ferris Owens's house, and yep, I did it again! Whooeee, run home Morgan. But Ferris convinced me to stay and I helped build something with the erector set. All was well until noon and I went upstairs to get something; his mother had stripped the bed and the sheets were hanging all over the room. I ran down the stairs, said goodbye to Ferris, and ran home. That was the last time I suffered from lack of control.

Back to age five: Mom decided I should go to school. Why at that age I'll never understand. Everyone started first grade at the age of six. As in all rural areas the schoolhouse was one room from first to eighth grade. Preschool didn't exist in those days, so I started first grade. I hated it; I was afraid of the bullies, the teacher, everything. Sister Katty was in third grade, but she had her friends, and our strict teacher, Lorna Jones, didn't in any way help me get over my fears. And besides, I was getting a bald spot on the back of my head. What a case! One of the happiest days of my childhood was in September 1924 when sister Frances sat me down on our little bitty front porch and asked me if I wanted to quit school. I know in ten seconds I jumped up and gave her a hug and screamed, "Yes, Yes, Yes!" I then ran down the steps, climbed up the maple tree and hugged the limbs and leaves. Hell, I'd have hugged a snake if one had been up there.

That year I occupied my time doing things little farm boys do with the exception of cutting out paper dolls with sister Katty. I didn't enjoy it, but she was three years older and while she was not bossy, I felt it better to try and get along. The rest of the time I watched Dad and Uncle Elias milking the cows and harnessing the horses. I'd sometimes get a chance to ride in the wagon to the cabin field to check on young steers. I did work a little feeding chickens and gathering eggs, mostly easy things I enjoyed doing.

You notice I mentioned the cabin field, which got its name from Squire Baker's cabin. Brother Clem told me a story about the squire, a Welshman. Mother's family came from Wales in the 1840's. She knew a few phrases but did not speak it as well as Elias. The story goes that Uncle Elias went back to the field during a cold winter day to check a rail fence. After seeing that all was well, he noticed there was no smoke coming from the squire's cabin, so he knocked on the door and the squire opened it and invited Uncle in. Elias found the cabin very cold and asked the squire why there was no fire in the fireplace. This dialogue was spoken in Welsh. The squire replied, "The Mrs. will no darn me socks, so I will no build a fire." Uncle Elias, speaking very firmly said, "You build that fire right now or you will no live here any more!" The squire built a fire immediately.

My free year passed happily. I went to an electrologist and he ran little blue and pink colored glass tubes with a round half ball on the end over my bald spot. Eventually the hair grew back in. I was then six years old and had to go to school. I still wasn't happy about it, but there were some other boys from my neighborhood that I knew and they were also going to school for the first time.

A few days after Labor Day, Katty and I joined Mary and John Milner who lived up the road from us on the mile walk to school. Katty and Mary were old hands at school. Katty had skipped a year and was now in the fifth grade. Things went better from the start except for John Milner; he had me buffaloed. He'd tell me to do things and I would do them. Sometimes we would tussle a bit and he would get the better of me. Finally, John told me to do something, and I said no. He grabbed hold of me and something popped in my head; I wrestled him to the ground, got him down good, and shoved his face in the grass and yelled, "Say 'uncle!'" He wouldn't do it. I pushed harder and yelled again "Darn you; say 'uncle!'" And by golly he did. And we soon became good friends. After that, I tell you, my life in school improved immensely.

A word about the general layout of the area; as one stood on the road, the view revealed a large schoolyard at the back of which was the main building. To the left was the coal shed and left of that was the girls' outhouse, farther left down near the creek was the boys'. They were all built of red brick.

The pump with a tin cup on it was placed directly in front of the school on a wooden platform. A few feet behind the pump were three cement steps leading to the front door and into the schoolroom. To the right of the front door was the boys' cloakroom, large enough to hang a lot of sheepskins and lunches in the winter. The girls' cloakroom, same size, was on the left.

A wide aisle ran down the middle with students' desks on each side and a big stove right in the center. A large blackboard that ran across the entire room with the alphabet in upper and lower case along the top was the decoration for the back wall. And, of course, Miss Lorna Jones' desk was in front of the blackboard. I once spent two hours blubbering away under that desk; I don't remember why. Thank goodness the room had many windows on both sides, so we had sufficient light to do our lessons.

Students from grades one through four were seated on the left of the aisle and five through eight were on the right. The school day started at eight and at ten we had a recess. At noon we had the hour to eat lunch and play games, such as May I, Blind Man's Bluff, Drop the handkerchief, and Black Man. That was the game where one person was chosen to stand in the middle of the field and the rest ran from one side to the other. When the black man touched one of us, we were on his team and we helped catch the enemy. All games ended promptly just before one o'clock, and we trudged back into school. Another recess was allowed at two thirty, then back to class, with the school day over at four.

In the winter we had snowball fights (no stone in the center, please). Another game, Fox and Geese, was played in the snow. A figure resembling a huge wagon wheel was drawn in the snow. The safe spots were where the spokes joined the rim and the large center of the wheel. The idea was to catch someone who ran around the rim or down the spokes. Everyone played this game. And, of course, angels were made in the snow. All these activities kept us in good health and mostly skinny; there was maybe one obese girl in the entire school.

The education was adequate. I learned to read, but not with the McGuffey reader. The one we used had a picture on the first page of a huge cloud-like figure with a fat face and big open lips and you could see the wind blowing out of its mouth. I believe it was entitled "The North Wind." I also learned a bit of math. You have two apples and you put three more down how many do you have? I'd probably count on my fingers and get five. Miss Jones had the great idea of asking the seventh and eighth graders to help us when she was busy with other students. During spelling bees we lined up on opposite sides of the room and fought it out.

There were always things happening at school. In the eighth grade Martha Owen was on a ladder doing something above the blackboard; she fell off and banged her head on the floor. She was unconscious for a while, finally came to, and then got sick. I don't recall how they got her home. She was better in a couple of days.

One time, some of the trappers came in with skunk stink on 'em and were sent home. Another time, when all was quiet in the room, Miss Jones admonished Harry Porter about something as she stood in front of the upper grade students. Harry, a fifteen-year-old eighth grader, yelled and threw a book at Miss Jones. I mean it was a pretty big book. I can still see it flying through the room, both sides flapping like a flying crow, until it crashed into the rear wall, missing Miss Jones by inches. Harry tore out of school, banging doors and cursing a blue streak. That was a most startling time. Classes were dismissed quickly! Harry dropped out after that.

There were many other happenings at the good old one room school, but I feel you get the idea of what went on. I must reveal one last incident. It was Christmas and several of the first graders were holding up perfect large letters spelling Merry Christmas. I was lucky enough to be holding one of the R's, but wouldn't you know, I held it upside down. My first attempt at show business and I screwed it up, and I've been guilty of that several times since. After our big final day party in May 1927, Sharon Valley School was closed down, and in the fall I entered the third grade at the Newark Township School. We rode a bus to school.

Naturally, the Township school was larger since it also took in students from Goose pond one room school and others from the area. The first and second grades were on the first floor. Across the hall were the third and fourth grades, and down the hall were fifth and sixth. The mighty seventh and eighth grades were up the stairs on the second floor. We had inside toilets! A large basement with a stage and curtains at one end had many uses: performances; school meetings; box socials (that's when you bid on a ladies box dinner and hope she gave the right hint for her box). Inclement weather found us in the basement playing Dodge Ball, Drop the Handkerchief, and other games.

Another wonderful thing about the Township school was the exercise equipment available, such as swings, giant strides, merry-go-rounds, basketball hoops, and a baseball backstop. During the good weather, they got a lot of use.

Anna Louise Craig (Craigie) was my third grade teacher; she was a lovely young lady. I approved of her right quickly.

Every morning Miss Craig put on a record and a tinny voice instructed us in physical exercises that lasted about ten minutes. The rest of the day, of course, we did math, reading, spelling, writing, and grading each other's papers. Craigie would say, "Change papers now." I would worry about other students finding out how dumb I was, particularly in math. I don't recall any outstanding event during the two years I spent in Miss Craig's room. I did what I was supposed to do in class, and managed to finish my homework with a little help from Katty sometimes. I was enjoying school and had some good friends. All was well.

Fifth and sixth grades with Miss Priest continued much the same way, except by now I was in love with Lucille Hartshorn and wanted to sit close to her; that never worked out, but I saw her every day and sometimes sat close to her as we rode the bus together. However, I was very shy with the girls.

A couple incidents remain in my memory. I developed 27 warts on the back of my hands. Mother, with her home remedies, couldn't get rid of them. Miss Priest noticed them and brought some salve, which I applied regularly, and the warts disappeared in two weeks. My gratitude knew no bounds. Miss Priest the healer. That's a good name for a healer. The other event I remember clearly was a county spelling contest. Our school had a contest and a few of us were chosen to go to Newark to compete for the county prize. I managed to stay afloat through 6 rounds, but the seventh got me: The word was Cincinatti. See what I mean? I still don't know how to spell it, CINCINNATI. Remember that, Morgan! Modesty almost forbids me to mention that I stayed up longer than the other spellers from our school.

On to the seventh and eighth grades, the top floor, the big men and women on campus. Our teacher, Verna Keller, was also the school principal and a distant cousin of ours. I really enjoyed those two years, for I was able to do so many things I loved doing: singing, performing, (I played Scrooge in *A Christmas Carol*), reading plays aloud in class, even some Shakespeare, and Orthography (defined as "Language study concerned with language and spelling." OK, now I know why I enjoyed it.)

Then, too, knowing everyone so well made it comfortable. Still, there were some kids that didn't fit in and were unconsciously shunned. (I hope I didn't do that too much. It still goes on even in adulthood, doesn't it? We need to take the time to find the good in every one.) I didn't have a Philosophy 1 course at this school, so let's get on with the eighth grade.

The time outside class was filled with all kinds of physical activities during recesses and noon hour: baseball, basketball, swinging on the giant strides. In the winter we played marbles in a small hallway leading into the basement or we walked down to Goose Pond and slid around the ice in our shoes, no skates. In the spring we jumped rope; the girls were included in this activity. I could jump with one rope, two ropes, and jump in with them going up or down, yelling as each jumper came in, "In with the doctor, in with the nurse, in with the lady with the alligator purse!" By this age I was a show off: Jumping up and down, I would throw my legs out to the side or any which way. I'm not going to be humble about it; I was a damned good rope jumper.

A few more interesting things happened during grade eight. One was rather unpleasant; I grew a dozen boils on my head. Luckily, I fell down and struck my head on the hard ground and popped a bunch of them open. I came back into the school and showed Miss Keller. She took me up to a first aid room and slapped a bandage on my head, and in a few days all the boils were gone—another healer. I also went through measles, mumps, chicken pox and various other childhood diseases. Does this sound like the bible story of Job? I didn't falter; from seven on, my Sundays were occupied by singing in the boy's choir at the Episcopal Church in Newark until my voice changed.

Grade eight was a very active year for me. I had a fight with George Daniels in the back of our classroom. I have no idea what it was about. He was bent over and swinging at me. I let fly with one from the floor and hit him on the forehead. At that point someone must have stopped the fight. I remember George coming to school the next day with a big knot on his forehead, and my right hand hurt like hell. I apologized and we patched up our sudden display of anger, for he was a good friend. Later in the year I banged Billy Speaks on the head and hurt my hand again; shame on me for losing my temper so quickly.

I was voted in as student body president at the beginning of the year and appointed Salutatorian for graduation, tasked with greeting the folks. Everyone, of course, knew that Lucille Hartshorn would be appointed Valedictorian. For the graduation ceremony, Mother purchased me my first long pants suit.

Until that time all we lads wore knickers and buckled them below the knee, which, according to "The Music Man," leads to trouble in River City. With the knickers came knee length stockings. Mother bought colored stockings for Katty and me. Johnny and Charlie Milner wore black stockings, so I wanted to wear black stockings, too, but mother wouldn't hear of it. One problem with knee socks was the ease in which they slipped down; I'd be running for a touchdown, or rounding third for home, and if one slid down, I'd stop and pull it up. I was a nerdy neat nick. Finally, I kept the socks in place with an inner tube rubber band.

CHAPTER 2

Life On the Farm

AFTER EIGHTH GRADE GRADUATION, there was life on the farm. I mentioned earlier that I didn't do any farm work. Katty and I were house slaves; we cleaned rooms, washed dishes, hauled wood and coal, beat rugs, and hung up the washing. I believe I moved on to outdoor work when I was twelve. My first work was milking cows. Our hired man, Stores Lee, with his two sons George and Earl, lived in a house our family owned about two hundred yards up the road from our home. George was seventeen years old and quite husky; he worked with his father on heavy lifts.

Mother helped Earl get through the eighth grade with me and even got him a long pants suit. I'm very proud of my mother for doing that. He was two years older than I. He and I did the milking in the evenings when we got home from school; in the summer we milked morning and evening by hand, no milking machine. We milked twelve cows, obviously six a piece. The milker sits upon a small three legged stool about eight or ten inches high and holds the bucket between his legs, leans his head against the side of the cow, grabs the teats, and milks away.

Most of our cows were Jerseys or Guernseys. They were smaller than the Shorthorn we had and were easier to milk. Shorthorn was red and white and had very little horns and big hard teats. I'd say she was a 42 or maybe even a 44.

Milkin' wasn't bad. Once a good rhythm was going, it was great accompaniment for singing a country song, "Oh hand me down my walkin' cane; I'm gonna' leave on the midnight train. All my sins are taken away."

Or " She'll be comin' round the mountain when she comes."
I left out some of the lyrics, but you get the idea. There were
always two or three cats hanging around, and we put milk in
a pan for them; I also enjoyed squirting milk straight at them.
They didn't mind; once in a while they'd get lucky and get a
mouthful.

In the summer of 1933, I was bailing hay with my friend,
Ferris Owen, when someone stopped by and said there was a
fire at the Stock house. Ferris and I jumped in his Model T
truck and drove to our place. The barn was on fire. A bucket
brigade was pouring water on it, but it was useless. A water
wagon used by the threshers was down at the crick, but we had
to get a team of horses to get the water to the barn. The barn
burned to the ground.

Luckily, it was in the summer when the horses remained
outside all night and the cows stayed outside until milking
time. The sheep were in a field and didn't come in at night, so
milking was done in the sheep shed. There was a haymow on
the second floor, and we managed all right.

After cleaning all the debris away, Dad and Stores started
laying cement blocks, and Skinny Hartman brought his Case
threshing engine and his saw- mill and placed it as close to our
woods as possible. We cut down trees, trimmed the branches,
chained the team onto the logs and hauled them to the sawmill.
It was harder to do than to write about it.

There were more workers than Dad and Stores Lee. Brother
Clem and Earl and George Lee helped; even Katty and I swept,
carried boards, and mixed cement. It was the height of the
depression and a neighbor, Lloyd Clagget, worked on the barn
for 14 cents an hour. That was probably the time Mother wrote
to FDR and received a $5000.00 loan. She was still paying it
off when she died in 1945. The barn was finished in a year. It
was a beautiful barn with plenty of room for cows and horses.

A total eclipse occurred one day when Dad and I were laying the cement blocks. It happened around 2:00 pm, and the first thing we noticed was the behavior of the animals. Naturally, they thought night was coming, so chickens headed for the henhouse and our dog Laddie, a brown Collie who loved to bring in the cows, went to the upper field to get them. Usually we give the order, "Go get 'em," and he'd be off like a shot. However this time he probably said to himself, "It's getting dark. I'll go get the cows on my own." When they came down the road, I decided to put them in the sheep shed until milking time. The sows went into their sties for a nights sleep. The ducks came up from the crick to march into their pen. That's what happens on the farm with the occurrence of the beautiful Ohio twilight.

In the   meantime, Katty and Mom had brought out some lemonade and cookies and some smoked glass, because the paper had warned us not to look directly at the sun. We sat on the block wall admiring the beautiful work of nature. The sun was completely obliterated, but some light spilled through.

A couple of hours later, the day was as bright as it had been before the eclipse. A rooster crowing was the first indication that animals and feathered friends figured they had a full nights sleep and began to emerge from their beds. I can imagine the chicken's conversation, "Did that night seem short to you?" The reply, "It sure did, I only laid one egg."

Perhaps this is a good time to relate the stories of Johnny Buck Sheep. He was kept in a field across from the house. The problem was that the field was full of wonderful places to play and the crick ran through it. We had dammed it up and had a nice little pool, which was about waist deep. We had an old washtub that we could sit in and paddle around. The incident with Johnny occurred near that hole. I was about six; Katty would have been nine. We were dressed to go visit Aunt Annie, but we had a little time before we had to get in the car, so we hurried off to the crick to watch skippers, dragon flies, and, if we got real lucky, we could see a little water snake.

The problem was we didn't keep an eye on Johnny. When we did see him, he was running straight at us. There were some small willow trees along the crick; consequently we headed for those and Katty, having three years on me, made it first and climbed to safety. I was just starting to get up the tree when he hit me and knocked me into the crick.

He had made his point and just walked off. Katty got down and helped me out, and we walked to the house with me blubbering all the way. The one good thing about this experience is that we didn't have to go visit Aunt Annie. That probably sounds terrible, but we were kids, and she always gave us sloppy kisses and sometimes cookies with ants on them. Bless her heart; she was treating us very nicely. In hindsight I'm grateful for her kindness.

The next troublesome time with Johnny occurred when Clem suggested we hit some golf balls in Johnny's field. Clem climbed over the fence, and said, "Come on, Morgie." I replied, "I'm scared Johnny will get me." Clem said, " Awe, come on. If he comes after you, hit him with this golf club." The club was what we called a mid iron with a wooden shaft. I climbed over the fence and here he came. I swung the club and broke the wooden shaft, then zipped back over the fence to freedom.

The buck didn't bother with Clem; he knew better. You see, Clem, at this time, was a lineman on the Newark football team and whenever he felt a need for extra practice, he donned his helmet, crossed into Johnny's territory, took up the lineman's three point stance, and the two of them spent time banging into each other. One had to see it to believe it.

We did all kinds of activities in the field across the road, for it was a very level, grassy field, good for all sorts of athletic activities. We entered the field with Johnny a bit removed from our territory and would start kicking and throwing the football. Bus Spencer, Frances' boyfriend from Columbus, joined us that day. Naturally, we forgot all about Johnny until Bus kicked the ball and, from out of nowhere, Johnny nailed him on the backside, tumbled him, and then walked proudly away.

We began to understand Johnny's behavior: When first entering the field, he'd pay you no mind and just calmly nibble away. But the next time you looked at him; he would have crept closer. Having forgotten about him, he would end up unexpectedly upon you—smart, sneakin' old buck. We suspect he ate Bus's necktie, too, for it was no longer on the fence where he'd hung it. I know about him eating cloth, for one time Katty and I stood by the fence, as she was wearing an old dress with a loose, torn pocket. As it blew through the fence, without a moment's hesitation, Johnny seized it, pulled it off the dress and ate it.

All the time I knew Johnny, from age five to eleven, folks told me not to show my fear, just walk into his field as a very brave fellow. Even Mother spoke about it, "Don't be afraid of him, Morgan. Just show him that you are the boss." Yeah, Mom, sure!

Finally, the day of reckoning arrived. Mother went to the coal shed for some coal and came out to be confronted by Johnny; somebody must have left the gate to his field open and he ended up in our yard.

By now Mother was screaming and flailing at him with the coal bucket. I heard her screaming and ran from the house to see what was happening. She yelled at me to go get Uncle Elias up in the sheep shed. Uncle heard her, for she had a voice that would split rocks, and was on his way. Somehow she worked her way into the garden and closed the gate so Johnny couldn't harm her. Uncle Elias arrived, grabbed Johnny by his wool and led him away.

When things calmed down, I didn't say what I thought, "Mother, don't be fearful. Just show that bully old buck sheep who's boss." No, no, that would be the wrongest thing to say. Instead I said, "I'll pick up the coal, Mom." She went back in the house to continue her work and I hung around outside for a while. That was the last I ever saw or heard of Johnny Buck Sheep. In all our brushes with Johnny, no one suffered any injuries because of one beautiful feature: He had no horns.

This is a good time to discuss relationships with the rest of the animals and feathered creatures on the farm. Naturally, there were pet dogs and cats; I've already mentioned Laddie. We also had a female Collie named Peggy. She used to accompany us part way to the one room school, but needed to be sent home when we reached the Keenan's house. We had a Persian house cat and a plain old Tabby. Sister Francie named the Persian, Mephistopholes. Sounds as though it's out of "Faustus." We called him Mefisto.

Anyone brought up on a farm that raises pigs, sheep, cows, chickens, ducks, and turkeys knows one will have to raise a runt pig, save deserted lambs, and prevent the baby chicks from smothering themselves if the fire goes out in the brooder house. Pigs and lambs stick to you like adhesive tape until you get them weaned off the bottle.

With calves it's different. Eventually they have to be weaned away from the cow because the milk is needed. I would teach them to drink from a bucket. The procedure goes like this: Take the calf away from the cow, put your finger in its mouth so it'll have something to suck on, and shove its head in the bucket. Sounds simple, doesn't it? The calves are quite strong by now and they do not want their head shoved in the bucket, so they fight and bruise your hand, or upset the milk all over. That's how I learned to cuss real good on the farm.

My wife, who was raised on a farm in Northern Ireland, said she got so mad teaching them to drink from a bucket that she threw the milk on them and said "Damn you! If it ain't in yuh, it's on yuh." She learned to cuss then also. Of course, by the second or third try the calves would come running when shown the bucket.

Pigs are different. Usually the sows would give birth in their sties, but for some reason one of them once came in the barn and birthed a litter of nine. While in the barn throwing down hay or milking I would check on the little ones as they were sucking away. I noticed there was a runt in the group. He'd get a faucet to work on occasionally, but more often a bigger one would toss him away. This went on for a time and I decided it was time to take him to the house and hand feed him. That was accomplished by getting a Nehi bottle, sticking a nipple on it, putting it in his mouth for him to suck away. In no time at all he was doing fine.

At the same time we had a deserted lamb. Dad brought it in hanging limp in his hands. The first thing we did to bring the little guy to life was put him in a box behind the stove, cover him with a blanket, and ladle some whiskey into him. Yeah, I know it was prohibition time, but we had to have some moonshine in the house for the animals, snakebites, and other medicinal purposes.

The lamb was left there while other duties were done. Usually, the next time we came in the house we'd hear a faint bleat, then a wee woolly head would rise shakily above the edge of the box. A short time later the bleat would get louder and the head shake less, and the lamb would climb out of the box and stagger around the kitchen floor, growing stronger by the minute until the tapping of the little feet became regular and healthy. Now it was time to get the Nehi and nipple again. I tell you, there is nothing so thrilling as to see those wee woolly souls come back to life. It's positively a miracle. Katty and I would grab each other and dance around the kitchen laughin' and cryin' for joy.

Now is the time to give more history of the Stock family. Mother, as I have said, was born and raised on the farm and learned all the work the farm ladies did: cooking, gardening, canning vegetables, fruit, jams, jellies, making soap, rendering lard, and on and on. She was encouraged to go to what was called Normal School for two years. Upon completion of school, she taught a couple of years. It was shortly after that she met and married Dad in 1902 or '03.

Mother was a high-class lady. She insisted that we children learn the rules and regulations of etiquette from the proper way to dine, all the social graces plus the proper way to address older folks: Always use the last name, Mr., Mrs., Miss, as in Mr. Owen or Mrs. Milner, never use the first name. When I was young, I was shocked when my friend Johnny Milner called my dad Jake!

Furthermore, Mother insisted that Katty and I take elocution lessons from Mrs. Rogers in Newark. Let me tell you that none of the other farm children in our neighborhood were given that opportunity. We learned and recited poems; Katty even delivered hers accompanied by a piano. Mother insisted we all go to college, and when the time came, helped Frances and Clem to do so. Katty and I had to wait a few more years to get our help. I am deeply grateful for the knowledge, help, and care Mother gave to all of us.

Dad was born in Germany in 1874. The family immigrated to Shawnee, Ohio in 1882 where his father and uncles went to work in the coal mines. This was natural, for the men in the Stock family had been miners and musicians for generations. It was not an unusual combination. In Germany, managers encouraged the miners to form a band. So, continuing that tradition, one was formed in Shawnee.

Dad finished the third grade in Germany and that was the end of his academic education. At nine he worked in the mine as a door opener. Later he became a full-fledged miner and an even better clarinet player. Sometime in his early twenties, he went to Columbus and joined the army. He was assigned to the military band, and in a very short time was in the Spanish American War and sent to the Philippines.

When the army went into battle, the musicians became medics and stretcher-bearers to help the wounded. After the war in the Philippines, his outfit returned to the states and was assigned to Fort Niobrara near an Indian reservation in Nebraska. During a visit a few years ago, it was said that the soldiers were stationed at the fort to prevent the Indians from stealing cattle from the ranchers nearby. The Indians probably said, "The soldiers are there to keep the ranchers from raiding our reservation." This fort is near the small town of Valentine.

With the stories he told us, you can imagine what a hero my dad was in my eyes. The stories never began with, "I did this" or "I did that." Dad would tell about helping the wounded, the earthquakes and typhoons in the Philippines, the terrible storm at sea the troops experienced coming home. He would say what a great feeling it was to get back to the states safe and sound. I could tell from his stories that Dad loved the army, but he was especially happy with the excellent musical education he received during his six-year enlistment.

After he left the army, his first job was in the orchestra of the "Al G. Field's Minstrel Show," which was one of the great ones that toured all over the US.

A slight digression here: I was in a play once with the old character actor Charles Coburn, and I remembered that he was from Georgia. The

Field's show also originated in Georgia, so I asked Charles about it, and he said he had seen it in his youth and loved it.

From the minstrels on through the rest of his life, Dad played and taught music. Living on the farm did not stop him. Probably the highlight of his musical career was playing in Washington D.C. for the inauguration of three US Presidents: Garfield, McKinley, and Taft. Naturally, those presidents were from Ohio. Indeed, Dad was first chair all the way!

Now we move on to sister Francie. She was fifteen years older than I, and she told me often that she practically raised me the first six years of my life; I don't doubt it. Mother was so busy that she was probably very happy to let Francie look after Clem, Katty, and Morg. Francie must have been home one weekend from Ohio State in Columbus the time she asked me if I wanted to drop out of first grade.

Francie had a beautiful soprano voice. Quite often she and Dad performed for organizations throughout the area. When she lived in Columbus, Francie played in a number of light operas.

After graduating from Ohio State, she married Bus Spencer and resided in Columbus for two or three years. I remember Katty and I visiting them once in a great while. I particularly remember the time Bus took us to see the WAIU building; I believe it was the tallest structure in Columbus then. We went to the top and walked out on the observation platform and Bus put me on his shoulders so I could get a good look at the streets below. Jumpin' Jasus that scared the hell out of me!

Francie and Bus divorced in about three years, and Francie went to New York to study with Estelle Liebling, a great vocal teacher. While in New York she met John Clarence Rockefeller who had been a child actor and now was an excellent pianist and comic songwriter. He was a very distant relative of "The" John D Rockefeller. Early in his career he changed his name to Jack Rock. Francie and Jack formed a vaudeville team and played around the New York area until the Stock Market crash in '29. With no work available in New York, they went to Canada and found plenty of jobs there.

Now, I've already told some stories about Clem; I will add a few more and let that be it. Music was the most important part of his life. Father, of course, taught him to play the clarinet and saxophone, and from the time he entered high school he performed in marching bands, orchestras, and jazz bands. Now, the last one leads to a story.

In our front room we had a large Victrola with hundreds of 78 records from Madame Schuman Heink to jazz, and a Yale fight song. I remember the lyrics to one that Katty and I played, "Ice cream, you scream, we all scream for ice cream. Rah, Rah, Rah. You want some chocolate? I'll take vanooola," something like that.

One time Clem was playing along with one of the jazz records and Dad came in and banged him along side the head and said, "You stop playing that nidden nadden (Dad's term for syncopated music) and practice your reading skills from the Lazuras clarinet book." Which Clem surely did, for he became an excellent musician on the clarinet and saxophone.

I was nine years old when Clem and I were driving to the YMCA in Newark. I noticed him falling asleep so I immediately yelled and tapped him on the arm. He certainly woke up and banged me on my chest right hard with the back of his hand. Clem was eighteen, weighed 180 Lbs, at 5-11, so I learned my lesson at waking him. From then on I would cough, sing, whistle—do anything but yell, "Wake up!" and touch him. What I don't understand is why Mother or Dad never said anything about it. Probably because when he was awake, he was the most energetic man alive, and it was difficult to remember that he would fall asleep the minute he stopped. Years later I heard a term that seemed to describe his condition: Narcolepsy.

I could fill a book describing the exhilarating life of brother Clem, but perhaps relating stories that come up as I progress through the years of my life would be a better way to do it. One last story before I move on to sister Katty. Clem had finished one year at Denison University in Granville when he received a call from Francie in Montreal telling him that there were good opportunities for musicians in Canada. That was the first goodbye I said to my wonderful brother; he was my hero. I remember that goodbye: We were standing in the dining room and Clem was hugging me, and I tried to beat back the tears. He told me he loved me and he would write to me. Then dad came in and said, "Let's go, Clem" and they walked out, got in the car, and drove to Newark where Clem took the Greyhound bus to Montreal.

Now, about Katty: I knew her better than Clem and Francie, which is only natural since we were closer in age. I was about four or five when Katty and I would crawl into a bed and she would read to me; girl books of course: The Bobbsy Twins, Alice in Wonderland and others. I didn't care what she read, just as long as she read something. I know that helped me learn to read, for I was anxious to start reading boy books. A few years later I was reading: Tom Swift and His Electric Run About, Tom Swift and His Electric Rifle, The Rover Boys, and, eventually, pulp fiction westerns. Thank the Lord for Katty's reading to me.

It wasn't all rosy between us when we were growing up. We played Old Maid and she would always beat me and I'd get mad and throw the cards. She seemed to get to stay overnight with friends often, and I'd say to Mother, "Why is Katty staying over night so often and I hardly ever get to?" Mother replied "Why, you just stayed with Ferris Owen last week; stop complaining." Yeah, OK Mom. I probably sulked for a while, but not for long.

Katty would say, "Let's go back to the cabin field and cut some red clay." I'd join right in and we'd get the clay, bring it back to the house and cut it in blocks and build houses. Or Katty would do a sculpture with it. She was a talented artist. She might suggest that we go to the woods and swing on the vines like Tarzan. We had a beautiful maple tree in the front yard and she taught me how to climb it.

It was fun to be with Katty. She had a wonderful sense of humor. She played the piano a bit and taught Mary Milner, our neighbor, for fifty cents a lesson. I never heard Mary play, but I sure heard her pedal the player piano. Oh, we had such wonderful evenings singing with the Milner kids.

Katty went to Granville High School, for our farm was in Newark Township and Granville Township, so we could go to either school. She walked two miles and rode the school bus for another mile to get to school, this being tough to do in the winter. I knew it well since I did the same thing. Katty graduated from high school the same year I finished the eighth grade. We had a good summer together before she left for Los Angeles by Greyhound bus.

Francie was now living in Los Angeles, and she heard there was a junior college in Compton, California. In fact, it was one of the first junior colleges in the state. With money very scarce on the farm, that seemed the perfect solution for continuing Katty's education.

That's sufficient information about the sisters and brother. Obviously, they will be returning often in this memoir. Now is the time for Morgan to get on with his story.

In my room there was a closet that contained all sorts of paraphernalia and clothes Uncle Elias used and wore: ties with permanent knots, old watches, stickpins, and two muzzle loader shotguns. One afternoon I came home from school and was getting into my work clothes, and I noticed the muzzle loaders in the closet. I decided to find out how heavy they were and lifted one out—pretty heavy. I raised it to my shoulder, pointed out the window, cocked it, and pulled the trigger. Then I tried the other one. It seemed a bit heavier, so I didn't point it out the window; I laid it on the bed cocked it and pulled the trigger. There was quite a bang, and the double bed burst into small flames.

Holy God, what happened here? I started beating at the flames with my overalls and called for Mom. She came running up the stairs, saw the problem, got a bucket of water in the bathroom, poured it on the bed and extinguished the flames. I was scared as hell; thank God Mom was home. I told her I would never touch those guns again. It seems someone left an ignition cap in the gun. I can say once again thank the Lord there was no powder in the gun or we would have really had a fire.

I was probably in the seventh grade when Mother got a phone call from Clem in Montreal saying he was ready to come home. It was late spring, so Mother persuaded the principal to give Katty and me a few days off to ride along on the journey to Montreal. The weather was beautiful, the car ran well, Sister and I sang, read, and probably came up with the age old comment, "Are we there yet?" We slept at motor courts until the third day when the car broke down. We made it to a small town, Varysburg, New York. Dad found a mechanic shop and heard that the repair work couldn't be finished until the next day, which meant we would have to stay overnight.

Our parents found a small hotel, and, once we were ensconced, Katty and I walked from one end of the town to the other. Later, at the hotel, we were talking to a nice elderly lady and she informed us that Varysburg was known as the "Flower Basket" of that part of New York. That was a good way to describe it, for there were hills on either side and the town was in the valley. Flowers were everywhere up the hillsides, along the main street, in the yards. It was absolutely a Flower Basket.

The next day Dad retrieved the car and we were on our way again. We arrived in Montreal that evening and finally located Clem's rooming house. Wouldn't you know he had left for Ohio a couple of days before?

Oh dear, why didn't we have cell phones in the thirties. I never did hear what caused the mix-up. I do know that Mom and Dad yelled at each other as we drove out of Montreal; Katty and I sat very quietly in the back seat.

We arrived home in three days, and I was back in school when Miss Keller received a phone call asking her to tell Morgan that Clem was home. He had hitchhiked back to Ohio. Once again peace descended on the Stock household.

In the summer of '33, members of the Welsh Hills Grange decided to produce a play. I had a very good part, playing the character Willie Worgel, a stuttering fourteen year old that helps solve the mystery. A couple of years ago June and I were back in our Ohio neighborhood, and we visited Mary Milner now married to Frank Anderson. As we walked into the house Frank said, "Hey, Morgan, I remember seeing you when you acted in the play, The Spooky Tavern." I had completely forgotten the title of the play, so I was grateful to Frank for giving me that information. The play was so popular at the Grange Hall that it was moved to the Granville Opera House, a much larger and better theatre. We only played a couple of nights there, but it was a boost to the ego.

One time a company from out of town was putting on a play at the Opera House, and someone was needed to do one line. George Lee happened to be walking outside the theatre and they begged him to come in and do the line. He didn't want to, but finally agreed. The line was, "The Queen is dead, I heard the pistol shot." George said it over a few times and they pushed him on stage. He said, "The Queen is dead, I heard the shistle pot, shostle pit, postle shit. Arrr, horseshit, cow shit, didn't want to be in your damn play anyway" and stormed off stage – probably apocryphal.

During this period in the summer, baseball was in full swing. Newark had a twilight league composed of players from the Heisey Glassworks, the Pharis Tire and Rubber Company, the Worley Stove factory, the Pure Oils, plus four or five more teams whose names escape me. The games started at 5:00 and drew good crowds to White's field. Of course, there were always favorite players; one was Scoop Bowie. Newark had one real, genuine nationally known hero, Woody English, who played for the Chicago Cubs for a number of years.

Pierce Packham, a neighbor, would pick me up in his Model T and we would head for White's field and enjoy the game. Summertime in the Midwest is baseball madness. Pierce played with the YMCA team. I probably would have gone out for some team, but I didn't have the time until Curtis Berry, Chief of Police in Newark, decided that we needed a team in Sharon Valley. He chose our location since he was related to the Joneses, our neighbors over the hill. The Daniels gave the use of a field, and someone hooked up a team of horses to scrape a level playing field. Another volunteer built a backstop, and we were in business.

The Chief bought us uniforms and christened us The Sharon Valley Juniors. That's what it said on the front of the uniform. Getting the pants to make one look like a real ball player took a bit of doing. I cut an inner tube into bands, pulled them up to my knees, put on my socks, put on my pants then dropped them down again and put the bands over the pants where they fit on the legs as far down as I thought looked more like a ball player. I was ready to take my place in right field.

I wasn't a bad right fielder, if I do say so. If the ball came somewhere near me, I would catch it or pick it up and throw it to the proper base. My problem was hitting. I could hit, but never a home run. I'd bang 'em through the infield or occasionally over second or third. I seldom struck out, which pleased me. Once we were playing on a diamond in the Welsh Hills, and folks sat in their cars and watched us; I caught a fly and they honked their horns. That made baseball even more fun. Actually, we were a pretty good team and won more than we lost, so it was a successful season.

We didn't want Chief Barry to foot the entire bill for our team, so we put on square dances at the Grange Hall. Johnny Milner became a very good caller and put us through our grand right and left and do-si-do.

Furthermore, we got to dance with all the pretty girls. I will close this section by saying a **Big "Thank You" to Chief Barry.**

Now a freshman at Granville High School, I had lots of fun experiencing the same two-mile walk and one-mile bus ride that Katty did. In the fall and spring it was a lovely walk. The winter, however, was something else. My costume for winter consisted of corduroy pants, a shirt, a pea jacket, a wool cap, and, when it snowed, four buckle artics. These were soft cloth rubber boots that reached to the calf of one's leg. To be fashionable, the two bottom buckles were fastened and the tops of the artics turned down so they reached just above the ankle.

Entering high school I was a little frog in a big pond. Not that there was a large student body, probably no more than 200. However I was alone at Granville High. All my friends at Newark Township went to schools in Newark. We all took the same classes: English, Algebra, History, Study Hall, Latin.— Vini vidi, vici or runny runora fally bumptus. That's the Latin

I remember.

One class I really enjoyed was band; it was directed by a gentleman, Harvey Williams, who had four jobs at the school —vice principal, math teacher, football coach, and band leader. He was Dad's good friend, so he called Katty and me, Jake. Playing clarinet in the band, along with Dad teaching me, improved my playing considerably.

I had a bad time with algebra, but thank goodness Mr. Williams helped me. I would be at the blackboard trying to solve a problem, and he would say, "$2x+3x$ equals, well, put it down, Morgan." Then I would put down the answer; in that way we would get through the problem. I can just imagine what the sharp mathematicians in class were thinking. With his generous help, and the fact that he wouldn't dare flunk his friend's son, I got a C in the class.

One night in January 1934 I went to a Marx Brother's movie, "Duck Soup", at the Granville Opera House. I left the theatre about nine and started home; driving down Granville road, I decided it was too early to go home, so chose to go on to Newark and see Clem who was playing in a café on Fourth Street. About halfway, I looked to my left and saw this terrific red glow in the sky. Holy Moly! Is that another barn burning somewhere, or a gas well? I drove on to Newark, went into the café, and told Clem what I had seen. He suggested that I call home; perhaps Mom and Dad would know something. I called and got no answer, so I then called the police and asked them if they knew anything about the fire. They didn't. At that point I told Clem I was going to drive on home, and I left.

I got out of Newark onto the Granville road and then turned off onto the Sharon Valley road. It seemed there was quite a bit of traffic for that time of night. When I arrived at our old one room school, which at that time was occupied by the Slaughterbecks, I couldn't drive any farther. Cars were parked all along our dirt road. I got out and started walking. Obviously, I knew then that the fire was on our road. I ran into the father of our neighbor, Jimmie Crombie, and said, "I don't wish you any bad luck, but I hope it's Jimmie's house and not ours." I think he mumbled something like, "I hope it isn't either one," which was a kinder thing to say.

There is a little rise in the road that prevents one from seeing our house or the Crombie's, but once that was cleared the view is unhindered. I was breathing heavy, perhaps even praying when we topped the rise and I saw that it was our house.

The sight was unbelievable; I still see it as though it happened yesterday. The flames had died down a bit, and I saw the studding and the roof timbers. As I watched, the studding, the roof timbers, and the whole top floor plunged into the basement with a great shower of sparks and flash of flames.

Oh, My God, where are Mom and Dad? Blinking back tears, I ran as fast as I could and entered our barnyard, which was full of neighbors, even strangers. I yelled at Roy Milner, "Where are Mom and Dad? Did they get out?" Roy replied, "They got out, they're OK. Your dad is up by the barn." I rushed to the barn and saw him talking to the neighbors. I ran to him and hugged him as hard as I could, and let the tears flow. Dad said, "Aw, Morgie, Morgie. Everything's gone, nothing left, nothing at all." I then asked him where Mother was and he told me she had gone to stay with Kitty Evans, a cousin just a couple of miles away.

I asked Dad how the fire started; he said he didn't know. As they came down the narrow stairs the walls were about to burst into flames; if they had delayed even a few minutes, they would never have made it. Neighbors said the fire was out of control by the time they arrived. Furthermore, no one from the fire department had time to do anything; they wouldn't have been able to get there anyway with all the cars parked on our road.

From that day I have never followed fire trucks to see a fire.

Finally the fire was nearly out, just glowing embers. People were leaving, assuring Dad that they would be available to help in any way they could. Since there was nothing anyone could do, Dad left for Aunt Kitty's and I went to stay with the Milners.

Perhaps this is a good time to describe the house and the surroundings. The front of the house faced the Milner road. A picket fence ran parallel to the road with a gate in the middle. A path of step stones led up a slight incline to four wooden steps leading up to the small front porch. I know it was small, for I remember Mom sitting in a rocking chair sewing or snapping green beans. That pretty much filled the porch, but we could all sit on the steps and enjoy each other's company. Three beautiful maple trees provided shade, which kept us cool on the porch during the summer.

Another step up led to the door that entered into the large living room, running from one side of the house to the other, probably about 35 ft by 20. There was a fireplace at each end, although the one on the left was never used. That area was originally the parlor with black horsehair settee and chair. A door from that area led into the downstairs bedroom. The right side of the living room was used winter and summer, particularly during the cold winter days. A fire kept the area nice and warm, and a comfortable couch and chairs, along with a table, surrounded the fireplace.

A door at about the center of the living room lead directly into the dining room containing a large table, an old church pew on one side, and an ironing space. There were two doors to the outside from the dining room. One led down some steps to the spring house, which was our refrigerator. The other on the opposite wall led to the side porch. From the porch one could enter the downstairs bedroom. Another door led to the pantry, where Mother stored all her canned goods, and to the cellar stairs.

The last door led to the large kitchen. There were two big cabinets reaching from floor to ceiling, a large stove, and a round table to seat six. There was an exit form the kitchen to the back porch, which contained a washing machine, and the separator, for separating the cream from the milk.

Let's get back to the morning after the house burned. After a fitful night's sleep at the Milner's, I walked down to where the house used to be. All that was left was the stone wall that formed the cellar. Dad was there and we stood looking down at the ashes. He informed me that our dog, Peggy, was burned in the fire. She slept in the cellar in the winter. What could be said at a time like this? I think I said again, "Thank the Lord you and Mom got out." Dad muttered, "Yeah, that's right. Well, let's go do the milkin."

I spent three weeks at the Milners. It was great fun. They had four kids: Mary, two years older than I, John, my age, Charley, a couple of years younger, and Grace, the youngest of the group. I really enjoyed it because I was sort of in love with Mary. I didn't have a chance, though, for she had a boyfriend. Interesting thing, at a firm request from their parents, all the Milner kids quit school at sixteen. I suppose when one considers that they had a large Grimes Golden apple orchard, about twenty milk cows (they did have a milking machine), and raised other farm grains, plus a big stand in the farmers market in Newark, the parents decided they needed the help at home.

My three weeks' stay with the Milners was fine; I hardly missed a day at school. I did, however, miss helping Dad with the milking. I could have gone down in the late afternoon and helped; I'm ashamed of myself for not doing that.

While I was living the good life with the Milners, Mom

and Dad were busy moving our renters out of the other house, the Red Cross was coming through with beds and blankets, and the Elks Club, in which Dad was a member, along with friends and neighbors, gave us enough necessary items so we could move in and continue our lives in a different house.

Believe me, it was different—no running water. There was a spring about twenty yards from the kitchen, so we walked out with a couple of buckets and brought water in to start the day. We had an outhouse, or privy. We sure missed our lovely bathroom in the house that burned down. Why did I complain? The Milners, the Packhams—most of the neighbors —had no bathrooms in the house. They got along fine; by God, we will, too, and we did. The Sears and Roebuck catalogue made excellent toilet paper.

The two hundred yard walk to the barn was a bit different on cold winter days. We had to get out our felt boots and sheepskins, but it was so wonderful to walk into the barn all warm and cozy. The horses and the cows in there really warmed the joint up.

The rest of my freshman year was uneventful. I got to know my classmates better and felt comfortable going to school every day. A couple of the girls even asked me to take them to a party. That was perfectly acceptable; if one of the fellows didn't ask them, they just stepped right up and asked someone to take them. I was happy to do so; maybe they weren't the ones I would have asked, but it would be very impolite to turn them down; besides I got a chance to go to parties. I also learned some social graces. I was fourteen and it was perfectly legal to drive the car then, so I would go to their front door and rap politely. Usually they were ready and I escorted them to the car, opened the door for them, and off we went to the party. I also got to practice my dancing (thanks to sister Katty). After the party I drove them home, escorted them to the front door, and bid good night. No kiss with those girls. I was too shy anyway.

During that summer I was a typical farm hand. I plowed a field full of rocks using a single furrow plow with our team of Fritz and Princes; Fritz was pigeon toed on his hind feet but it didn't slow him down a bit. They were Belgium horses and a wonderful team. I also plowed up weeds in the cornfields. I loved that, sitting on the plow and placing my feet on curved foot pedals to guide two sets of three small plows on each side of a cornrow. Back then corn was planted about three feet apart. Now it's planted very close together.

On Sunday I would usually go swimming in the creek down by the Heil's, beyond the little school. A bunch of us young neighbor fellers dammed up the creek, so we had a pretty good pool about four feet deep. Of course, it was a skinny in place. We played games like floating on the water and yelling, "Hey guys, look, pickle on a dish and two olives." The older guys were bank strollers, you know, showing off what they had. We younger ones stripped down and were in the pool fast. We also played follow the leader, doing different kinds of dives from the bank. There was no diving board.

One particular dive I remember very well. Willie Milner demonstrated a sailor's dive by putting his hands behind his back and diving in headfirst. The rest of us followed. I put my hands behind my back and dove straight down. Suddenly I heard a click, and I realized I couldn't feel a thing, nor could I move a muscle from my head down. I started to float to the surface and got to where the water was at my mouth and I yelled help. Willie thought I was kidding and shoved me under. Great Scot! After what seemed an excruciating long time, I floated to the surface again and screamed, "Help me!" This time, thank God, Frankie Noolon put his arms under me and laid me on the bank.

I remember it as though it was yesterday; a hand appeared

on the ground near my face. I thought it was Frankie's, but as I continued to look it became familiar and I knew it was my hand, but I couldn't move it. I don't remember what I thought. Perhaps I wondered how I would get home. The guys were all standing around me probably wondering the same thing. After about a half an hour, I felt a tingling in my hands and arms and I could move them slightly; in an hour or so I was able to walk home. Unbelievable!!

The only ill affect I suffered was not being able to stand anything touching my back from my waist to my head, so it meant I had to go to Doc Kennedy for electrolysis treatment with his pretty little tools. One good thing about the whole escapade was that I didn't have to shock wheat, so I sat in the beautiful shady front yard and read The Virginian by Owen Wooster.

I may have felt too poorly to shock the wheat, but when it came to threshing time around the community, I was back to my job of pitching wheat sheaves on to the wagon. Father would get a call from a neighbor who would say, "Jake, we are threshing (always pronounced like an A in cat in Ahia) Thursday. Would you please send two men and a team?" Of course, he would, for in a week or so we would need the same thing from the neighbor.

We had two gentlemen in our neighborhood that owned threshing machines, John Jones, who was also a Newark cop the rest of the year, and Skinny Hartman who had run the sawmill to cut the wood for the new barn. Both of them had large Case steam engines that pulled the separators from farm to farm. The farmer then told the operator where he wanted the straw stack, often in or near the wheat field, and then John or Skinny hooked the engine to the separator with a long belt, and we were ready to start threshing.

We usually sent three men on the job. Earl Lee and I pitched the sheaves up on to the wagon, and George stacked them. He had to load them carefully so they didn't slide off on the way to the separator, especially if there was hilly land to drive over. Pitching was hard work particularly when the load was nearly finished. One had to stretch up the whole length of the fork so George could grab the sheaf and place it where needed.

George then drove the team near the separator where the sheaves were thrown on to a sort of treadmill that swallowed them and spit straw out a long pipe and the beautiful wheat down a shorter pipe at the side of the separator where it was captured in a burlap bag on the ground. When we threshed, our cousin Charles Evens, who suffered from polio as a child and had difficulty walking, always handled the wheat as it poured into the bag. His upper torso was tremendous; Charles could lift those eighty or more pounds from the ground on to a wagon all day long. Wherever he threshed, that was his job. Threshing usually took a day or a day and a half, and about a week later, Dad would hire a truck and take the wheat to the mill in Newark.

The thresher's dinner was something to behold. At noon everything stopped; the horses were fed and watered, the men all gathered at our spring, pumped water into wash basins, washed, combed their hair, and entered the dining room. Other peopled have described these dinners better than I. Suffice it to say that there were three or four different types of meat, all the vegetables and fruit that grow on a farm, four or five different kinds of dessert, coffee, juices, spring water, and, maybe the best of all, the neighbor ladies who helped prepare and serve the meal. Furthermore, practically all the food was consumed. There wasn't even enough left for us to have a good supper.

I do have to tell about coming home from a threshing day. Coming slowly out of the field we'd be tired as hell, as were the horses. Now the horses thought they were going to pick up another load, so they would plod along. Then we would turn onto the paved road and they would start to perk up a bit. Finally, we would hit the dirt road that leads to our house, and the horses understood: Hey, we're heading home!! Sometimes the horses would break into a trot. George, Earl, and I would be jumpin' up and down on the wagon singin' "She'll be comin' round the mountain when she comes." Vigor was restored; oh man, oh man, that was life! (We have to keep finding those wonderful moments, don't we?)

I must explain the processing of wheat from the beginning. The seed was placed in a drill with several channels reaching four or five inches in the ground along with fertilizer. The wheat was planted in the fall, in the spring it came up in little green shoots. By the summer it turns golden. Our hilly farm provided a beautiful sight when the wind came up, for the wheat swayed and bowed resembling waves.

In August it was time to get the binder out of the shed, oil it, and check all parts to be sure everything was working properly. The next day the team would be brought to the shed, hitched to the binder, and taken to the wheat field. Once at the field the large bull wheel that runs all the mechanical parts would be lowered to the ground, and the binder would cut the wheat and pass it along until a sheave was formed and automatically tied with twine. This would continue on until there were four or five sheaves on a carrier. Then Dad would trip the carrier and the sheaves fell off. We stood them up, and took two and folded em' over at the grain end, and placed em' over the standing sheaves to keep the rain off, and the shock was complete. (I feel kind of sorry for wheat farmers today who have those air-cooled combines. They don't get to do that lovely hard work with the binder and the shocking on a miserably hot, sweaty day.)

We shall now return to my sophomore year at Granville High. It was much easier as I knew most everyone. I continued the same classes: US history, Geometry, (Thank you, Harvey) English, and Latin. I really enjoyed attending Latin class, for we had a beautiful practice teacher from Denison University, which is located in Granville. Occasionally, she wore a sort of metal belt that had a part in front that hung down and pointed toward, well, you know. It was quite appealing, not to mention a bit arousing. She must have worn that belt around the college, because one day walking home, I passed a diddle park on our road and there she was in a car with a nice looking college lad. It was broad daylight, probably just a philosophical discussion. Oh, sure, certainly! I should have said to her the next day, "Vine, Vide, Vici."

One night I was alone in the house studying assignments for the next day. We had no electricity in our second house, so we used coal oil, or kerosene, lamps. The light was fine while next to you, but the room was dark away from the lamp. Here I was at the dining room table deep in brain work, when I heard someone knocking on the window to my right. I looked over and saw the most frightening face I had ever seen: A hair-hanging-down dirty face.

I looked over in a corner of the room where my shotgun stood. Oh, Jesus, what do I do? Go for my shotgun? I looked at the window again and he was gesturing for me to come out. I decided to go to the back door, open it just a bit, keep my hand on it, and if he made any false move slam the door in his face and lock it. My heart was pounding as I opened the door and yelled, "What do you want?" He growled, "Let me in, let me in, I'm John Innes, Morgan." I nearly fell flat on my face with relief. John Innes attended Granville High with me. The Hi-Y inducted him into their club, and he was dropped on this country road for his initiation. I brought him in and he washed his face and made himself look presentable. When Mom and Dad came home, I drove him to his home in

Granville. Wheeooo, man, that was frightening!

Fall is the time for football, so I went out for it. There was no "B" team, no junior varsity, and just one team. That year I weighed 130 lbs; Pete Boggs played tackle at 180. I'm sure I wouldn't have made the team if it weren't for Harvey Williams, the coach. I tried half back, end, finally tackle. I got to ride along to different schools and watch my friends play. We played Pataskla the last game of the season. There were three substitutes on the bench, one of our players was injured, and I thought I might get in the game; but no, coach put in John Innes. That was the end of my football career at Granville.

I had some other successes, though. I still played in the band, and I got in a one-act play directed by our English teacher, Miss Sullivan. I can't remember the name of the play however I remember one line from it: "Cowards die many times; a brave man dies once." Or close to that. (Sounds like Shakespeare, doesn't it?)

Every year the school had a Spring Festival. There were several categories: singing, reciting poetry, speeches, original short stories, all memorized. I decided I would sing On the Road to Mandalay. However along with that song, we all had to sing Flow Gently Sweet Afton. The whole student body was in the audience, and Morg was very nervous. The accompanist played the introduction, and I started singing, "Flow gently sweet Afton among thy green braes. Flow gently—la la la la." The words left me. I left the stage.

Later that year, I was the end man in a Minstrel show. We put burnt cork on our face and were ready to go. "Mr. Interloceter, Why does a chicken cross the road? Well, I don't know, Mr. Bones. Why does a chicken cross the road? Why, to get to the other side!" Hee, hee, ha, ha. I also had a song in it and didn't forget a word. Dad loved the show.

About half way through the semester John Stewart, a senior

and a good piano player, formed a jazz band. He asked me to play sax and clarinet. I was happy to do so. At the same time a freshman boy wanted to learn to play the sax, so I taught him during noon hour. I think I received 75 cents a lesson. For once, I beat Katty.

Our first gig was for a school dance in the gym. We weren't very good. I don't think we were much better at our next job. It was a student's private party. They all seemed happy with us; however the next week one of the students who had been to the party told me that some of them went to another room and danced to the radio. We practiced a lot more and got a job playing for a service club in Newark. We must have done all right, for they paid us $2.00 each. Our last gig was playing for Alexandria High School's senior prom. John added another clarinet and a trumpet. I knew we needed one more good man for this one, so I talked Clem into coming with us. We sounded great.

At Granville High, sophomore boys and girls were invited to be waiters for the junior-senior prom. That was really quite an honor. The boys were supposed to dance with the junior and senior girls, who were sitting forlornly, waiting for an invitation to dance. I don't think I danced with anyone; I was so preoccupied watching stodgy Miss Sullivan, my English teacher, dancing her legs off with the superintendent's son. Thus ended my sophomore year at Granville High.

The summer of '34 was fun. Katty returned from California on the Greyhound bus. Clem had left home again and was playing with a group in Detroit. Unbelievably, Clem sent us a hundred dollars a month for three months. Mother had gone to California in late spring, so Katty, Dad and I ran the joint. Katty did the cooking, and Dad and I (along with a couple of men who rented houses that Mother and Dad owned in Newark) worked the farm. We cut corn stocks with corn cutters, or big machetes, stacked it, tied it with twine, and made corn shocks. We then had fresh corn on the cob to eat.

We were living in the other house and still had the pig and the lamb, so we moved them in to a shed just off the back porch. They would spend the day playing with each other, mostly running around the house. The lamb's feet could be heard clicking as it ran across the back porch, and in a very short time the pig would follow along. The porch had a large flat door on it, which, when raised, revealed steps leading to the basement. One day the lamb ran across the porch, and I, ignorant they were on their game, opened the door to the cellar. At the same time the little pig ran across the porch and plunged straight down ten feet into the cellar. Oh, my God, I thought, I'd find poor little pig out cold, so I hurried down the stairs, and there was Porky happily chewing on a potato. I brought him and the potato back up and closed the cellar door.

Eventually Porky and lamb were weaned enough to join their proper groups. I kind of missed them; they were fun to have around. A few days later, though, while slopping the hogs, I saw Porky was having trouble walking. Something was wrong with his hind legs. (Incidentally, he was a she.) The other pigs probably attacked her; they do that sometimes. She lived in the barn from then on and followed us all over the farm with her slow walk. When she got tired, she sat down and rested like a human.

CHAPTER 3

Adventure, School and Work

ABOUT THE MIDDLE OF AUGUST 1934, I started on a great adventure. Dad, Katty, and I began our drive to California in a 1931 Model A sedan. Dad and I were going to bring Mother back home in time for me to start my junior year.

We packed our bags and set forth. The first night we stayed in a motel in Indiana. The motels all looked similar. It consisted of a row of rooms adjoining a garage with no door on it. The roof of the rooms served as the roof of the garages and so on down the line. Not very beautiful, but the rooms were clean —on good old Route 66.

I can't recall very much about the trip, except it was uneventful. We must have driven all night once, for I remember going through Oklahoma on a washboard dirt road. I discovered that it is better to drive faster on that kind of road to hit just the top parts of the washboard. Large jackrabbits would lead us right along this road. One would get going in front of the car and eventually peel off, but right away another one would jump right in.

From Oklahoma we hit the northern section of Texas and on into New Mexico. For some reason I remember the town of Raton. Why I remember that town I don't know. I recall that we had to go up a mountain to get there, and I realize now that it was the first time I had ever seen a hill that high. It is close to the Colorado border. What we were doing that far north when we were heading for Los Angeles I'm not sure.

A bit of a detour from the road trip is rather interesting. We move to the present. The date is May first, '05. We are celebrating son David's and wife Kathy's 33rd wedding anniversary at the Fandango Restaurant in Pacific Grove, and I am talking about remembering the town of Raton. There was a pause in the conversation and a gentleman at the table behind us said, "My mother-in-law lives in Raton and she is here with us." I saw this elderly lady at the table and asked, "Am I right in saying the town is on a mountain?" She replied, " Yes, it is at six thousand feet." I then said, "I know a girl from Raton named Mary Alice Harnish." She exclaimed, "Oh, yes, the Harnishes, I know of them." We were on our way out, so I thanked her and we left. Is that another "small world" incident?

On the road again (there's a song in there somewhere). We traveled on through New Mexico, Arizona and into California. Finally we arrived in Pasadena and I saw palm trees, the first I had ever seen other than in the movies. I surely must have seen some before we hit Pasadena, but for some reason that's the town I associate with seeing palm trees. We drove on and finally arrived at sister Fancies' house, which was located on a small alleyway just off Silverlake Blvd. It was a grand, interesting trip.

It was the first time I had seen Francie and her husband, Jack Rock, in three or four years. His real name was Rockefeller, and he was a distant cousin of the wealthy side of the family, but it was too long a name for a vaudeville man. Anyway, it was wonderful to see them all, and Mother looked fine, probably rested up from all the cooking she had to do on the farm that summer.

The second night Francie and Jack took us to Santa Monica, and I had my first view of the Pacific Ocean. It was beautiful but also a bit overwhelming, with those waves rolling in and crashing on the shore. Of course, I soon got used to it and always enjoyed trips to the seashore. Two years later Katty and I lived in Santa Monica for a few months.

After showing us many interesting spots in LA, time came for Mother, Dad, and I to head back to Ohio. One afternoon, Francie and I were in the tiny back yard where a fig tree was handing us ripe figs. I had never tasted figs before so I was having a ball eating them when Francie said, "How would you like to stay here with us and go to school in LA?" I gave her a very surprised look and said, "What did you say? Stay here and not go back to the farm? Well, yeah, uh, no, I can't do that, I should go back and help Dad and Mom." She replied, "I've already spoken to them about it, and they think it's a good idea." I exclaimed, "They do? Holy Moly! I'd love to stay here. No more milkin', and I'm right here near Hollywood and can become a movie star." I gave her a big hug. Francie came through again; I felt as though I didn't have to go to first grade anymore.

Mother and Dad left for Ohio, and a couple of days later we got a telegram that they were hit by a train in Nebraska. No one was hurt, but the car was totaled, so they took a bus on home. I never heard much about that wreck; I don't recall either one of them mentioning it again. It was evidently something they didn't want to talk about.

The first thing we had to do was find out what school I should attend; we found out John Marshall would be my school. We also discovered that I would be riding in a city bus, so we had to go to a station that gave passes to students. I was about to enter a new school of about 2000 students where I knew no one. I floundered around and ended up enrolled in French, California History, English, Orchestra, Drama, and Chemistry. I remember learning the initials for about 90 elements. It was a good experience; the ride to school and home in a bus was better than walking the four miles back home.

Ah, yes, Fall. FOOTBALL. The school had three different teams: varsity, junior varsity, and the B team. I somehow understood that the B team was my proper niche. I had to go to a sport store and buy my football shoes. At least Granville's were free. I lasted about a week and the coach said, "Farewell, Morgan." I think I shared a locker with another B man, and he complained that I had left the locker unlocked and someone stole his shoes. He demanded that I reimburse him. I said, "Hell, take my shoes, and stick 'em where the moon don't shine; I'm leaving anyway." That was definitely the end of my football career.

There was one very bad thing about John Marshall; the school didn't have an auditorium. Where am I going to do any acting? Even little old Granville had an auditorium. We did have a regular classroom for our acting and put on scenes for each other. I remember doing a scene with Peggy Moran who had to spit in my face. I didn't mind all that much since she was quite lovely. A couple of years later she signed a contract with Warner Brothers and performed in a number of "B" movies. I did get a chance to act before an audience; we took a one-act play to Thomas Star King Jr. High and had a good crowd who enjoyed it.

I met some very nice classmates at John Marshall, but I didn't date any of the girls. I didn't have any money or a car, and besides I was too shy. Milton Delug was the piano player in the orchestra and a few years later I happened to be watching the late show (I'm not sure if it was Johnny Carson or the one before him) when who should be leading the orchestra but Milton.

I did get a chance to do some acting later on. My brother-in-law, Jack Rock, had written a detective story called, "The Green Joker," which was aired on a local radio station before I came to Los Angeles. It was off the air for a time when someone decided to make half hour transcriptions of it and Jack wrote in the part of a cub reporter for me. Sisters Francie and Katty (Oops, sorry, she is now Kay) were in the cast as well, including some acting students from LA City College whom Kay brought in. She had transferred from Compton to LA, as it was much closer. The transcriptions were not a success.

Radio acting was different from anything I had done and it was a great experience working with the professionals. I also tried other avenues to get in some acting. I read in the paper that a theatre was having auditions, so I rushed on down and read for them. A very pretty lady came out exclaiming how well I had done, and they wanted me for a part. Then came the blow; I had to pay them to be in the play. Many of the amateur theatres did that. I did however get to sing a solo for some kind of celebration for the John Marshall Library. I remember some of the lyrics: "I dreamed I was a pirate, a pirate brave and bold. I dreamed I sailed the seven seas in search of yellow gold." Thus ended my junior year at John Marshall.

I knew I had to get a job for the summer and Frances came through again. She knew the manager of the Paramount Theatre, which was on the corner of 6th and Hill in downtown LA. The first day of summer vacation I went to the theatre (probably spelled theater), and landed a job. The next day the tailor fitted me with my usher's uniform, and I went to work. It was not hard physical work, but it was certainly a long day, a three way split shift: ten to twelve, one to four, five to eight. There was also a later shift that ran until ten at night, or whenever the last show ended. When we had large crowds, we didn't stick to any kind of schedule. I made seventeen dollars a week, and Francie charged me twenty dollars a month rent. I was happy to pay it. One of the head ushers made twenty-five dollars a week and rented a two-bedroom house and raised his family. When one considers bread was five cents a loaf, a two pants suit was twenty-eight dollars from one of the better stores, you can understand how we coped on our salaries.

Senior year at John Marshall was much the same as junior year: History, English, Orchestra, and Voice. I went the fall semester, then found out I had enough credits to just go mornings for the spring semester, which I did. This gave me time to work as an usher again. At this time Mother and Dad rented the farm and moved to Los Angeles, and Clem (from now on his name is Jake) left his job in Detroit and brought some musicians from Ohio and got a job at Santa Catalina Island. The whole family ended up in Los Angeles or close by.

Mother and Dad got a job managing a seedy rooming house on Figueroa. She went to night school and studied apartment house managing. Kay was enrolled in Santa Barbara State College majoring in education. Francie and Jack did their vaudeville show two or three times a year at a large theatre on Main Street that had seen better days; I was pleased that I got to see them. Francie sang light opera songs like "The Italian Street Song." Jack did his comic songs. They were very good, but their act was going out of style. Jack had another job working as an arranger with Raymond Paige, the orchestra director for Hollywood Hotel, a national radio show with Dick Powell and Francis Langford and Hollywood guest stars. I listened to it every week.

When I caught the bus at noon at the school, I had the same driver practically every day, and much of the time we were the only folks on the bus. I must say he was a talker and mainly spoke about his conquests with the ladies. Whether he thought he was teaching me something, I don't know. I got tired of it and tried to change the subject, but he would always get it back to the ladies. I usually left the bus at Silverlake and Sunset and caught the Big Red Car to the Fifth and Hill station. Sometimes

I would get off the bus earlier to get away from his bragging.

In those days, the public transportation in LA was wonderful. One could travel to Monrovia, Balboa, San Fernando Valley, or Long Beach on the Big Red Car. There were streetcars for the downtown area, and a double-decker bus with the top deck open to the elements on the Sunset street area, and of course, reasonably priced.

I continued with school in the morning and ushering afternoons and evenings. One big improvement, though, was the purchase of a car. With the help of Kay's boy friend, Kenny Mastain, we checked some used car lots. I found one car I liked very much, a '32 Model B ford coupe, but Kenny said, "I don't think you should have that, it's too hot a car for you." I shrugged and we went on looking. We came upon a '31 model A Ford coupe, the last year of the Model A's. The price was right, $100.00, so I bought it. There was just a slight problem: It was all white with a large 81 printed on the back. We found out that a Globe A flour salesman had used the car. Anyway, we had a perfect name for the car: "81" or more often, "Old 81," or "Damned Ole 81" when it was on the blink. Actually, it was one hell of a car. Francie and Jack used it during the war because of gas rationing. They couldn't afford to drive their De Soto.

Now, to the ushering experience: The job was very interesting; not only did we see the first viewing of Paramount Pictures, we saw live stage shows as well. And some of those shows were terrific. Fanchon and Marco ran the theatre. In their youth they had been quite a dance team, so it was only right that there should be a chorus of twenty girl dancers called the Fanchonettes: Sound familiar? The ushers had a dressing room under the stage; the dancers had a dressing room in the basement also. We would exchange hellos with them.

A few of the stars who appeared on the stage were Mae West,

Eddie Cantor, Rudy Valle, Ted Lewis, Me and My Shadow, Eddie Peabody (a great banjo player), Olsen and Johnson (a wonderful vaudeville show), Pinky Tomlin who wrote "The Object of My Affections," and many others. There were also a number of name bands: The Dorsey Brothers, Harry James, Duke Ellington, Phil Harris, and more. Frank Sinatra sang with one of the bands. I must find out which one. When the famous bands were not there, a house band was there led by Rube Wolf, an excellent musician and comedian.

A singer named Kenny, I can't remember his last name, auditioned for a job with the house band was signed, and became a terrific hit. A year or so after he left, he became a singer with Guy Lombardo. Then a couple of years later I read that he wed Guy's daughter. The lesson here is: Do the auditions, go for that job interview, go to your boss and apply for the better job. In other words don't say, "Oh, I probably won't get the job. Those other people are better qualified than I." Do not put yourself down! One never knows how things will go until he or she tries. All of you remember that!

Ushering is easy: Stand at the head of the aisle with a flashlight in hand, lead the patron to an empty seat and return to the head of the aisle for the next one. The job would get tougher when there was a hit show. There was a partition behind the last row of seats and a standing room area. If there are no empty seats and the standing area is filled, a standing area in the lobby is roped off. Some folks would want to go to the balcony; if the balcony were full, people would wait in the balcony lobby. There would be four thousand patrons seated and perhaps two hundred waiting. Ushers would seat people from the inside waiting group, allowing a few people from the lobby group to move inside, and more patrons would come into the theatre, joining the lobby group. The situation continued until the end of the movie. Those were the times the ushers would stay on the floor much longer.

My fellow ushers were a great group of young men. We aisle ushers had our own dressing room. Three men we called captains had their own dressing room. They stood under a spotlight in the center of the theatre and directed patrons to the different aisles. The assistant manager, Ken Bushey, (that last name has a familiar ring to it) loved sports, so we formed a softball team. There were four other large theatres: Warner Bros., RKO, Lowes, the MGM Theatre, and the Orpheum, within a few blocks of the Paramount. These were our opponents on the diamond, so we played our games on Saturday or Sunday mornings before the theatres opened. I was again in right field. We won a few and lost a few, but we all played and it was great fun. Auction bridge was a favorite card game when we were off duty. If we didn't care to play bridge, we walked down the hall to another room and engaged in a fierce match game of ping-pong.

Come winter and basketball season was upon us, we continued our matches with our theater brethren. We had a couple of good players; all I did was guard and throw the ball to the sharpshooters. One time I did sink a basket and maybe won the game. Whatever, I was very happy and looked forward to getting a ride back to the theatre in a new Airfloat Chrysler, a brand new body structure. The car looked so different, sweeping up in the front and down in the back.

One of the ushers, Don Nelson, had borrowed a car from his uncle. I wanted to get a ride in it, so I asked him if I could come along, and he said, "Sorry, Morg, I have a load." I replied, "That's OK, I'll get a ride with Bushey," which I did.

The next day the LA Times had a headline which read something like this, "Four ushers from the Paramount Theatre were killed on the Pacific Coast Highway." I was stunned and rushed to the theatre with the feeling that I must be with friends to talk about this. I couldn't face it alone. One of the group was a close friend; I had been in his home, met his parents —Wheeoo, rough! I went to our locker room and talked to those who were there. We wondered why they were on that highway out beyond Malibu. Perhaps it was to check out the car's speed. I felt better talking about them and reminding each other of funny things that happened when we were all happily together.

Time to go to work; interestingly, several of the patrons told us how sorry they were about our loss. Among them was Bob Hope. I was working in the balcony and he came up to me, shook my hand and commiserated with me.

Four funerals in three days is a bit much, but I must say the fellows looked as though they were in a deep, peaceful sleep from which they would never waken. (However, that is not true, for they are awake in our memories as long as we live.)

I would like to relate a few more ushering job experiences. When one watches and hears a movie over and over again for a week or two, the lines are memorized with no effort at all. Consequently, we would recite the dialogue to each other, and sometimes ham it up atrociously, or play it straight. Hell, we obviously were as good as the pros and sometimes better. At least that's what we thought.

I saw a lot of movie stars come into the theatre: Gary Cooper, Bing Crosby, David Niven, Marlene Dietrich and many others, but Mae West was the one that I remember best. The head usher would get a call that Mae was coming to the theatre. We knew that she came to the exit doors on Hill street, so we would stand by one of the doors until we heard a rattle, then open it and lead her down the side aisle and get her seated. I enjoyed seeing her beautiful Rolls Royce. It was one of those where the driver sits outside and passengers sit inside. I can't leave Mae without giving a line from her act when she was on the Paramount stage. She is relaxing on a chaise lounge and a servant runs in and says, "Miss West, there are ten gentlemen downstairs waiting to see you." In that "Come up and see me sometime" voice, Mae replies, "I'm a little tired tonight; one of those boys will have to leave."

I was in love with one of the cashiers in the box office; her name was Inez Garrison. How come I remember that when I forget more important things? Anyway, we ushers had passes to go to the large theatres I have mentioned, so I went down to Warner Brothers and went up to the balcony to sit in the loge section. Who comes in but Inez and sits next to me. I say hi; she says hi, and I spent the next two hours shaking like a leaf in a high windstorm. I'm sure she didn't know I was going to be there. The picture ended and we went our separate ways. Some guys are kinda' stupid, aren't they?

One last usher story: Ken Bushey decided we should all go on a night horseback ride, including the lovely cashiers. We drove to a stable in San Fernando Valley and picked our horses. There was one horse that the stable man said had been a racehorse, so it would be good if a more experienced rider would ride him. No one stepped forward, so I said I would ride him. We mounted up and rode down a paved road for a bit then turned and rode in the dry Los Angeles riverbed, which was nice and sandy. The stable man was right about my horse; he wanted to race all the time so I would let him go for a while then I would rein him in, which wasn't easy. Everybody was having a good time with lively banter going on, and horses walking, or once in a while trotting, until we headed back to the barn.

It was as if one horse yelled, "We're going home gang" and they took on new life. Some of then even galloped. I was reminded of our old farm horses. If a horse passed the one I was riding, mine would break into a wild gallop and pass it. In the middle of one of these races we reached the paved highway and my horse slipped and fell on my left leg. Suddenly life went into slow motion. I felt my mind saying, "Morg, get your foot out of that stirrup, or you'll be dragged on the road." The horse got up and started for the barn, and I struggled and worked to free my foot. Finally, after what seemed an eternity, the horse and I parted company. I was dragged just a few feet and was able to limp back to the barn. I went home, took a hot bath, but the foot kept a hurtin'. I had to lay off working for about a week until I could walk better.

In June of 1937 I graduated from John Marshall. We had the ceremony in the Greek Theatre in Los Angeles. I don't remember much about it. I listened to the speeches, and got my diploma, but mainly I was just happy to be through high school. Francie and Jack took me to a cafeteria for my celebration dinner. I suppose we should have gone to a more fancy restaurant, like The Brown Derby. However I liked the cafeteria as I'd been there several times before, and for me the dinner represented the completion of four years on the road of life.

About this time Kay and I were living in a two room apartment in Santa Monica. This was just before she left for Santa Barbara. I believe she was working in Sears and Roebuck. I moved in with Kay for I loved the beach and this was a good chance to swim and get a tan. Mother and Dad were running a pleasant rooming house on Santa Monica beach not far from Marion Davies' home.

Jake, Katty, Francie and Morgan, 1920.

Mother and Father.

Morgan in front of the family home before the fire.

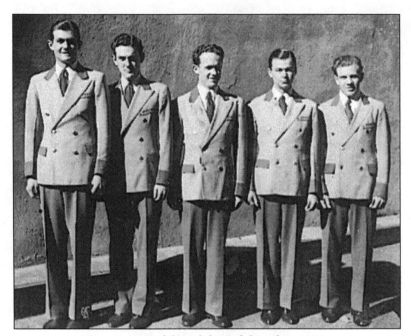

*Morgan, second from left, and friends ushering
at the Paramount Theater.*

Young man Morgan.

Brother Jake

Sister Katty

Sister Frances

CHAPTER 4

The Pasadena Playhouse

WHILE I LIVED IN SANTA MONICA, I worked the late shift. This gave me a lot of beach time. It was quite a drive to the Paramount, but I felt it was worth it. Kay went on to Santa Barbara in the fall, and I moved back to Francie and Jack's new place on Vendome Place just off Sunset Blvd. This had more room than the old Randall home. It was two stories, three bedrooms, and two baths – very comfortable.

In remembering where the members of the family were located, I recall Jake was still in Santa Catalina. I visited him once there. It was my first boat ride. I walked around the Island during the day and listened to his band at night. I had to sneak around and stand off-stage because I was 18 at the time, and they were very strict. Later Jake and the piano player had a fight, and the piano man left for Detroit. Jake got in touch with the agent and he sent a replacement that turned out to be a young woman named Grace Nelson, a wonderful pianist. Jake and Grace hit it off and stayed together the rest of their lives. Kay was finishing her education in Santa Barbara. Mother and Dad were in Santa Monica, and I was with Francie and Jack.

I ushered until September 1938 when my life took a wonderful turn. I wanted to go to an acting school, and I read about one called the Pasadena Playhouse. All the family encouraged me to march to my drummer, so I drove to the Playhouse and had an interview. The dean of students told me to show up for registration with $600.00. I had saved $200.00, and Jack had just sold a song to the Yacht Club Boys and loaned me $400,00. I was all set and showed up at registration with my money.

The next problem was finding a place to live. The Kral dormitory was a place for young men like me. They charged $40.00 a month for a room and three meals a day. Of course, I didn't have the money, so sister Kay sent me the funds from her teaching job in Bakersfield. See what I mean by family support? I'm eternally grateful to my wonderful family.

The opening day we juniors gathered in a room just off the patio and heard a welcoming speech by Gilmore Brown, the founder of the Playhouse. Then we broke up and went to our classes. I recall that half the class had rehearsals in the morning and classes in the afternoon. The other half did the opposite. I was a morning class student.

The subjects were voice and diction, costuming, theatre history, makeup, eurhythmics (the teacher beat out a rhythm on a hand held drum while we students did exercises and dance steps), and fencing, for which we trained with foils. The latter two were held at four o'clock on the 6th floor roof of the playhouse. Someone had hung up a basketball hoop, so at leisure time we could get some exercise that way. There was also another smaller section where we played badminton. One of the best parts of the roof area was a neat little coffee shop where one could buy food and drink.

The directors for the main stage productions rehearsed us in the afternoon. We did scenes from the Greeks, Romans, Shakespeare, the Restoration, early Melodramas, and more modern plays on the main stage in front of scenery for the Playhouse production that was on at the time.

I wish to return to the present now and write about Sunday, June 5, '05 before it leaves my memory. A month ago I received a letter informing me that the Playhouse Alumni Association chose me Man of the Year. The award was to be presented at the annual luncheon of the alumni. June and I flew down on

Saturday. Sunday morning I dressed in my gray sport coat, blue pants, black shoes, striped shirt, and a blue cravat. I had modeled these for June before we left Monterey. All went well until I tried to tie my shoes; you know how sometimes one lace is longer than the other. I kept trying to find the right one to loosen and then tighten to make them even. Finally, I asked June to do it. By now it's getting late and I'm so nerval and excital I feel as though I have opening night jitters We grabbed a taxi and made it to the Brookside Country Club in plenty of time.

A very nice lady greeted us and took our picture, and I started to relax. We found table four, and sat down beside an old classmate, Bill Irwin, the only one I knew in all 200 people. (At the luncheon two years before I knew two, Bill Irwin and Jack Beardsley.)

The luncheon began with an address by Ross Eastty, president of the Alumni Association, followed with a talk by Sheldon Epps, artistic director of the Playhouse. There were a few more talks about the work the staff and volunteers were doing. The Mistress of Ceremonies was Sally Struthers. Remember her from "All in the Family?" Steve Vinovich was the Master of Ceremonies and he introduced me as "Man of the Year." As I stepped onto the speaker's platform, Sally met me with a very nice kiss on the mouth. I said that was almost the best part of the award.

I thanked them then digressed and recited, "For a month to dwell in a dungeon cell" from "The Pirates of Penzance" by Gilbert and Sullivan. I did this because a man named Ray Lynch had written to "Stage Whispers" (sometimes called stage whimpers), a semi-monthly news sheet written by the alumni, asking if anyone had a copy of The Busy Speakers Pocket Practice Book, which was written by our voice and diction teachers, Belle Kennedy and Patsy Chalgren. I purchased one at the Samuel French drama catalogue store in Hollywood and took it with me to the luncheon to give to Ray if he didn't have one. It turned out he did have one, so I suggested they auction it off and left it with one of the volunteers.

I used the Gilbert and Sullivan piece, since it is a practice selection in the book. I thanked them again and said I had many good things happen to me in life, and the two years I was a student at the Playhouse was right up there with the best of them. I then walked off the platform and forgot my lovely glass award. Sally yelled at me and I returned and the man handed it to me. I walked on back to my seat, pointing my finger at my head.

I now return to 1938. In one of the early class meetings each one was asked to give our name and a wee bit of information about ourselves. When I was called I said, "My name is Morgan Stock, and I was a director at the Paramount Theatre in LA." I paused a moment to let this statement sink in, then continued, "Oh, yes, I directed people down one aisle and then over to the next one." I got a pretty good laugh with it. The most fun for me, though, was to see the expressions on their faces during the pause; some with utter disbelief, others with a look of, "My God this guy must be very talented to be so young a director."

The junior year went very swiftly probably because we were kept so busy. It took me a long time to read plays for the drama lit class. Then we wrote a short synopsis of several of them on a single page. In order to do that I had to shrink my hand writing and it affected my grade. Finally, a good friend in Krahl's dorm, John Alvin, said he would type them for me. The typewritten pages improved things considerably.

Frayne Williams, a heavy set Welshman, was our teacher. He peered through his monocle at the role sheet, and then looked at the student, and would draw out the ends of our names as he spoke the role. One I remember in particular was

Chandlaaa McCluraaa. Chandler taught me a lesson one day. He broke wind in class rather loudly then looked accusingly at me. Oh, sure, every one thought I was the culprit. Remember that one gang!

For costuming I made a Roman toga. I put a bunch of designs on the bottom of it. Fairfax Proudfit Walkup was our teacher. She wrote a very good costume book we used for our text, which was popular in colleges and other theatres. Besides the class work, we were always busy learning lines.

Every two weeks the junior and senior class students gathered in the balcony of the main theatre to watch the current productions. We saw Dana Andrews, Victor Mature, Steve Reeves, Laird Cregar, and Gig Young (original name, Byran Barr). I saw Robert Preston (original name, Preston Meserve) around the Playhouse, but I never saw him act on the stage there because the members of the Screen Actors Guild and the Actor's Equity, the union for stage actors, were forbidden to work with amateurs. I'm sure he didn't mind that too much, for he had just signed a lucrative contract with Paramount Pictures.

At that time the Playhouse was staging a Gilbert and Sullivan musical and one of the leads got sick, so someone had to take his part with about twenty-four hours to learn the lines, including songs. Gilmore Brown said, "The only one I know around her who can do this is Pres Meserve." And do it he did! Never missed a cue, lines, or music. He was perfect. I'll bet he went out with the cast and celebrated after that performance.

Jack Joly was quite a character himself. He and Laird Cregar were working off their tuition at nights during their junior year. Jack, however, got mixed up with one of the girls in his class and they tried all sorts of things to keep her from getting pregnant. Thank heavens the effort worked, but somehow word reached the dean that he was playing around with this young lady. He was kicked out of school for the remainder of the year, but would be allowed to start over as a junior again in '38. That's the beginning of our friendship that lasted for sixty-six years.

The junior class had a tradition of producing a musical at the end of the year. Luckily, we had a very talented group of musicians and writers who developed a clever show called "Backdoor to Heaven." Mary Alice Harnish and Tom Gregory wrote the music and lyrics for most of the songs, several students' songs and lyrics as well. There was a four-piece orchestra, and a few characters in the cast: God (the perfect voice of Bill Griffin), Satan and his wife, Hitler and Mussolini (a pair of lovers), the Ladies from Hades, and Gabriel played by Morgan Stock. I remember only a few words from my song, "I Play a Shiny Trumpet." The show was a real hit. Thus endeth my junior year.

Years later I heard someone had made a silent film of our performance, and five years ago the fellow who played God made a VCR from it, and gave each one of us a copy. There I am a skinny 19 year old, overacting my heart out.

I had to find a job for the summer so I could pay the $400.00 tuition for my senior year. Phyllis Benbow was in our class, and her folks owned the Benbow Inn in Northern California, near Garberville. I asked her if I could get a job there. She replied. "I don't think so; we are full up. However there is a bus boy job at Knapps Coffee Cup Restaurant in Garberville." The next week I packed my clothes, hopped on a Greyhound bus and arrived in Garberville and reported for duty.

There was a small two-bedroom shack back of the restaurant, and another bus boy and I were assigned the rooms. I don't remember any living room or kitchen in the place, but there was one bathroom with a shower. We were on a three-split shift: 7 a.m. - 10 a.m., 11 a.m. - 2 p.m., 5 p.m. - 9 p.m. Sounds like the ushering job. Of course, if we had a big crowd, we worked till they cleared out, at no extra pay.

Phyllis also got Leola Berger, another playhouse student, a job working at Richardson's Grove, a beautiful resort among the redwoods on the Eel River. Our three hours in the afternoon were spent at the Eel or any place we could get to without a car. Sometimes we would get a ride with Phyllis and go to Scotia or anywhere else of interest. Later, Leola's boyfriend, Leslie Stuart, came up in his new convertible and we bummed rides from him.

Many of the young people working at the restaurant or at other jobs in Garberville were college students: A third busboy was president of the sophomore class at UC Berkeley; a pretty young waitress; a student at Humboldt state college; a sturdy young man working on a road repair gang was the quarter back at UC Davis. They were all working to save money for the next school year.

Richardson's Grove created entertainment around a campfire two or three nights a week and I sang at a couple of them. It was fun and gave me a little more experience before an audience. Speaking of an audience, Phyllis had been most interested in creating a summer theatre near the Benbow Inn. She had written a play that would work outside in a natural setting. I couldn't be in it because of my work, but I did go see it with a few other folks. It was a short play, sort of half improvisation, not bad, not good. It did, however, make her decide to bring more actors the following summer and continue with her idea.

The Rotary Club held their weekly meeting at the restaurant. That meant hard work on that day. There was a large room off the main dining area, and we had to set it up with the dishes and silverware and other things to make it look attractive. Except for the young waitress, the others were forty or older, and I was surprised at the rough language some of them used. In fact, that was the first time I ever heard a woman use the "F" word. I thought the chorus girls used some pretty strong phrases, but nothing compared to the waitresses. You understand this was during the setting up and tearing down for the lunch, so there was no one around to hear them but we who were working. As I look back on it, it probably gave them a chance to let off some steam.

I finished work at Knapps about the first week in September and moved to the Benbow Hotel for the next few days. Leola was there and Phyllis thought it would be fun to ride horses back through the country where two old brothers lived. Phyllis had a young male friend who was a good horseman ride with us.

We set out one morning fairly early, since the brothers lived about six or seven miles from the Inn. The ride was fine, the weather and scenery beautiful. We arrived at one of the brother's house at noon, and Phyllis brought out the sandwiches and soft drinks she had packed. We met the old man, a tough looking one. What was remarkable was the piano he had in the one large room of the house. He told us they brought the piano in by horse and wagon, since the only way one can reach the house is by horse or walking. I never heard such an out of tune piano. Phyllis had informed us that the brothers moved into the house together, but there had been a falling out and the other brother built a house a couple of miles away and they never saw or spoke to each other. That wasn't good, was it? We all have our differences, but we should talk them out and move on.

We rode back to the Inn, and when I got off the horse, I wasn't sure my legs would hold me up, but I girded my loins and made it inside, up three flights of stairs, and flopped down on the bed for a much needed rest. We were on the third floor with no paying guests nearby, so later on that evening we were running up and down the halls and one of the others knocked one of those large fire extinguishers over and it started spraying. Everybody just stood there looking startled. Finally, I grabbed the thing and rushed into the bathroom and let it empty itself in the tub. I felt pretty heroic and expected some kind of a decoration, but no. Somebody did say, "Good work, Morg." Sure, I'll take that.

I nearly forgot; one exciting thing happened while I was at Knapps. Joan Fontaine and Brian Ahearn spent their honeymoon at the Benbow. I was a little disappointed that I didn't get invited for cocktails. Years later, I met Joan during a film festival in Monterey and told her about being in Garberville when she was on her honeymoon. She replied, "I wish it had been you instead of Brian there with me." I thought damn, one more missed chance.

A couple of days after our horseback ride, Francie and Jack wanted to get a look at Garberville and the Benbow Inn, so they drove up from LA. I showed them around the interesting spots, and then we drove home. I preferred that to the Greyhound. A few days later I was back in Pasadena ready for my senior year.

I plunked down my $400.00 and was eager to begin my last year at the Playhouse. Now came the time to find a place to live. A fellow classmate, Lee Lemon, who hailed from Columbus, Ohio, and I decided since we had something in common, coming from the same state, we would try living together. We found a room over a dry cleaning establishment that was large enough for two single beds, with a bathroom down the hall. The rent was $20 a month, which was fine.

It had a little two burner electric stove and a small fridge so we were in business. There was a lady down the hall from us, and, after a month or so, she complained and the landlord warned us to keep the noise down. We tried, but young guys are naturally noisy; throw in that the young guys were studying

acting and going over lines and occasionally singing loudly—
we were warned again. Lee had a dartboard and some darts,
so we hung it on the closet door and spent free time flinging
darts. Naturally we missed the board sometimes and stuck the
darts in the closet door. One day while we were at school, the
landlord looked in our room, saw the holes in the closet door,
waited for us to come home, and kicked us out. We moved
the next day and found a temporary place to stay with Arlee
Steere's mother until we could find a permanent room.

Lee Lemon, Jack Joly, and I were in the same play at the
time. Jack wanted to find another place to live, so the three of
us decided to rent a place together. Jack and I found a second
floor room in a house on Herkimer Street just a few blocks
from the Playhouse. It was a large room with a double and
single bed. Again, the bathroom was down the hall, and we
shared the kitchen with two older women. The kitchen was
fully appointed, but we did have to time our meals with the
ladies. We flipped coins to see who got the single bed. Jack
and I lost so we had to sleep in the double bed. I hadn't slept
in bed with anyone since brother Jacob, but at least Jack didn't
have the frantic nightmares and slam his fist into me. We were
finally all set for the remainder of the year.

The seniors did their productions in the small lab theatre,
which was upstairs from the patio leading into the main theatre.
The senior stage was at one end of the room and the laboratory
stage was at the other. The seating capacity for this theatre was
about seventy, and the audience sat on folding chairs.

We performed in full-length plays with costumes and good
lighting on a small stage about twenty feet wide and fifteen
feet deep. Instead of furniture, we used different sized boxes
made of wood. One could stack them up to look like a chair,
table, or bed. When needed, a cloth covered the boxes to make
them look more realistic; it worked quite well. Of course, the

audience really had to suspend their disbelief.

The plays ran for five performances, evenings at 8:30 and a Saturday matinee at 2:30. My first play was, " The Lowells Talk Only to God." With a cast of twenty-nine. Wheeoo! That's a large cast; however it was necessary to give all the actors a chance to do some acting. Six other students were the production staff; they would act in the next play.

I kept a few programs from this era, and here is a list of some of the plays we did that year: "Ulysses Sailed By," "Finder's Luck," "The Frod1," 'Lady Windermere's Fan," "Snow in August,' and "Vanish The Years." I never heard of any of these plays except for Oscar Wild's 'Lady Windermere.' The others were probably written by amateurs and read by a play reading committee. That way they didn't have to pay royalties and could pick large cast plays to give us students more acting experience before an audience.

I never played a romantic lead in my life. I was a character actor; consequently, makeup was essential; I became quite good at ageing myself. From sixty on, though, I needed no makeup. I said I never played a romantic lead that is not true. At the end of our junior year we all did one-act plays, directed by third year students. The title of our play was, "Lonesome Like," and I played a shy fellow who finally got to kiss the leading lady. The student was Barbara Lee, a lovely young girl. In real life we both were shy, so our kiss was not very passionate.

One time another student, Bob Rockwell, happened to be watching a bit of our rehearsal, and after it was over, he took me aside and said, "Morg, why don't you really kiss her?" I answered, "I thought I did; I put my lips against hers." Bob, replied, " Yeah, you did, but you gotta hug her and kiss her with some vigor." I said, "Ok, next rehearsal I'll put some more vigor in the kiss." And I did. Ah, it felt much better.

I stage managed the play *Ladies in Retirement* at Gilmore

Brown's Playbox Theatre with a capacity of about sixty people located in front of his house. A fellow named Byron Barr played the lead. He was a very good actor and a very nice young man. Later on, he changed his name to Gig Young. William Holden was discovered at the Playbox. Neither Gig Young nor Holden were students there. Anyone who wanted to act at the Playhouse came to Sunday night auditions in the lab theatre. Other actors who did were Robert Preston, Dana Andrews, and Vic Mature.

I often get asked if any one in my class became famous actors. The answer is no. There were, however, a few who made a good living in theatre and films. The aforementioned Bob Rockwell played Mr. Boynton in the TV show " Our Miss Brooks." Louise Allbritton played the lead in a few movies, and would maybe have reached stardom, but she died at a young age. Others from my class who did well in films were: John Alvin, Maudie Doyle, Jane Cowan, Russ Arms (who was soloist for many years on the radio show, "Your Hit Parade"), Bill Irwin from the PG class, Jack Beardsley and David Breneiser. Many others in the class made a good living as teachers or working in the movies or TV in other capacities aside from acting.

I believe it was early March 1940 that I felt a pain in my lower left side. Lee Lemon and I were walking along together and I said, "Lee, I have a pain here." He looked at me and stated, "It's probably your epididimus; I had that once; it is a bit painful." I replied, "What the hell is an epididimus?" He went into a long explanation. I told him to forget it; I'm going to see a doctor. I had to get Mother's approval. She gave it quickly, and I went to see Dr. Davis. He told me it was appendicitis and we should operate as soon as possible. Mother gave her permission, and I had my appendix removed at the Huntington Hospital in Pasadena. I spent a week in a room with about eight other patients; that was the first time I heard a nurse say,

"I'll wash you from your head down as far as possible, and from your feet up as far as possible, and then you wash possible." I was discharged in a week and went to stay with Mother and Dad for a week in San Fernando Valley.

Back to the Playhouse and walking on egg shells for a time. In another week I was fine and ready to get back into the swing of things. Ollie Pricket, the head of publicity and all other writing for the Playhouse, decided that the Playhouse needed a basketball team. He would be coach, and a bunch of the lads showed up, among them was roommate Lee Lemon. I had no desire to play any more basketball. It was fun, though, to attend the games. Lee was a darn good player. They won a few games and lost a few, but everyone had fun.

The school year was fast drawing to a close. There were two things left to accomplish. The first is the senior production of the final play performed on the main stage with a full set, lights, sound, and costumes—our graduation play. The second thing was graduation itself. That's very easy; walk up and receive your diploma when your name is called.

"Lost Horizons" by John Hayden was our last play. We auditioned for it four weeks before the performance. Hershel Daugherty, the youngest director at the Playhouse, directed it, and Lee Lemon was the assistant director. Lee told us what parts we would have before the cast list was posted. He swore us to secrecy and we zipped our lips. It was fun having prior knowledge of what parts the rest of the class was playing. We performed the play two afternoons. The first afternoon Jack and I had good parts; the second afternoon we had bit parts. I was happy to see that one of the best actors in our class, Russ Arms, and I played the same part. That made me feel maybe I had a bit of talent. The play had thirty-five actors in it, so the two productions provided parts for all our class.

The graduation ceremony was a rather sober affair. World

War II was on and Germany was winning battles, so even with some of the girls performing Grecian dances in lovely costumes, we had a tough time being light hearted. Then when Charles Boyer, the main speaker, tearfully said that he wished he could be in France fighting for his country, we really felt the sadness of the occasion. All graduations are kind of like that aren't they? One is happy to complete something, and appreciates the education and challenges, but with our small class, we knew and enjoyed everyone and realized this could be the last time we would see most of them. That deepened the sadness a bit. Anyway, my name was called and I walked up to Gilmore Brown, received my diploma, and returned to my seat. I opened the cover that contained the diploma and read, "Morgan Stock, The Board of Trustees of the Pasadena Playhouse Association Forbids The Management To Issue A Diploma Until All Accounts With The Association Have Been Paid In Full." Mercy me, talk about being sad! I paid in full the money I owed, and received my diploma. I was happy again.

Jack and I decided we would double date for the graduation dance, which was held at the Huntington Hotel. Jack borrowed a large old car from his dad and we picked up our dates. Jack was with Harriet Freeman and I took Kate Vosburg, and we danced the night away.

Ordinarily, that would have been the end of the Playhouse for now, but Maxwell Sholes, one of the faculty directors, asked me to show up at a reading for James M. Barrie's play, "The Professor's Love Story." I read for the play and got a very good part, playing a Scot laborer in competition for the hand of a Scot housekeeper. What a great experience; there were three classmates in the play, and a very good cast. And I got good reviews in the Los Angeles papers. This gave me a bit more confidence to tackle New York and become a STAR!

CHAPTER 5

New York

GOODBYE PASADENA. HELLO NEW YORK! Well it's not quite as simple as that. Jack's father had two sisters back east. He and his wife Celeste decided they would injure two birds with one stone. We would all go back and see the sisters, and that was a perfectly cheap way for Jack and me to get back to New York. From here on I'll call Jack's father John, so as to distinguish between the two of them. John had been a very successful building contractor in Bellingham, Washington, until the depression hit and he lost the proverbial hat and ass. He and Celeste came to Pasadena and John worked in real estate. All by way of saying he knew how to design and build anything made of wood. So John spent the last month in Pasadena building a trailer that slept the four of us.

The top bed under the roof of the trailer was John and Celeste's. A big drawer below their bed became Morgan and Jack's bed, so we slept in the open under the stars. The first part of the drawer gave room for cooking utensils, food, and a small two-burner propane stove. I felt it was a most remarkable trailer, and it worked very well.

The trailer was pulled by a 1933 Rio, and the gearshift was a small lever about 4 inches long under the steering wheel. That was the first time I had ever seen a gearshift there, but it worked fine, and took us to New York with no problem.

We left Pasadena about the middle of July with John and Celeste in the front seat and Morg and Jack in the back. We rode to New York with that arrangement; John drove the entire trip. Actually, Jack and I were happy to sit in the back seat enjoying the scenery and occasionally break into song. We first drove to Monterey. Jack slept all the way. The reason for the big sleep was he had spent the night with Dolly Hancock who owned a music store in Pasadena, and Jack worked for her as a bill collector when folks were late on a payment. Her husband had died a couple of years earlier, so she wasn't cheating on anybody. This was the first time they were intimate. This led to a beautiful romance and they were married when Jack returned form New York. She was twenty years older than Jack, kinda like today, with older women marrying younger men.

In Monterey, we saw brother Jake and his wife Grace and their baby, Jay, who was the first of nine. We spent a pleasant day with them and then drove on to San Francisco and visited Jack's brother Bill and his wife Tony. We stayed a couple of nights with them and visited some interesting places in San Francisco. The most interesting was the 1940 Worlds Fair on Treasure Island. The exhibition Jack and I found the most interesting, aside from the great fan dancer Sally Rand, was on making a movie. A Hollywood studio produced it; they had all the equipment needed to make a movie, and filmed a few scenes to show us how it was done. The fellow who played the director was a friend from the Playhouse, whose name escapes me. I remember he was a prematurely gray haired handsome dude—a perfect character for the part.

I'm sorry I didn't get to see very much of Bill, Jack's brother, as he was busy working. I would have enjoyed getting to know him better, for he was a very likeable guy and a great personality. I'm sorry to say I never saw him again as he was killed in World War II, flying in the South Pacific.

One evening Jack and I and Tony were sitting around, and I remembered this stupid joke that Ward Wood, an actor at the Playhouse, told me. A man was employed in a factory whose job was to stand at a machine tightening a couple of nuts eight hours a day. One day the foreman came in and watched the man doing his job and decided he could do more, so he told him to tap a spring with his left hand. Well, you can see where this is going; the man ends up with arms, legs, and head moving constantly. The foreman comes through again and the man looks at him and says, sarcastically, "Just shove a broom up my ass and I can sweep the floor, too." Why is it I can remember that story and the people involved, but forget someone's name I met two days ago? Yeah, I know, "You are old, brother Morgan, you are old."

Back to the trip: We left San Francisco on a lovely day and drove through a number of towns and cities. This was before freeways, so we drove right down the main street of these places. Finally, we got into the Sierra Nevadas and found a lovely place to camp by a river. We pulled out the long drawer, took out the cooking utensils, and Celeste cooked us a good dinner. Jack and I washed the dishes, and we all hit the rack. That's a perfect name for the beds, but we did have good mattresses. It was a bit close quarters, but we all slept well.

After a good breakfast, we headed for Salt Lake City. The trip was a bit warm since cars had no air conditioning back then. The Salt Lake is impressive, but I was even more impressed by the City; the buildings, the trees, and the streets so wide and clean. A very pretty city. We stayed the night, then up and on to Wyoming.

We took the Northern route to New York; it was called the Lincoln Highway. There were three things I remember about the drive through Wyoming: First, the argument Jack and his dad got involved in. I don't remember what it was about, but after the words waxed hot and heavy, we stopped for a drink of water out of the canvas bag hanging on the bumper. That's how the water was kept cool in those days. We all got out and drank our fill, and Jack started walking down the road to New York.

Wait! What the hell is going on here? Am I going to end up going to New York alone? There he goes disappearing over the hill. The rest of us got back in the car, and John drove slowly along and stopped abreast of Jack. I opened the door, and said, "Come on, Jack, get in." And he did, thank goodness.

Second, we were driving along happily singing songs, something with Cheyenne in the title, when a car passed us and cut in too close, nearly hitting us. John immediately stepped on the gas and the old Rio and trailer took off after it. Celeste yells, "John, what are you doing?" John yells back, "I'm gonna catch that son of a bitch and stomp the hell out of him." I'm pleased to report that we never did catch him; the old Rio filled with four adults and dragging a trailer couldn't do it.

I must interrupt Wyoming and go back to Jack and Morg in California. I call this bit "Like father like son.' Jack and I are in his old Model A roadster, driving along Los Feliz Blvd in LA, and someone must not have liked the way Jack was driving, for he honked his horn and gave us the finger. Like Dad, the son stomped on the gas and the chase was on. Thinking this is not worth having a fight over, I tried to talk Jack out of it—no use. The man turned off Los Feliz and headed for Glendale, and then pulled into a service station. Jack pulled in behind him, jumped out of the car, and ran to him. The man was a short, swarthy, muscular fellow; Jack didn't even take off his coat. He assumed the boxer's stance, ready to do battle, whereupon the man backed up a couple of steps and took a mighty swing at Jack; he only missed him by about three feet. Jack looked at him, dropped his fists, turned to me and said, "Come on, Morg, this guy doesn't want to fight." While all this is going on, a friend of Jack's opponent and I squared off, but he didn't want to fight any more than I did, so Jack and I got back in the car and headed for Pasadena with the swarthy man yelling obscenities at us.

Back to Wyoming. Third memory: We were driving on a high plain after all the excitement between John and Jack, and it was time to stop for the night. John pulled off the road, and we set up camp. The evening was beautiful: "Big Sky Country." Celeste made us a great meal; the sunset was astounding. It was as though someone were telling us, "Alright you folks, enough tight jaws for the day, kick back and relax." We did, we did! And the hurt feelings slid right on down with the setting sun.

In Nebraska, we stopped at a public park for lunch, and were sitting at a picnic table enjoying our food, when a group of male teenagers sitting at a table nearby were heard uttering an expletive. It may have been "bitch." Up springs Jack, ready to do battle again. We all got him to sit down. He was really angry that anyone would say a swear word in front of his mother. Jack and I went over to the boys, and Jack told them he would appreciate it they wouldn't use swear words in front of his mother. They said, "Oh, sure, we're sorry!" That was the end of that. I thought, "Jumpin' Judas, Jack is gonna' get me in a fight yet."

I remember two things about Iowa; we were driving along a lovely country road when we came upon a one-room school. As it was time for lunch, Celeste said this was a good place to stop. Oh my! Nostalgia time. There was the pump in front of the main door with a tin cup on it. Over to the right was the girl's outhouse and to the left was the boy's. I'll bet they played some of the same games we did at recess and the noon hour. We ate our lunch and drank the cool water from the well, sitting on the school steps. A feeling swept over me, for I could just see the kids running out of the school and playing exactly as we did at the old Sharon Valley one room.

The second thing I remember is that all during the trip John suffered from pain in his neck and shoulders. He would have Celeste massage him in the evenings. Finally, he removed his suspenders and that cured him. While we were sitting on the school steps, he announced in a pain free voice, "I'm healed!" We yelled back, "Praise the Lord." And headed for Chicago.

We arrived in the windy city, however that July we named it "The Hot City." After driving around quite some time, we found John's sister's house. I don't recall her name. We didn't do anything that first day, but on the second day Jack and I decided we would see Chicago. Off to the Art Museum. The only art I remember was the beautifully sculptured pair of lions that graced the sides of the entryway. Later, we went to the Loop and saw Pinky Tomlin. Two years ago I had watched him for a week at the Paramount. That was enough for one day. Next day we all took in the view along the lake—no visit to the Palmer House or the Drake Hotel.

On to Indiana and we camped one night there. Then away to Ohio, which is called the State of Presidents, since seven U.S. presidents were born there, and, furthermore, the birthplace of that most famous Buckeye: Morgan Stock.

I showed the Jolys around the farm and then we parted company. They went to Buckeye Lake for three days while I caught up with cousins and neighbors. The damndest thing happened while I visited cousins Charles and Gerty Evans, on the farm next to ours. I finished talking to them and jumped off the porch. Their Collie dog Spike got excited and bit me on the back of my leg. I pretended it didn't hurt and left.

I remember that son of a bitch (that's really what he was, isn't it?) from when I lived there five years before. He was always a mean bastard. Luckily there was a thicket nearby with a stream running through it, so I took off my pants, seized the handkerchief, and washed off the blood. Then I dressed and headed for Buckeye Lake Park to meet up with the Jolys.

We had arranged to meet in front of the big dance hall, where brother Jake used to play with Leo Reichert's orchestra.

Everyone was there on time, so the "Joads," Celeste's name for us, all piled into the good old Rio and headed for Pennsylvania. Nothing untoward happened through West Virginia or Pennsylvania, so it was on to New York, by way of New Jersey, for we had to get to the Lincoln tunnel to arrive at the Big Apple. If driving to New Jersey was untoward, going through the tunnel with John at the wheel was very toward. Of course, we arrived at the height of traffic, and the cars sped along on the approach to the tunnel and continued on through just as fast.

John kept up with them, but inside the tunnel he kept hitting a foot-high curb along the right side. Jack and I kept looking at each other and grimacing each time he scraped the curb; we knew we dare not speak. Celeste didn't hesitate; she spoke right up in a loud voice, "John, you are hitting the curb." John's answer was to shove his head forward, grab the wheel tighter, and continue bumping the curb. By now Jack and I had visions of the trailer bouncing off the curb, turning over and spilling all the contents in the tunnel, blocking traffic, cars ramming us. Jesus, what a ride!

By God, Jesus must have been with us, for we made it through in one piece and drove on North to Hartsdale. There we met Jack's Aunt Mary, John's other sister.

We did it. I don't recall how many days we traveled, but, by George, the old Rio brought us through safely. Aunt Mary and her husband had a beautiful home, and a servant brought the meal to the table at dinner. I had never experienced the like before. We stayed that night at their house; it was wonderful to sleep in the luxurious beds

After a good night's sleep, a refreshing shower, and a bountiful breakfast, we left the trailer behind, and Ma and Pa Joad drove the young lads to 608 E. 17th St., Brooklyn, where my brother-in-law's father had a three-bedroom apartment.

This was to be our home, rent-free, for a short time.

We arrived in Brooklyn near the end of July. Seventeenth Street appeared to be a nice, quiet, tree lined place. We said goodbye to John and Celeste and carried our luggage to the second floor of the apartment building, which was to be our home for the next four months. We met Papa John Rockefeller, an eighty-four year old gentleman, and Tony (no relation) who worked in a local bakery. These were our housemates.

Our room was okay. I mean, after all, it was free; one should not complain about it being a bit small for two young men. We spent a couple of days walking around Brooklyn, getting used to the ambience of the place. We checked out Flatbush Avenue. I was glad we didn't live there, people yelling at each other from across the street, mostly women. Not unhappy talk, mind you, but at a pretty high volume.

The second morning some lovely music wafting up from the street awakened us. We raised the window and right below us a German Band was giving it the old, "Ein, zwei, drei, so, vier, fünf, let her go." We tossed some change down, not enough folding money to spare. What a pleasant way to wake up. "Maybe this Brooklyn isn't going to be so bad after all," we thought.

We went to see the New York version of the World's Fair. I must say, it appeared a bit sexy, for a large ball with a tall tower behind it marked the location of the fair grounds; it resembled a phallic symbol – tsk, tsk. The Fair was interesting with many fascinating things to see; our biggest thrill was jumping from the tall tower with a parachute. Two world fairs in one year was a bit unusual, I would say.

The next day Jack and I took the subway to New York. We got off at Times Square and walked around a bit, getting a feel of the place. We were impressed; I mean, my God, Jack, look at those tall buildings! We had just left the LA area, and at that time buildings over twelve stories were not permitted, probably due to earthquakes. And the bustling activity of everyone, packed sidewalks with people walking rapidly. It wasn't long before we joined right in and walked swiftly along with the rest.

So this was it. Here is where we start on our way to stardom. Well, others have made it, why can't we? Throw in the wonderful energetic flow of the city, and the feeling was reinforced that, damn it, I can do it. On top of that, we walked by some playhouses and saw who was starring in what show: Ethel Merman in "Panama Hattie," Jose Ferrer in "Charlie's Aunt," the Lunts in "The Guardsman," and many more, which set our desire on fire.

Finally, it was time to return to good old 608 E. 17th Street and fix dinner. This was Jack's duty for he had done that in Pasadena, and I did the dishes; we saw no reason to change that. After dinner, we borrowed Papa Rockefeller's phone book and made a list of theatre agents so we were set to go in the morning.

Next morning, up, shaved, bathed, looking as neat as possible, off we go to the Newkirk subway station to catch the train to Times Square to start our great adventure. The William Morris Agency was the first place we picked to start our adventure. We walked in and said hello to the receptionist and were told to sit down until one of the underlings was free to see us. An agent named Robert Goodhue called Jack in first. It was a very short meeting, sort of a get acquainted time. I didn't see anybody.

Then it was on to the Paramount Building where we met the agent Laura Arnold. She told me that if there were any acting jobs, she would take them herself. We saw another agent on Broadway, and decided it was time for lunch.

We went to the Rockefeller Center milk bar and abated our

hunger a bit with a sweet roll and a glass of milk. There were many places in New York to get a cheap lunch. We went to a couple more agents on one of the side streets and decided to call it a day.

We followed this routine for about a week, then Jack suggested we split up and see the agents alone. I wasn't sure I liked this idea, for it was fun for me to see Jack getting to see the agents; whereas I usually wasn't permitted to go any farther than the receptionist's desk. It was quite humorous to behold. We would walk in together and report to the receptionist. In the big agencies like William Morris, the receptionist would phone into the office and say we were there. In a short time Bob Goodhue would come out and speak thusly: "Jack, How are you doing? Come on in, I have something you may be interested in. Oh, hello there." (That's to me.) Then the two of them would go into the office and leave me sitting there twiddling my thumbs.

It is perfectly understandable; Jack was very good looking, blonde, 5' 10, with an okay figure. He was the typical juvenile type, maybe the friend of the leading man. He was perfect for coming on stage, a tennis sweater hanging around his neck and swinging a racquet, uttering the absolutely stunning line, "Tennis anyone." While old long faced Morg sits there ready for a character role, which I played my entire life, I could have been the leading lady's homely brother. Ah, well, in another life.

From that point on Jack and I would ride together to New York, part company, do our own thing, and join up again in Brooklyn. The separation was a good thing. I never felt rejected watching someone walking into the important offices. I just kept in mind that I was a pretty good actor and my time would come. One afternoon my ego got a great boost.

I went to the Leland Hayward Agency. Now Leland was

one of the great ones. He was Mr. Theatre. At the time he was married to Margaret Sullivan, a very well known actress. He stole her from Henry Fonda, The great man called me into his office and talked to me for several minutes. He asked me questions concerning my theatre experience, and I told him about my role in the "Professor's Love Story" at the Playhouse and showed him my review from the LA Times. He said he wasn't casting anything at the moment, but he would be starting very soon and asked me to leave my resume with the secretary. He was so nice and kind and seemed genuinely interested in my talent that I left his office walking a foot off the ground. I celebrated by going to Central Park and talking to or even singing to the animals.

It was about this time that Jack also got a big boost; he had a parting of the ways with Bob Goodhue. It turned out that Bob was gay and made a move on Jack. When he rebuffed Goodhue, Jack got another agent and hit pay dirt right away. The agent informed Jack that a producer was doing a new play and needed a good looking juvenile, so he would send Jack to a casting director.

That night, back in Brooklyn, Jack excitedly told me he was to meet the casting the next day. If we had enough money for a drink, we would have popped a cork. Since that was not to be, we wished each other "break a leg" over a cup of tea.

The next morning we both set off in good spirits, for Jack's high was contagious. I thought I might even get beyond the receptionist. I couldn't wait to get back to 608 to hear how things went with Jack. Everything was going fine, the casting director liked Jack and said he would send him to someone else. This went on for a week, and Jack worked his way up to the director. By now, Jack walked on air; I was happy for him and, of course, a bit envious.

A day or two later we were sitting around the apartment

in the late afternoon and Jack got a phone call. I was "all ears" as I watched him. The conversation went like this from Jack's end. "Hello, oh, hello there, Jim, how you doin'?" (His agent, Jack, had a big smile on his face.) After a bit more opening chatter, Jack asked, "Anything to report?" A long pause, Jack's smile fading as he continued. "Oh, yeah, uh huh, yeah, I see. Oh sure I understand, yeah. Thanks for calling." His whole body kind of slumped and he turned to me and said, "I didn't get the part." I reply, "Oh shit!" He says, "Oh shit is right!" It seems that the director had someone else in mind. Of course, rejections go with the territory in theatre. One learns to handle it and move on or out of theatre. I used Jack's collapse in acting classes I later taught. If the student didn't measure up to Jack's performance, I'd say I don't believe you.

Incidentally, the play was never produced. The curse we laid on it worked. For the life of me I can't remember the name of the play.

There were times we went to an audition without the help of an agent. One I remember very well was "The Corn Is Green" starring Ethel Barrymore. I appeared at the proper place and hour and joined actors about four abreast on the sidewalk. After a few minutes, we were all inside the building, and climbing four flights of stairs to the office. The audition went like this: a secretary called, "next," at that command we walked into the office and stood in front of the casting director. He asked our name, said thank you, and we walked out of the office, down the stairs, and out of the building. The young lead in the play was named Morgan Evans (obviously Welsh). My name is Morgan Evans Stock, so I left out the Stock when he requested my name. It didn't help; I was never called back

We met a few Playhouse folks when we were in New York. The closest friend was Norman Brooks. Between the three of us we could manage a decent wardrobe when auditions called for it. Norman's sister, Phyllis Brooks, was a good actress who did a lot of movies. However, she was playing in "Panama Hattie" with Ethel Merman when we were in the Big Apple. I wonder now why Norman didn't get us comps for the show. We didn't see one play while we were there; we barely had enough money to eat let alone go to a play. Other friends in town were Werner Klemperer and Jean Knudson who were co-habiting long before it became popular.

Speaking of eating, I remember one famous dinner Jack cooked for us at 608. He read a recipe in the paper for a meal that was called Weiner Crunch. He thought, and rightly so, that he should make a big pot of it to last us a week, plus it was cheap to make. It consisted of wieners and oatmeal. One made it by placing a layer of oatmeal on the bottom and then a layer of split wieners and so on until the pot was full. It was then heated properly and voila, tres bon or ser gut meal. We looked forward to eating this delicacy; I'm sure Jack cooked it right, but the taste was not commensurate with all the work put into it. In fact, it was terrible. We had one meal of it and flung it out.

To return to auditions, I recall Jack going to one for a musical; they were holding tryouts for the chorus- labeled a cattle call. Jack didn't know diddly about dancing. The voice work he could have handled since one time I put my hand on his throat and shook it so he would produce a vibrato, and he could carry a tune. Anyway Jack somehow sneaked in with about a hundred real pros and lurked in the background. Eventually came the moment of truth and they asked him to dance. He did a silly thing where he shuffled his feet a bit, ended with a flourish with one foot in front, arms extended and bowed. The choreographer, without a moments hesitation, said, "You with that ingenious time step, goodbye, goodbye!"

About the same time, I tried out for "New Faces Of 1940."

It was fun for I got to see all kinds of wonderful acts. I had to get an accompanist, so I asked this fellow that I had seen playing for other folks to accompany me. He said he would for a dollar. I told him I only had 50 cents; he said okay. I sang the old Harry Owen's Hawaiian song "The Princes Poopooly (if that's how one spells it). I didn't hear anything from the New Faces folks.

One more tryout I really must mention. It was 1940, and Wendell Wilke was running against President Roosevelt. Moreover, Wilke was making a speech in Brooklyn, so we decided to go and hear him. The speech was inside and by the time we arrived there was quite a crowd waiting to get inside. I saw that it was hopeless that we could make it, so I said, "Come on Jack, let's go." Jack replied. "No, I came down here and I'm going to get in." I knew that when he was in this mood there was no use arguing with him. I told him to go ahead, I would wait for him outside. I was pretty sure they wouldn't let him in since there were two or three security men at the door. He disappeared into the crowd, and I didn't see him for an hour. When I spotted him coming out the door, I asked him how he got in, and he showed me a sloppy press card he made and walked right in.

With this kind of nerve and guts, he should have made it in the theatre. Don't cry for him; those two qualities made him a millionaire in the music store business.

I had a couple more auditions, one for a third rate traveling company, another singing on the radio, but I was never called back to sing. I hocked my watch; I think I got two dollars for it. I even tried to get an ushering job at the Radio City Music Hall. Can you believe it! They turned down, the best usher at the Paramount Theatre.

An incident occurred in an agent's office that made me think more about this theatre career. I was sitting patiently when an elderly gentleman next to me said, "Waiting for an interview, huh?" I said, "Yes, I hope..." He interrupted. "They don't always turn out well, you know." I replied, "Oh yes, I certainly know that." He said. "But I've had some turn out well. Here, I want to show you these." He showed me reviews of plays he had been in. I didn't bother to read them, for he went on, "I was supposed to be in a play with Katie Hepburn, but she really likes to take stage and doesn't want any one else to do that. I like to take stage, too, so we didn't get along, and I didn't get the part." At that time I was called in by the agent and informed no work now. I thought about that scene as I walked down Broadway and said to myself, "I don't want to end up like that. It's time I think very seriously about my future."

By November I had had enough; it was cold and I was hungry most of the time. The Milk Bar, Nedick's orange stand, Horn and Hardart's automats were reasonable, but not too filling. When we both got hungry enough, Jack would call his aunt and get an invitation to dinner. Those dinners were to die for.

I went to a travel bureau and got a ride to Los Angeles for fifteen dollars. Car companies would get their cars delivered to cities that way. It was a new car, so I suspect it would show up in the proper dealership with the mileage rolled back and sold as a spanking brand new car.

The fellow who arranged for the car wanted to see a lot of friends on the way to LA. He and his buddy did the driving. First we went to Nashville, thence to Dayton and on to other cities in a most circuitous route. Thank goodness there was a sailor on leave in the group, and he and I sat in the back seat and talked, slept, and finally arrived safe and sound in Los Angeles.

Jack moved out of the Rockefeller apartment and moved in

with Norman Brooks for a time. He got a job at the Algonquin Hotel as a bus boy, and, surprisingly, got his really big break in theatre. This is what he told me when we met again in LA several months later.

"The Man Who Came to Dinner" needed a replacement for the young son in the family, and, glory be, Jack was picked to play the part. However, they didn't want to take time to rehearse him with the rest of the cast, so the stage manager told him to learn the lines, sit in the balcony, watch the play, and get the blocking down properly. When the young man left the cast, Jack would be ready to step in and do the part. This was Jack's big chance to conquer BROADWAY!! He was within a couple of days of filling the part when a very official letter came from the US government. It began, "Greetings, you are to appear at your draft board on such and such a date." Shot down again, Damn, Sheister, F, Merde, BS, ETC!

Two days later, instead of reporting to the theatre, Jack reported to the Travel Bureau and got a ride to Pasadena for five dollars. One more time he beats me. How is it possible that we can stay best friends for sixty-two years? I guess even with all his faults and foibles, and his winning ways, I love and respect the old fella'. I firmly believe that his reason for good luck is that he is a Yankee Doodle Dandy Born On The Fourth Of July.

My long ride ended with me convincing the man who was the leader to take me to Burbank, where Francie and Jack had purchased a house. When we arrived, I opened the trunk, drug out my suitcase, and bid farewell to my road companions. I walked in the house, greeted Francie and Jack, fell into bed and slept for nearly twelve hours.

I awoke, showered, had lunch, and conversed with Francie; we talked of my New York experience. She was very supportive and mentioned what a wonderful experience it was for me. She was right, it was a wonderful experience. I learned a lot and I realized that I needed to put that experience to good work and think about my future.

First, however, I got in old 81, the 31 model A coupe I had bought, and drove out the San Fernando Valley, and saw Mother and Dad at the chicken ranch. I stayed with them a couple of days, and caught up with all the family: Kay was still teaching in Bakersfield, Jake and Grace were in Ventura, playing in a nightclub. All were happy and in good health.

It was then I thought, "Morg, what are you going to do? I didn't really know what to do , except get a job right quick, and the quickest place to get a job would be with my brother-in-law, Kenny Mastain, who owns a couple of service stations in Los Angeles. I called him and within two days was a service station attendant. We did the regular work: pumping gas, checking oil and tires, cleaning windows. Kenny added another job; he told us to use a whiskbroom and sweep out the floor at the front seats. The patrons seemed pleased with this extra effort.

A week or so later I attended a Sunday night tryout for an original play, which would be presented in Gilmore Brown's Playbox Theatre. Back in the saddle again! I got the part of the butler. I thought maybe I wasn't such a terrible actor after all. We opened in January and had a successful run.

It was wonderful to get back on stage again. The cast was nice, and we talked about everything. I told them stories of my time in New York, and they spoke of their experiences in the theatre. Most of the stories dealt with work in nonprofessional theatre. I began to get an idea of how I might change my life.

I considered doing amateur theatre for the fun and enjoyment of it and putting my education and experience into teaching drama. All right, if that was the way to go, I had to return to school and get a degree in theatre. Now the question was which college to attend? After thinking it over for a few days, I remembered how much I enjoyed visiting sister Kay when she went to Santa Barbara State. I met some of her friends and liked the beautiful small town, so I cranked up 81, drove to Santa Barbara and discovered that the spring semester started shortly after we closed the play.

A couple of weeks later I quit my job with Kenny, packed my huge wardrobe and toiletries, drove to Santa Barbara, and rented a room at the YMCA. On registration day I signed up for several classes: English, Us History, Physiology, Speech, and some kind of a dance class. In the speech class I told Dr. Snidecor about my theatre work and he asked me to work with students who were reciting poetry for another class. I worked with a lad who chose, "Casey At The Bat." It was enjoyable; I believed I was going to like this here teachin'.

I attempted to find a job so I could move out of the Y. The college had a list posted of available jobs. One seemed interesting: a family needed someone to help out in the kitchen and take care of two children—a boy eight and a three year old girl. I drove out to the address and met the fellow who was leaving. He told me it was a good job and the nights were usually free so I could try out for plays. I met Mrs. Hancock and she told me my duties, and that I'd be sharing a bedroom with son, Robert. I agreed, so I checked out of the Y and moved in with the Hancocks.

It was a two bedroom one bathroom house—a bit dicey at times, but I was happy. I seldom saw Mr. Hancock; he worked in an office downtown. Mrs. Hancock was my boss. I remember a few things I had to do. Every morning I squeezed orange juice and set the table for breakfast. When the meal was finished, I cleared the table and did the dishes, then off to class. Often I took the kids for a walk up the street toward the mission with Sarah in her little buggy and Robert running back and forth all over the place. On sunny days I had to remember to put sunscreen on Sarah so she wouldn't get freckles; Mrs. Hancock insisted on this. When I had free time in afternoons, we played games or I read to them. Dinnertime was much the same as breakfast; I helped as much as possible and after all things were spick and span, I was free in the evenings.

Naturally, this freedom gave me a chance to read for the first play of the semester, which was Shakespeare's, "Merchant of Venice." I got the part of Antonio from whom Shylock wanted his heart cut out for not paying his debt. Oh, great Scot, Morgan, what are you going to do? Never fear Portia is here! You may cut out his heart, but do not spill one drop of blood.

The cast was a wonderful group. The head of the drama department, Fred Hile, played Shylock and did a good job, and the rest of the cast did well in their roles. I enjoyed the experience. During rehearsals, I met Irving Manspeaker who became a very good friend. He was not in the cast, but at one of the early rehearsals I noticed this huge man lying along the aisle in the auditorium. He resembled a beached whale. I saw him later and found out his folks owned a cafeteria in LA where we dined quite often. I think it was the very one where I celebrated my high school graduation night.

Irv had a new Ford roadster, so we traveled around with the top down during that wonderful spring in Santa Barbara. I was amazed by his hobby: Irv was nuts about pistols. He even made his own shells, or I should say put them together. Irv would order the shell, powder, and bullet and then assemble them at his workbench. I watched how he put the exact amount of powder in the casing, placed the bullet in the casing, and crimped the casing around the bullet.

Once in a while we took pistols out to a remote area and fired at tin cans. Another time Jack Rock was with us and I handed him the pistol, he took it, started to raise it up, and

BLAM the bullet broke a rock on the ground just ahead of us. Irv forgot to tell Jack he had reset the trigger so that a light touch fired the pistol. Luckily, the bullet or flying rocks hurt none of us.

The classes went along well. Thank goodness I wasn't taking any math. Physiology was interesting and fun due to my lab partner. He was from Watsonville and, once again, humor sort of saved the day during an experiment. We were handed an instrument that had a sharp knife-like point on it. The instructor showed us how to work it, and said, "Try to get a little blood out of your ear lobe." The gadget was set to get a reading on how deep the point would go. The point wasn't pushed in; a little trigger was pulled and the point quickly thrust forward. We practiced with it on a piece of cardboard and figured we could do it properly. I said to John, "Go ahead, try it on me." He did and it worked fine. I gave him a bit of blood and wiped it off with a Kleenex. John said, "Okay, my turn." I put my finger behind his ear lobe; placed the instrument against the lobe and pulled the trigger. The knife went beautifully into his lobe and right on through into my finger. We both had some blood to wipe away. I must have unintentionally changed the distance. We laughed about it. What else could I do? Sue for shooting my own finger?

The semester went along very well. Along about April, three fellows I worked with in "Merchant" invited me to move in with them in a large house, and I accepted. They were a good group, although one of them had eyes that went back and forth very rapidly. It was kinda hard to look him in the eye, but I got used to it. I bought an old army cot, borrowed some sheets and stayed with them the rest of the semester. The Hancocks and I parted friends, for they understood that I needed to be on my own.

The move meant that I would have to earn a bit of money

to add to the funds family members sent me. A lady who knew me from the Hancocks asked me to help her with her patent medicine route. I collected money from the patrons and sometimes took new orders and delivered the medicine. I felt like the snake oil salesman at the county fair, but I wasn't cheating any one. And they were happy with the results.

Another something, another show, auditions, time for the next play: "Night Must Fall" by the Welshman, Emlyn Williams. The story is about a young fellow who murdered a lady and carried her head around in a leather hatbox. I wanted very much to be the villain because it was a hell of a part. Again, it was not to be; I was the detective that tracked him down. Fred Hile did get a very good young man to play the lead. It seems strange to call the murderer the lead, but he was. I remember Robert Montgomery played the part in the movie. Until that time, he usually played young romantic leads, but this part showed that he was a fine actor. The play went very well; plus the leading lady Lucille Chester was a beauty.

I got up nerve enough to ask her for a date and she accepted, so I drove her down to Ventura in old 81, and we had a fine dinner with live music. We danced and talked and drove on back to Santa Barbara. I stopped along the way and spoke: "Lucille, may I kiss you." She replied, "Morgan, don't ever ask a girl, 'May I kiss you.' Just do it." So I did. We had a short little necking session—quite nice. I kept learning things every day.

CHAPTER 6

Private Stock

IN JUNE I RECEIVED A BEAUTIFUL LETTER that began "Greetings, you are to report to the induction center in Los Angeles in July…" I finished the semester and said goodbye to all and drove to Mom and Dad's chicken ranch, stayed there for a few days then on to Burbank to stay with Francie and Jack until that fateful day.

I reported to an army office in LA July 9th, 1941, one day after my 21st birthday, and had a physical. A doctor checked my blood pressure, checked my throat, listened to my heart and breathing and said, "You have a malocclusion." "Holy Jasus! What in the hell is a malocclusion?" I asked the doctor. He replied, "It may be serious enough to keep you out of the draft." That part was good news, but I was worried about what he said I had. Was that something in my heart or lungs? What did he see or hear that made him say I had that thing? At that point he told me to open my mouth; I thought oh, oh, it's in my throat. He said, "Bite your teeth together," which I did, and he looked and tapped my teeth and finally said, "You only have six teeth that don't come together, so you are in good shape for the army." Oh, Lordy, what a relief! I had already pictured myself in the hospital ready for an operation. Shoot, I always knew that my upper and lower teeth didn't come together in front. I didn't know that problem was called a malocclusion, if that's the way you spell it. Why did he have to scare me so?

Many are called but few are chosen. That does not work in the draft. Many are called and a whole bunch are chosen, so we were loaded into a bus and traveled to Fort MacArthur on the outskirts of LA. There we were issued our army clothes. They had us take off our shoes and pick up two buckets of sand to get our proper size. Mine was 9EE.

We spent two or three days at MacArthur, taking IQ tests and seeing movies about how not to catch a venereal disease. Then we boarded a train and chugged up the coast to Camp Roberts, which is near Paso Robles.

We were assigned to the 2nd Battalion training program, and for a week we were kept busy doing odd jobs until the battalion had the proper number of soldiers for the training program. One job we worked on was marching out to the rifle range and digging postholes. Camp Roberts is very hot in the summer, so we had to bury the long crow bar to keep it cool enough to pick up the next time we used it. Obviously, it was just busy work; for the eight months I was there no fence was ever built.

Finally, the battalion was full and we began our basic training. I believe we were paid twenty dollars a month. I remember some smart ass saying, "Oh yeah, I got a hell of a job. I get $20.00 dollars a day once a month. We arose at 6:00 and fell in for our sergeant to report all present and accounted for. Fifteen minutes of exercises followed, then in to the mess hall for breakfast.

The first week we spent a lot of time learning how to march and handle the rifle. Our rifles were 1903 (commonly called thirty ought three) bolt-action single shot, same as the WW I soldiers used. They were perfect for our training. One time the supply sergeant ordered five of us to report to the supply room and unload some new rifles from a large case. We opened the case and dug out the rifles and they were covered with this very thick grease. The sergeant gave us some liquid and some rags and told us to remove the cosmoline from the guns. What a job that was! We spent hours rubbing the grease off the rifles and then hours rubbing it off our hands. This job made me understand the expression, "He's a revolving, cosmoline-covered, son of a bitch." One can scrub and it won't come off, and no matter which way you look at him, he's still an SOB.

Our barracks were two story wooden buildings next to the dirt parade ground. I was on the second floor, which was okay, except about three o'clock a stiff breeze would come up and blow the dust from the parade ground through our windows that covered the floor, our beds, and any clothes we had hanging.

We left the windows open in the morning because Roberts was such a hot place. At noon, if we were in for chow, someone would yell "windows!" and we would close them. If we were not in, we put up with the dust until we could brush it away.

Now, the time came for firing the rifle. The range was about a mile away and we walked the route with our rifles hanging from the sling on our shoulders. We tried several games to relieve the heat and boredom: spelling, filling in words, definitions. Interestingly, almost every one in the early days of the draft had graduated from high school. At least that's how it seemed in our battalion.

My first job when we reached the range was in the butts, marking the targets. The firing line was 200 yards away. The trainees fired one shot and we told them how they had done by holding up a piece of round tin on a long stick painted black on one side and white on the other. If they hit the bull's eye, we waved the black. If they missed the bull's eye, we showed the white over the hole they made in the target, so they could zero in their rifle. When they missed the target, we waved Maggie's drawers. I can't remember what we used for that, maybe a red piece of tin.

Captain Butts, our company commander, was in the butts with us one day, and he loved to tell jokes. His name is

a joke in itself – Butts in the butts. I remember one of them.
A lady was driving along a country road in Minnesota and she
noticed a husky lad plowing in a field along the road. She asked
directions to a place and he picked up the plow with one hand
and pointed it down the road She thought, "Wow, he's one
strong fellow, I had better enjoy a bit of intimacy with him." So
she went into the field and got him on top, and he didn't know
what to do, so she said, "Alright, now push it in. That's right;
now pull it out. Now push it in; now pull it out." She kept this
going for a time. Finally, the young lad said, "Lady I wish you'd
make up your mind. I got to finish my plowin' today." Why in
the world would I remember a joke that wasn't very that good I
heard sixty-four years ago? It's probably the situation I was in.

The next day I was on the firing line. I fired the first round
and was surprised at the heavy kick of the gun. I noticed a few
of the soldats had swollen lips from the recoil of the 03. I had
made marksman which was one degree above a bolo. The other
two categories were sharpshooter and expert.

The training went along with firing of different weapons,
long hikes, KP, and night hikes and problems. The night
problems were a bit chancy because of the presence of
rattlesnakes and tarantulas. I understand now that tarantulas
are not dangerous, but it's a bit disconcerting to have them
crawling on you. After about a month of training I was assigned
a new task.

One of the lieutenants checked our biographies and found
out that three of us had been in theatre, so we were ordered to
put on a show for the battalion. We met after the day's training
and tried to figure out something to perform. One of the GI's
wanted to write a musical. I didn't like that idea—too much
work. Another one suggested we read a play. I didn't think
the boys would enjoy that. Finally one of the members of our
team said, "Come on guys we're wasting time here. Let's have

Sergeant Owens train some of us in a fancy rifle drill; we have a good pianist in our company, and some good singers, and I'll tell a few jokes, and Voila, we have a show." We all agreed, and that's what we did. It went over well, and we were even asked to perform the show for another battalion.

We finished our thirteen weeks training in October, and I was promoted to corporal along with my good buddies Gene Erikson, Carl Bomberger, and John Shepherd. We got to tell new recruits how to perform as soldiers. Besides that, we got a raise in pay; I now received 54 dollars a month. That helped considerably to pay for my weekends back in Burbank, when I could get them.

The trip to Burbank was something else. I would find someone in our company that was going to the LA area and bum a ride with an offer to help with the gas bill. We would leave on Saturday morning, drive to Paso Robles, turn left and proceed to Blackwell's Corner, which contained a gas station and a grocery store. We would turn right at Blackwell's and drive to Taft, then left to 101. A right turn at 101 (there was no highway 5 back then) took us partway up the grapevine highway, properly named since the two lane highway turned and twisted dangerously up the mountain to Gorman, then on down and eventually into LA. The trip took about three hours. It was always worth the ride to get to spend time with family.

We kept on doing the usual training. I didn't mind the infantry, but I did think about joining the air corp. However, when I inquired about joining up, they said I had to have two years of college. I stayed in the infantry; there were some good buddies there and interesting incidents kept occurring.

I was on guard duty one night. As corporal of the guard, I walked the men to their posts and brought the ones relieved back to the guardhouse. After making sure everything was proper, I would try to sleep a couple of hours. This night was different; I was awakened by a guard yelling, "Post number one reporting. There's trouble at post four." I grabbed a pistol and a flashlight and ran to number four. I saw the guard kneeling down holding his wrist, his rifle on the ground. I asked what happened. He said he accidentally shot himself in the wrist. I yelled to post three to have the sergeant get a jeep and meet us at four. I saw blood on him, but, from what I could see, the wound didn't seem too bad. He kept telling me it was an accident. The sergeant arrived and put him in the jeep and drove him to the first aid station. I returned to the guardhouse, and didn't remember hearing what happened to him. I often wondered if he shot himself to get out of the army.

Another time I was getting the guard duty troops together outside our barracks when one soldier didn't show up. He was regular army, perhaps in his late thirties, so I went back into the barracks to look for him. There he was, drunk as a skunk, trying to put on his leggings. He tried to stand up and nearly fell over. I said, "You can't go on guard like that." He replied, slurring his words, "Oh, yesh I can; jush hep me legs put up." I responded, "I can't do that; the officers and sergeants would give me hell for allowing you to come like that. Besides, you can hardly stand; if a dangerous situation occurred, you wouldn't be worth a damn." He kept begging me to let him come; I was afraid he'd start crying any minute. I felt bad about it, but I walked out and left him struggling with his clothes.

Speaking of drinking, once we were on a night hike and I noticed one of the older regular army boys was a bit boisterous, having a good time, but keeping up with the group. I discovered later he filled his canteen with whiskey and enjoyed the walk more than the rest of us. Truly, there was very little drinking during the week, maybe an occasional beer at the PX. We didn't want alcohol interfering with our very busy days.

On weekends I stayed in camp; Bomberger, Erickson, and

I played golf near Paso Robles. Once I went to Santa Barbara with a good buddy, and looked up some of the folks I knew. We were invited to a party; I met up with a gal I remembered from my college days. We hit it off quite well, drinking a lot, and kissing and fondling, when suddenly I had to head for the bathroom and heave, and passed out. I don't remember anything after that. I guess my buddy loaded me into the car and drove us away. I do remember very well the terrible hangover. That was my first experience with one of those things.

December 7th, 1941. I remember the absolute shock of Pearl Harbor. The next day we stopped training and sat on a hillside and listened to Roosevelt's "Day of Infamy" speech. After that, many of us were assigned to guard duty at strategic places throughout Camp Roberts. We remained on alert for a couple of weeks, and were then brought back to our company barracks. It was at that time a group of noncoms started talking about going to OCS, Officer Candidate School. We filed our papers, passed the test, and Erickson, Bomberger, Stock, Edwards, and Shepherd were ordered to proceed to Fort Benning, Georgia. While we were on the train, we heard that a Japanese submarine set off some kind of device in the ocean near Santa Barbara—no harm done.

Thinking of Pearl Harbor reminds me of a change in the treatment of soldiers by the civilian population. Before the Japanese attack we just all blended in. But after it, the civilians would tell us," Go get 'em, tiger" or "Bless you, soldier." If they spotted us in a car, they'd yell and wave. It was quite remarkable and made us very proud to be American.

We traveled by troop train across the country, sitting in seats day and night. I think we went to a dining car for meals or maybe had K rations. Whenever we stopped in a city, we got out and walked around a bit. I do remember very clearly stopping in St. Louis for a couple of hours one evening, and there was a nice bar nearby. Well, of course, we partook of the libations offered there. I was impressed with the dashing figure the young pilots cut with their white scarves and billed caps as they came into the bar. I was even more impressed and a bit envious to see the young ladies crowd around the flyboys. One can't blame them; when they looked at our olive drab uniforms and silly little caps, they preferred the colorful air force boys. I think the only one of us to enter a conversation with one of ladies was the very smooth, handsome, Stanford graduate, Corporal Bomberger.

We continued on, reached Fort Benning, were assigned to the Harmony Church area, and began our training as Class 15 of the Officer Candidates School on February 19, 1942. I was assigned to 4th Company student training regiment.

I won't bother you with all the details of the training; suffice it to say that the instructors were all excellent. We fired all the weapons again. However, we had the M1 rifle by then which was much better than the old '03. Just pulling the trigger fired eight shots. The training was hard physically; we usually sat in bleachers for the lecture then the instructor would give an order, "Fall in over here and double time to that red scarred hill over there." Believe me, there are many red-scarred hills and valleys at Fort Benning. I guess it's red clay. Well, at least the red lent a bit of color to the place.

We spent our free time in various ways: a couple of times they had dances, and I went to them. I was very surprised at the ages of the girls. I asked some of them and found out they were fourteen or fifteen, but they looked in their late teens or early twenties. I had heard that southern girls matured faster than those in other parts of the states—probably just a myth. There was a large open space on the way to the PX, and often trainees practiced their commands in a full voice, "Platoon, halt!" It startled me so I would stop walking and wait for the stentorian tones of, "Forward, march!" I went to Columbus, the town nearest Fort Benning, a couple of times. It was too crowded and busy. One weekend I went to Auburn with a couple of buddies and stayed in a nice quiet old hotel. That was very nice. Find the name of the town where Auburn is located

At times, while sitting on the bleachers waiting for an instructor, one of the group would get out in front and lead us in songs, or a stand up comic would do a routine. During lunch breaks, the Benning kitchen crew played records for us. I remember a few of the songs: The Chattanooga Choo Choo, Don't Sit Under the Apple Tree With Anybody Else But Me, The Boogie Woogie Bugler from Company B, Drinkin' Beer in a Cabaret and was I Havin' Fun, etc. Fill in any others you remember. I just remembered that sister Francie gave me a little record player and some records, so we had music in the barracks in the evening. Didn't Will say, " If music be the food of love, play on?"

The last month of training the weather warmed up considerably, and we came in from the field hot and sweaty. There was a small building near our barracks that was loaded with cold soft drinks, so, after we were dismissed, we walked rapidly to the building, stood in line, and paid a nickel for a coke or whatever. Those were the best cokes I ever drank.

A couple of weeks before our graduation, a men's clothing store salesman brought samples of officer's green coats and gray trousers and laid them out on beds in one of the barracks. I selected Hart, Shaffner and Marx, and was very satisfied with it for the rest of my army career.

I jump to the present now, August 26, 2005, and tell you that three days ago I received a complete record of my army career from the National Personal Records Center in Washington D. C., so I will be more accurate in most dates from now on.

The first date from these records is May 25, 1942, and I quote the information contained in that record, "No disabilities or defects noted on final physical exam. Discharged at Fort Benning, Georgia, May 25,1942 for the convenience of the government to accept appointment as 2d Lt. in the Army of the United States."

May 26, '42 we graduated and accepted our crossed rifles and stuck them on our shirt collars. Then tradition has it that one must watch carefully for the first time he is saluted and pay that individual a dollar. That wasn't hard at all; about three minutes after graduation— mission accomplished.

We all received ten days leave before reporting to our next assignment. My next duty station was Camp Wheeler, Georgia some miles up the road from Fort Benning. "Whee! I get to come back to Georgia for the lovely summer weather." However, before I report to Camp Wheeler, I wish to report on my leave.

Gene Erickson—oh gracious, I forgot!—LT. Erickson and I took a bus to Birmingham and caught a plane to Los Angeles. The other lieutenant went up North and I went to Burbank and stayed with Francie and Jack. The first good thing that happened was the loan of a car from Ken Mastain. A Japanese family lived next to Ken's station and they were transported to an internment camp. The father of the group asked Ken to keep his car for him until he came back, so Ken loaned me the car for the ten days. I would have used 81, but Jack needed to drive it because gas rationing made driving his De Soto nearly impossible.

I had a great time visiting Mother and Dad. They were so proud of my promotion to lieutenant. Dad stood up, clicked his heels, and saluted me as I walked in their home, shades of the Spanish American War. I was so happy to see them running a lovely cottage hotel on Hollywood Blvd., near Grauman's

Chinese Theatre. I saw friends at the Pasadena Playhouse. One special friend was Arlie Steere, whom I escorted to a fine dinner, and we agreed to write to each other. I was pretty much in love with her.

Time to return to the army. I flew out of LA, landed in Birmingham, and reported in at Camp Wheeler on or about July 6. I don't have a specific date for it. The job was the same as I did at Camp Roberts, training new enlistees. The weather was hot and humid, and we had a couple of men overcome by the heat, but not seriously, thank the Lord.

I enjoyed going in to Macon with a lieutenant I met at the camp. He was a recent graduate of Tulane and a southerner, so he instructed me how to behave when we went to a Presbyterian church one Sunday. It was communion day and they sipped grape juice instead of wine. The real treat was an invitation to an elderly lady's home for Sunday lunch. The house was beautiful; it may have been Ante Bellum. The table setting was something to behold: a lovely tablecloth, perfect plates, silver ware, glasses, and napkins. An impeccable black butler served us so wonderfully I was almost afraid to eat. I watched Lt. Jones to make sure I used the right silverware. I have attended fancy meals, but this one was the best. After the meal, our hostess took us to what she called Lee Hall. Every single space on those walls was filled with pictures of General Lee and his horse Traveler. We thanked our gracious host and returned to our mundane barracks.

I saw what I thought was very near cruel punishment at Camp Wheeler. One of the soldiers was forced to walk around the parade ground with a pack and rifle on his shoulder in the heat of July. I don't know what he did, but I decided right then I would make the punishment fit the crime.

My next tour of duty was with the Co F 118th infantry at Fort Jackson, North Carolina. I reported to them July 27 '42.

The 118th was a regiment of the 30th Division, a National Guard outfit. Our regiment was separated from the 30th, and we were ordered to entrain to New York where we boarded the Batory, a passenger vessel turned into a troop ship, and joined a convoy. The voyage was interesting for several reasons: first, the officers were quartered in nice cabins; we were served excellent meals in a dining room with full proper table lay out. I need to explain that the ship's crew were all foreigners and treated officers with much respect, even lowly second lieutenants. Our trip was similar to a lovely cruise. However, the enlisted men lived under different conditions. They had cots for beds, but the worst part was the food. Our mess sergeant told me we had to do something about the meals. I stayed with my platoon and ate the slop they were fed for dinner. I tried to talk to the foreign crew about the problem; that helped a bit, but not much. One puts up with all sorts of things whilst in the service.

The convoy, escorted by US destroyers, zigzagged over the North Atlantic for a number of days. The zigzag course was to avoid any U Boat attacks. Once, while doing some exercises on the deck, two large anti-aircraft guns on an upper deck opened fire and startled the hell out of us. No one told us about gunnery practice.

The Batory left the convoy and slid into Eyjafjord and traveled almost to the end of the Fjord, and on August 19, 1942, dropped anchor at the village of Akureyri on the north coast of Iceland. Can you imagine coming from all those hot states in the south to Iceland in the middle of August. It was a bit of a change, but the summers in Iceland were not cold. As I recall, summer came on a Tuesday that year.

As we disembarked, I remember seeing a large, blond haired young man peddling his bike around on the dock. He was the first Icelander I saw and I was impressed. Most of us made the long voyage in good physical condition, and I'm sure the enlisted men were looking forward to some good food. I do have to mention that Lt. Jim Martin was seasick the whole trip, and when he came down the gang plank, he could barely carry his bag, so one of us offered to carry his 45 pistol to lighten his load— anything to help a buddy out.

Trucks arrived and drove us on a dirt road to camp Lonsbrue, which was to be F Company's home for a number of months. We were about four miles out of Akureyri. All inside activities took place in Quonset huts, those buildings that resemble a rainspout upside down: we lived in them, ate in them, went to church in them, had lectures in them, and watched movies in them. Well, you get the picture.

Our regiment relieved the British in Northern Iceland. The Brits occupied Iceland at the beginning of the war to prevent the Germans from using the fjords for their U boats. I suspect, though, that they occasionally did use them to surface at night and make any adjustments necessary.

When we arrived at Lonsbrue, two British officers greeted us and gave us a tour of the camp. The captain, a very sturdily built gentleman, walked with our company commander, captain Eison, and I walked with the British Lt. I remarked to him, "The captain seems to be an excellent officer and certainly appears to be in good physical condition." He replied, "Oh, indeed he is, and he insists that we keep up our exercises and climb the mountain once a week." I enquired, "What does he weigh?" The lieutenant. said, "He weighs 15 stones and all muscle." I was puzzled to say the least and said, "What do you mean stones?" He answered, "Aw, that's right; you Yanks don't use that weight measure. You see, a stone equals 14 pounds, so if you want to get the captains weight in pounds multiply 14 x 15 and it rounds out to 210 pounds." Well, well, learn something every day. I was up to thirteen stones in a few months.

Following our walk and the detailed explanation of

Lonsbrue, the captain left. The lieutenant remained with us for a week in case we had further questions about the camp. I saw his batman bring him a cup of tea first thing in the morning. I didn't think our orderly would do that.

We set about moving in. We knew the workings of camp perfectly in less than a week and discovered the mess hall was too small to seat the whole company. Captain Eison called our battalion commander who contacted the army corps of engineers and within three weeks we had a very nice large mess hall, which was used for many activities besides feeding the troops, including movies, classes and lectures, and church service. Speaking of church, F company's church day was Wednesday; each camp would have a different day for Sunday to be sure that troops were available every day of the week.

In Iceland, infantry troops performed many jobs we had never done before, such as reporting to the quay with thirty men and unloading telephone poles off a boat. In the winter, the holds in the ships were very cold—an unpleasant task. We also reported to the food distributing building and helped separate the food and load it on trucks to be delivered to the companies.

The training in Iceland was much the same as we did in the States. We had company problems, platoon in the attack, squad problems, long hikes, short ones, and the firing range. When it came to the firing range, private Henry said, "Lootenant, there's just no use me goin' out there shootin' this damn gun. I cain't hit the side of a barn." I answered, "Come on now, we're going to do triangulations and when we get on the range, we'll take our time; you'll do okay." He replied, "If I get any better, I'll low know sompin," his favorite expression. His first day he boloed again, the second he got better, and by the end of our session on the range he was sharpshooter. He couldn't believe it; he kept saying, "I made sharpshooter How'd I do it?

Sharpshooter by golly. Yeah, I low know sompin'." We asked, "What do you low know?" He replied, "Jus don't give up; keep a tryin', keep tryin'." The rest of us had been pulling for him so hard that he made us happy as well: very good for our morale.

I'm going to make a switch at this time and write, verbatim, from a diary I received for Christmas 1942. The selections I chose from the diary explain our training and social life from the time we arrived in Iceland, though the diary was not started until the winter; in Iceland the sun is seen about two hours a day, if that much. So here we go.

I received a diary for Christmas from the one and only Arlee Steere. Being in possession of a diary, I see nothing to do but jot down a few incidents, which took place on this island. This is done for a purely selfish motive. I have no other in mind than the fact that I get a few hours of enjoyment by reminiscing over the odd things that happened to a soldier. I am writing this for my own amazement and also as a note to show people who will not believe my tails (I wonder what my mind could be on that I should spell that word in that manner). I like the truth, of course some exaggeration is permitted, but it must be basically the truth. TO THE TRUTH!

Jan. 2, 1943: From here on I'll delete the '43. First, I must go back to New Year's Eve. I went to the hospital and visited some of my men. Then I went around to the dance the nurses were throwing. Everybody was having a good time, what with a shipment of liquor in. It made everyone quite friendly. Me, I stayed cold sober because of a detail the following day—damn it. Very drunk out tonight.

Jan. 1, New Years Day: Unloaded telephone poles from 8AM to 7PM; had dinner with Lt. Vallelonga, a good Joseph. Damn near froze down in the hold; General's idea, one officer in each hold. I can think of better ways for spending New Years Day.

Jan. 2: Here we are, up to date; nothing new, cold as hell, followed inclement weather schedule. Saw a show tonight,

"Yokel Boy." Entertaining; I get a boot out of Joan Davis, and Albert Dekker was good too. These shows are practically the only entertainment we have and they're worth their weight in gold. Got a couple of letters today. God bless them! You may have Iceland.

Jan. 3: Got up to go on detail, it was called off. Carried on with training. This afternoon had a patrol problem, made up triangles, gave the men yards and azimuth and let them carry on from there. Most of them came within fifty yards of the point. Not bad considering difficulty with compasses here. The declination is 18 degrees off true north. Dropped about fifty Kroners in a black jack game this evening. I'll get it back sometime. I'm D.O. tonight; that's a pain in the tokus.

Jan. 4: Same old stuff, this morning had some work on target designation, range estimation. Men need some more work on that. This PM had eight men for training. I told them to go do their laundry. After supper had NCO school. Captain Eison lectured on coordination of field artillery and infantry—interesting at times. I dropped 30 K's to the good capn' in a casino game. This is getting to be a habit.

Jan. 5: Inspection this morning, the Colonel himself paid us a visit, found most things to his liking. Major McKeown was also here and he stayed for dinner. This afternoon Doc. Hall had physical inspection, so I took a shower. It was a darned good one, plenty of hot water, but the trip down is awfully rough in this cold weather. It is 11 degrees below today. I started wearing my long johns. Doc, Lt. Smoak and I had a domino game. The boys took lessons from me. Too bad it was free gratis. Had a show tonight, "Courtship of Andy Hardy." Very entertaining. Beautiful night out, it makes me think of love, but where does thinkin' get you?

Jan. 6: Rest day today, slept most of A.M. This P.M. went skating down by Lons, a very nice place. I got the skates at the Red Cross hut. Some of the boys from Wyoming are very good. This evening batted the breeze with the boys in the Orderly room. Every *subject was covered from politics to fights, lot of fun. Right leg is sore, too much skating.*

Jan. 8: This morning had security outpost, sent the platoons out then visited them using the bug for transportation. This P.M. had combat patrol. This evening had a show; two shorts shown, "Screen Snapshots," in which my old acquaintance, Vic Mature, was seen escorting Betty Grable to Maxie Rosenbloom's. The name of the feature was, "Castles In The Desert." And who played a good part in it but my good friend Ollie Prickett. Seven thousand miles from home and there is Ollie big as life. Who would have thought in this damn place I would see some of my friends. I sure wish I could hold a conversation with them. It makes me both blue and happy, if such a thing could be.

Jan. 9: Nothing much exciting, made a reconnaissance in the A.M. Major Baron was over checking on training. P.M. air raid red, no excitement. Men worked on target designation. This evening Lts. Reeder and Nylen were over. We engaged in a game of chance. I dropped one hundred K's. I must be going to be lucky in love. At nine o'clock, Lt. Reeder and I went to the Gulfoss. There was a lot of talent there in the way of women. I tripped the light fantastic. I really enjoyed myself. It's the first time I've been down there in about three months.

Jan. 10: This morning had squad in attack, this afternoon squad in defense. The captain went to the hospital for his tonsillectomy. Lt. Hubbard dropped in to let us know he would be back from the glacier day after tomorrow. He's been up there three weeks doing winter warfare training. This evening had a show, "Sing Your Worries Away." Musicals are really appreciated up here. The King sisters are quite pulchritudinous. This morning I sat up in bed and my damn cot ripped and dumped me on the floor. Oh, for the feel of a beautiful feather bed or at least a Simmons mattress.

Jan. 12: Inspection in the huts this morning, it was snowing too hard outside; fairly good inspection. This afternoon took first and second platoons around the loop a distance of about four miles. We made it in an hour and a half with no breaks and a fast pace. Commando Hawkins got a bit sick on the way due to overeating at dinner.

After the hike I went down to the Red Cross hut and drew fifteen pair of skates. I had to sign my life away to get them, but anything for the men. Don't let anyone tell you private is just a number. Maybe to some people it is, but to us who work with them they're men just like you and I or our brothers or fathers. Anything I can do to help these men spend some happy days up here, I'm going to do it. I'm writing this down so as to remind me if my duty to my men ever becomes lax, I shall give myself a kick in the tokus and get on the ball.

Let us leave Iceland for a moment. I'm afraid that quoting the whole diary as I have been doing is just as boring for you to read as it was to live it. From now on I shall just relate what I feel would be of more interest.

Back to Lonsbrue: A very nice rest day, church in the morning, followed by Lts. Stock and Hall tearing up a few numbers; Doc accompanying on the peddle organ. Got some mail today: one from the dream girl and several family members. Morale is way up today.

This day the company is all gone on details. I had the few men left dig a ditch for a pipeline to the kitchen. We'll have running water there yet. Digging a ditch doesn't seem hard work, but in Iceland during the winter the permafrost is four feet deep, consequently, pretty tough work. We got a new pump today, maybe I can have a shower here come spring. Incidentally, it has gotten quite warm here, but there is still ice all over the place. It took absolutely no imagination to name this country.

Again men on detail; had the ones left finish the ditch. In the afternoon went to Akureyri and bought some paint for the officer's mess and brooms for the men's mess. In the evening Doc Hall and I went down to the Gulfoss. I danced with a gal wearing a corset. It felt like I was dancing with a plank. There was a party there and I saw women in evening dresses, first I've seen since I left the states.

Lt. Smoak reminded me of an incident that happened a few nights ago during my tour as duty officer. Control room called and wanted me. I tore down and talked with them. Two days later we received a letter to reply by endorsement why the D.O. took eight minutes and 5 seconds to get to the phone. Smoaky tells me he'll write up the endorsement. A couple of hours later he presents me a copy.

"To so forth and so on. Lt. Stock states that he was duty officer and went to the show. During the show he received a call from control room. Having received the call, he dashed out of the mess hall like a scared rabbit, slipped on the ice and knocked himself cold for at least five minutes. Upon regaining consciousness he continued the mad flight to the orderly room and answered the phone." Two days later I found out he hadn't really sent that as an endorsement.

Had a great show tonight, "To Be Or Not To Be." Pretty too good you betcha. A great shame Carol Lombard met such an untimely end. She looked better in this picture than any I have seen her in; winkin', blinkin', and nod.

A couple of days later we were scheduled for a show in the evening. The operators dropped in around 6:30, but they couldn't get the engine that runs the generator started. After a long struggle, the film was started about 7:30. Then a fuse blew out in the projector that couldn't be fixed. They went after another projector and had a hell of a time getting it started, but we finally did have a show, "Twin Beds," at 9:30, a screwy film but entertaining in spite of itself. Came back to my quarters to go to bed, but Hub and captain had a couple of Icelandic stulkas in the captain's quarters, plus a bottle of rye and a phonograph. I don't think there is much sleep for me tonight.

Jan. 23: A new rate of march came down from headquarters; we are supposed to cover four miles in 45 minutes. That is going to be plenty hard. We did the four miles this morning at about 130 paces a minute, but it will have to be stepped up before we reach our goal. In the evening Lt. Reeder called and we decided to go to the Red Cross hut and see the variety show. It was quite enjoyable although I will go for a period of time before seeing another one. Upon making our exit the following phrase was appropriate, "Put the cover on the corncrib mother; we've shucked enough for tonight."

Took Platoons on the 4-mile march, getting ready for the big race. We covered a little over two miles in 29 minutes, and if you don't think that's walking, you should try it. Tonight we had another show, "Born to Sing," another "Babes on Broadway," but, hell, I enjoyed it. I haven't seen one I haven't enjoyed up here. I even find pleasure in seeing a shoot 'em up western. I'm easily pleased. I just had quite a nice session with my clarinet; it's amazing what playing an instrument will do for morale. I'm greatly cheered.

We had a good inspection this morning. In the P.M. we took the company up the mountain to the ski camp and had a good hard pull getting there. It's a distance of 4 miles making a total of 8 miles round trip. The trip down is a lot easier than the trip up.

This morning took the company on the obstacle course. The ice is terrible up here; the men fall down with amazing regularity, including old Morg.

Had a show this evening, "Torpedo Boat," a very minor picture, but nevertheless it was something to break the monotony of this life.

I just dropped 250 K's to the capn' in a crap game, so I'm not in too good a humor. I think I had better give up gambling until I have a change in luck, or give it up altogether. I'm afraid I'm a bit down in the dumps tonight so I'd better write it out of my system.

I'm going stale by stages; come on, Stock, get a hold of yourself.

Try to greet each day and its training, schedules, memorandums, poop sheets, endorsement notices, etc., with a spark of enthusiasm. If you feel stale, disgusted, fed up with the routine, how are the men going to feel? Even though it doesn't feel like it at times, those men look up to you. Maybe I shouldn't say up, that would be putting myself on a higher plane. I should say looking toward you and if you give any hint of your condition, the men will let down. Come on, "Jake," let's be getting some of that old indefinite stuff labeled Morale into this joint, OK? Right you are, son! I feel better now; I think I'll shave and go to bed.

All day hike today, dinner in the field. Went a ways up the mountain, got so misty couldn't see two feet in front. Snow was knee deep.

Went to the Gulfoss, had a nice time dancing with the stulkas. I think I've got a little blond on the line. Next time I go down I'll try to take her home. Came back out in the jeep, terrific snowstorm. Jugged the Capn' 50 K's.

Lot of snow and wind today, followed inclement weather schedule. In the evening played Black Jack with Lts. Hubbard, Smoak and Capn' Eison. I jugged the boys for 350 K's. I'm beginning to get back what I lost. Morale is good tonight.

Next day I grabbed a jeep and plowed my way to Sugar Beer where I had dinner with Lts. Ponick and Briggs, a couple of swell fells. Lt. Ponick hasn't changed a bit; he was going to be a very neat cadet, as he puts it, and clean up his pinks. He took some gasoline and rubbed it on said trousers, a very unusual effect was noted; instead of a few little splotches of dirt, he now had some big dirty circles on his pants, something wrong in his method of application no doubt.

The sun was out about a half an hour today, the first time I've seen it since November first. This morning took a quick tour around the loop, five miles in 73 minutes. This afternoon had training films; one of them was on 60mm mortars and an old friend from the Playhouse, Jim Seay, played the main character in it and did a good job. However I would have busted him down to yard bird for shooting an azimuth with his steel helmet on. Had a Hugh Herbert movie tonight, soooo corny, but there was another friend from the Playhouse, plump, pretty little blond, Jane Cowan. Rather amazing to see two friends in one day.

February 6: Same old training grind during the day. Went to the Gulfoss in the evening; little blond wasn't there, but several other stulkas were present. Eight of us sat around a table for two; you couldn't even see the table for coffee pots, cups, and all accoutrements.

Comments '05: This is a good time to explain why we never saw wine glasses or beer bottles in the hotels in Iceland. It was against the law to sell any alcohol just anywhere. Liquor was only sold in government stores, and only at times of national celebrations or family celebrations. The strong spirit sold was Aqua Vit. There may have been others. Those were the liquor laws when we were there. Perhaps things have changed by now.

While I'm on comments, I may as well explain how children are named in Iceland: a daughter is given a first name; my blond was named Disa; for her last name she uses her fathers first name and adds dotter to it, Disa Jonsdotter. A son would be Ingo Jonson.

Iceland '43: In the morning had platoon in attack; darn near froze me vital organ off and that's no kidding. It probably wasn't dressed left or something—pretty painful you betcha! It's like Sgt. Hawkins said, "Haulin' two inches of the vital through three inches of clothes ought to do some good, but don't do it when it's ten below zero." We received 1050 cans of beer today, so I sold some beer to the men.

I had my platoon problem today. I must say it was well attended. For an audience we had Colonel Sherbourne, Colonel Cooper, Major Baron, Major McKeown, Captain Gestefield, and Captain Eison. There were, of course, some mistakes, but that's what we have these for, so that there will be few mistakes when it really counts. I was very pleased the way my platoon responded-very reassuring. Lt. Coakley said it was one of the best platoon problems he has seen up here. Maybe his comments will help us get off that well-known list. A good movie tonight: "Pvt. Buckeroo" with Harry James on the trumpet and the Andrew sisters on vocalization.

We've had some mighty bad snow and windstorms the past week, but tonight is beautiful, very cold with a blue moon shining on the snowy mountains. The whole effect reminds me of the Valley of the Blue Moon in Hilton's "Lost Horizon."

We had an inspection with Major McKeown doing the honors. It snowed to beat hell most of the day; along about four o'clock a damn awful wind came up. It's a very warm wind, that's one consolation. We had a good steak dinner tonight and played cards after that until two .m. No one felt like going to bed due to the high wind. This is without a doubt the most changeable climate in the world. When I stepped out of the officer's mess and blew over to my quarters, there was hardly any snow on the ground. The warm wind and slight rain melted it almost immediately. Before the wind, the snow was about a foot deep. Capt. Eison weighs near 125 lbs. He jumped up during one of the heavy gusts and was blown about 15 ft. If we get any more winds like that, I'm going to tie a rope on his ankle and anchor him down or we're liable to wake up without a C.O.

Whole company on duty today, I spent the day censoring the mail. This was another boring job. Here is a brief example of what men wrote. " The news here is scarce as frog's tales and hen's teeth." In another one the writer got mixed up with his Rs and Ls, "I'm glad to hear you was elected prelliest gril in the shrit factory."

Comment '05: Officers had to read every letter the men sent home because of an order forbidding us to mention our location. That makes one feel we were on a secret mission. We heard through the grapevine that Sonja Heine was in a movie where the word

Iceland was mentioned, so we all told our folks to go see the movie. I can't remember the name of it.

Comment '05: I have mentioned that a lieutenant came back from winter Warfare Camp. That camp was a very vigorous exercise on a glacier where everyone stayed for three weeks, living in small tents with little heat and eating K and C rations, and practicing winter warfare all over the glacier on skis. I never attended that camp. Lt. Overmeyer, who was in H Company at Knightsbridge camp just up the road from Lonsbrue, had, and was so enamored with Winter Warfare that he created a simple camp up on our mountain. In our local camp every one slept in pyramidal tents, had coal- burning stoves, three good meals, and skied all day.

Sun. Feb 21: Nothing much in the A.M., but in the P.M. Wheeeeooo! Started out for Winter Camp up on the mountain at 1300 hours, got to Knightsbridge, put some coal in our haversacks, and started up the mountain. As we left K.B. there was a hell of a wind blowing. We couldn't distinguish the trail; we couldn't even see three feet in front of us. Ice particles, snow, and everything else blistered our faces. Clothing was very little protection. I ordered the outfit to turn around, go back down, a deed for which I was truly grateful, for when we got back to camp, it turned into the worst blizzard we have had here. A number of people couldn't get beyond our camp on the way to K.B.

Tonight was our night for a show, but we figured no luck. However, the operator made it through at seven, and we had our show. At the time the wind was worse than ever, we were unable to get to the mess hall due to drifts, so we had the show, "Juke Girl," in the canteen. Oh, what a deal—there was a leak in the roof right in front of us and a steady snowstorm continued throughout the performance. I damn near froze my feet and legs; even Ann Sheridan couldn't warm me up. After the show, the roads were so bad the operators stayed here.

The next afternoon we stopped at K.B. and picked up coal. I got a bag that must have weighed 50 pounds and we headed up the mountain again. On the way we gathered up stores, provisions, tents, etc. that had been left by other parties that couldn't make it. The hike was difficult because the snow would give in and you'd sink anywhere from ankles to knees. I won 400 Ks. Ah, yes, a beautiful night.

Today is the prettiest day we've had in three months, sunshine practically all day. Spring is really coming around. The next day the wind came up again and it's snowing. As I said, this place has changeable weather. We had a black jack game and I jugged the boys for 700 Ks. I believe that puts me even. Last night I heard a rumor, which I pray God is only a rumor. It seems that the Icelandic ship, the Asia, went down on the way to Rekjavik with some of my best friends, Lts. Ponik and Smoak, on board.

Mar. 1: Inclement weather, talked on various different subjects. Tonight went down to North Camp and listened to a correspondent with A.P., Pat Congor, talk on conditions in Germany at the time of Pearl Harbor, a really interesting lecture.

Next day same old crappid inclement weather, it's been snowing and blowing all this week. That rumor about the Asia going down turned out to be just a rumor. I went to the Gulfoss, all kinds of talent; I really enjoyed myself.

April 30: I've had a six-week layoff in diary writing. Nothing too exciting happened during that period; I'll give a brief resume of the events. I was up at the winter camp from March 16 to April 3rd learning how to ski. It was a great deal of fun, but at times it was some of the toughest work I have ever done. Of course, we don't have lifts to get us back up the mountain. We ski down and then herring bone back up. We had two Norwegian soldiers for our training. They were terrific skiers. One of them was called five pound because that's what he offered the whores when he was in London.

One time we were all practicing stationary kick turns with the younger Norwegian teacher standing to one side when old 5lb. came flying down the mountain and ran smack into our teacher. The officer in charge phoned for a sled to be brought up to get the teacher down off the mountain. Thank goodness he wasn't badly hurt, just a broken bone or two.

The Norwegian kept encouraging me to take a snow bath, so I did. Don't let anybody tell you that this is not something to write home about. I rolled in a snowdrift for maybe three minutes absolutely stark naked. Before I took the snow bath I was dead tired; after taking it, I couldn't feel a thing—frozen I was—not really. It is one of the most exhilarating experiences you can imagine. I advise a good snow bath before and after each meal.

Another exhilarating experience is taking a dump in a snow slit trench. The wind is blowing like hell; your body parts are freezing. You wipe your bottom and try to get rid of the tp, and it blows around and finally slaps you in the face. Oh, great! Yes indeedy, that winter camp experience was something else.

A couple of weeks later in our camp, it was warm enough to have a softball game. I think I may have scored with a stulka, at least she has been out to camp twice the past week. Hub has found himself a home, if you know what I mean, Gene. We got our ETO ribbons today. I'll be getting round shouldered with all these ribbons—all two of them.

May 2: Training as usual, but with a few complications. About 5 a.m. I aroused from my slumber with a dreadful set of cramps and an intense desire for nature's call. Afterward, I stood reveille and found out that two thirds of the camp had diarrhea. One of the men told me that in the latrine at 2 a.m. he was greeted with standing room only. Another soldier who had been making the trip at five minute intervals walked in and somebody yelled, "A regular customer boys, give him a seat." Luckily it wasn't bad and all men were feeling normal by the end of the day. It sort of helped break the monotony of life here.

Making the best of it!

Ski Patrol.

"5 lb"crashes into the Norwegian instructor.

Winter Warfare Camp in Iceland.

*Pack all
your troubles . . .*

Making camp.

*Mealtime at
the Mess Hall.*

*Entering the
Supply Room Hut.*

A couple of days later I had one of Eleanor Roosevelt's "My Day." The colonel chewed me out for not wearing a necktie. This afternoon we were coming in from a hike and the general stops his car by me and tells me to jump on the running board. Since it is a 42 Plymouth, I see there is no running board, so I say, "Sir, there is no running board." He then opens the door and says, "Get in." With which order I immediately comply. He says, "I want troops when marching in route step to be in step and walk as though they were going somewhere." We talk back and forth like that for a couple of minutes, him talking, me listening. Then he instructs me to get out and snap the company out of their stuff. I, of course, got in the last words, "Yes Sir!" Ah yes, today was truly one of great broadening experience. After today, I'm liable to remain a shavetail for the duration. Life has many pitfalls, especially for a G. I. lieutenant.

We had four stulka's out and Disa and Bibba had made us some curtains for our club and they now grace windows of Lonsbru and they look beautiful. That was damn nice of them. It touched me deeply. Went to the Gulfoss, Disa was there. We danced, talked until closing time, which is 11 p.m., and I tried to get her to come out to camp by herself, but no soap. She evidently believes in safety in numbers.

May 16: Training, storming, snowing, hailing, raining, and blowing. What a place! Off and on all day the same like this. Next day had an 18-mile hike and made it in 5-1/4 hrs, on the ball, eh, lieutenant?

May 21: Training in the morning and parade in the afternoon. Wonderful, gave me a big boost up. We were the color company and when they uncased that beautiful flag and brought it up to us, I felt chills up and down the backbone. That's the first time I've seen the flag since we arrived. Yes, indeedy, most beautiful sight I've seen in Iceland. My platoon and I were alerted today that we would move to Bragholt. Talk about an outpost, 17 miles from town, but I think I'll like it.

Sat. May 22: We took over Bragholt today; Lt. Hubbard goes in as camp commander. Not bad, I think I'll like it very much after I get used to the place. Went to bed with the sun shining in my eyes. Spent the next morning straightening up the camp. In the P.M .walked down the hill almost to the fjord to Fort George where a US coast guard group is stationed. I met some of the lieutenant fellers, a very nice bunch. In the evening am going to bed and sleep the sleep of the pure unbeguiled soul who is miles from nowhere and doesn't give a damn!

May 26: Nothing exciting; same old policing up, showed the boys at Fort George a movie. To bed at ten o'clock, this country life is getting me down. Congrats, one year as a 2nd lieutenant. Took a hike this morning and waged a war on rats in the P.M. All kinds of British boats in; Doc Rosenak got some whiskey and we all three had a cheerful little session. First whiskey I've had since New Years. It didn't taste badly, either. Today we straightened the camp in the A.M. In the P.M. I went to the village, got paid off and had my pictures taken. I hope they come out okay. Disa works in the photo shop, so I kinda' killed two birds with one stone. Last Sunday it was our turn to pull a patrol downtown, so Sgt. Harvey and I went down to report for duty. These damn patrols are pretty silly. We are supposed to see that men keep buttons buttoned, salute officers, don't hold up buildings, keep hands out of pocket, and various and sundry other items.

Sgt. Harvey and I are patrolling very hard, walking up and down streets. We go down to the quay looking out to the fjord when Lt. Lashek, who is transportation officer, drives down the slip in the amphibious jeep. He drives right on out into the fjord where he proceeds to doodle along for five or ten minutes.

He then comes back in and asks Sergeant and I to join him. We pile into the jeep and go out in the fjord were there is a British destroyer anchored, and nothing would do but we must go aboard,

*so we hove to, tied up, and stepped aboard. Then we must step
down to the officer's mess; of course now we must drink some scotch.
That was the first scotch I had ever tasted. We bat the breeze with
the commander on the ship and stood around first on one foot and
then the other. All the while I'm not feeling so good about it because
we are supposed to be patrolling.*

*Finally the skipper decides he must drive the jeep in the water
and also on land then he will have seen everything and will be
facing death with complacency. Incidentally he had the DSL,
whatever that means. Sgt. Harvey and I see our chance to get back
on shore, so we round up Lashek and three more British officers and
they drop us off on shore. The last I hear of the skipper he's muttering
to himself: "mawvelous, ripping, and I cawnt believe it."*

*On another patrol one of our soldiers, Jesus Gonzales, got in a
fight with an Icelander, and he had to have a company punishment.
In a case like this some officers sit as judges. It is not a court martial,
just a simple decision to make the punishment fit the crime. There
was one of the soldiers who was with him explaining about the
fight, and he said, "Well, this here Fishhead feller shoved Jesus, and
Jesus hit him." That kind of stopped me; I thought Jesus told us to
turn the other cheek. Ah well, what do I know!*

*About nine o'clock Monday night, something unusual
happened. We were playing bridge and the CQ came in and told us
there seemed to be quite a fleet coming in the fjord. We grabbed the
glasses and stepped outside; here come three battle ships, two heavy
cruisers, two light cruisers, and four destroyers. We were just about
to go inside when an aircraft carrier came into view and eight
more destroyers. There were nineteen ships in all. That, my friends,
is quite a fleet. Two of the battleships were American: the South
Dakota and the Alabama; some of the destroyers were American,
all the rest were British. They left early this morning. I wonder
where they are going? Do you suppose it has anything to do with
the second front? I hope so.*

June 25: An interesting happening causes tonight's diary entry. Those gold bars on my collar, shoulder, etc., have changed color; they've become silver. I knew if I blitzed them long enough I could polish them up to the correct shade. I didn't get the promotion because of outstanding work or some brilliant tactical move. I got it for serving one year as a 2nd Lt. and serving 10 months of that year in Iceland. No matter how I got it, I am now Morgan E. Stock 1st. Lt. Inf. SIR!

I'm now sporting a black eye acquired during an engagement of fisticuffs with one Lt. Hubbard. We thought we would have a workout with the gloves; I caught a sharp left hook with said shiner the result. Lt. Hubbard had a dislocated jaw, so you see we're just a couple of very tough hombres. Speaking of boxing, I have Guard Wyatt, the boxing champion of Fort Jackson, South Carolina, in my platoon. He is really a tough hombre. I would never put on the gloves with Guard.

Another day, the boys caught a wild duck that we are now in the process of training to be a tame one. After that, we are going o teach it the manual and close order drill. Out here on the Bragholt farm all sorts of strange things are happening. A sheep with two lambs has adopted our camp as the best place to live during the summer months. Of course, living consists of eating and it is bound to bring about an excretion of fecal matter. It's nothing to be playing ball and go for a grounder and come up with a handful of sheep dung. Ah yes, life on the farm presents its little problems.

I got some mail in a couple of days ago; the one and only still writes me very encouraging letters. I'm drinking two beers tonight in honor of my promotion. Such riotous living is my downfall, I'm sure.

Censorship rules have been changed; we may now tell folks our location, send pictures, and souvenirs home. I sent a sheepskin rug to sister Francie. Furthermore, I will not have to censor any more letters.

The war seems to be progressing nicely. I hope it keeps up; our motto here in the FBI, Forgotten Bastards of Iceland, "Back alive in '45!"

I went aboard the Alcoc, a British ship in the fjord, to see about showing them movies, and met several officers, including the captain. As I have related before, the first place they take you is to the wardroom or officer's mess and ply you with strong drink. I'm easily plied; I'd keep saying no thank you after the second drink, but that didn't phase them. The only way I could get them to quit was leave the boat. Actually, I didn't mind this little escapade; as a matter of fact I must go back there sometime. This is a rather weak attempt. I shall write again when I feel sharp as a marble. Good day to you!

Aug 31: Long time no write. Yesterday we were pulled in from Bragholt to Krosistadir. We now have five officers living together; it seems very strange after being used to only two officers in camp. Oh, happy day, the time has come when we are to leave Iceland. We don't know where, when, how, but we are leaving and does that make me happy. Oh, Joy and Happy, Happy sailing from this Lovely Island! I'm not going to write much tonight. I'll keep myself posted in the future. I will now take a shower. Thus endeth chapter 23, verse 17 of Stock's diary on life in Iceland.

It's not the end of Iceland yet, just the end of the diary. I must now, with the help of my Army records, remember the rest of my journey through WWII. We left Akureyri sometime in September and rode in GI trucks over a lousy road to a camp near Reykjavik, the capital of Iceland. We spent two months there doing all sorts of activities, but very little military training, mostly cleaning up the camp and other places that needed work.

The Borg, a classy hotel in Reykjavik, seemed as though it were just the place to attend and meet some beautiful stulkas. Consequently, three of us Os made the trip and walked into the Borg. It made the little old Gulfoss look very dinky. There was a big dance floor and good restaurant. The only drawback, no beautiful stulkas. We found that to be true the few times we went there. We probably just hit it the wrong nights. Anyway, we got together and sang this song to the tune of "Deep In The Heart Of Texas." "The Hotel Borg, is like a morgue, deep in the heart of Iceland. The stulkas fair, are just not there, deep in the heart of Iceland."

Before I leave Iceland, there are some interesting things I should impart to you. There were no trees in Iceland. I believe the whole battalion decided then to piss on the first tree they saw, sort of claim it, the same as dogs. When I was at Bragholt, I took my platoon to see the national forest; it consisted of about three acres of Birch trees maybe twenty feet tall. The early settlers chopped down the trees for buildings and firewood. Also, there is a bird in Iceland called the "Key Bird" about the size of the great Horned Owl. It could be spotted over the tops of mountains spreading its wings, diving straight down and screaming, "KEEEEERIST IT'S COLD!"

Speaking of early settlers, I now quote from Island y Mindum, (Iceland by Camera). "It is believed that Irish monks were the first inhabitants in the seventh century. They were, however, never numerous and moved away after the coming of the Norsemen in the latter part of the ninth century, for they did not wish to live among heathens. The entire country was colonized by the Norsemen in a few decades... Many of these Norse Vikings had previously raided Scotland and Ireland and carried away with them both men and women whom they used as slaves, and these they brought with them to Iceland, later giving many of them their freedom. It may be said, therefore, that there is considerable Celtic blood in the veins of Icelanders."

"In the year 1000 Leif Ericsson, son of Eric the Red,

discovered America, and attempts were made to colonize the east coast, both from Greenland and Iceland, but these attempts failed because of the animosity of the aborigines," Well, so much for Columbus. "In the year 1000 also, Christianity was adopted by the Althing, the legislative assembly, as the religion of Iceland."

One more comment: A group of officers were invited to attend a lecture by a city councilman, and he told us that so far this year there was one man in the Reykjavik jail. I don't even remember a jail in Akureyri. I hope they continue to this day as free of crime as they were in 1943.

GOODBYE ICELAND! I do not know the exact date; however my Army records tell me that I arrived in Scotland 4 Nov 43. Iceland is five hundred miles from Scotland, so I suppose I left the cold country about the first of November.

We sailed into the Firth of Forth at night and disembarked to be met by a number of Red Cross workers who gave us food and drink. What a pleasure to meet those wonderful folks. We then boarded a train and traveled to Yeovil, England.

On 6 Dec. 43: I was transferred to 3rd Bn. 118th Inf., still listed as platoon leader. I recall my first job with the third battalion was as Trial Judge Advocate. Thank goodness the trials I was responsible for were simple ones. Both trials concerned soldiers who had gone AWOL; therefore, all we had to do was get the first sergeant of the company to show the morning report to prove that they were not present at roll call. I do not recall the punishment, probably a couple of weeks in the guardhouse. I'm grateful there were no serious crimes during my term as TJA.

I read in my army records that I attended Instructors Refreshers Course #1 7 Dec 43 at the American School Center held in the city of Swindon. At this school I discovered that the 118th was a singing battalion not a fighting one. We came down a broad staircase and, while waiting for the dining room doors to open, we sang. "Lay That Pistol Down." That was the favorite. Then on to other popular songs or old favorites. We harmonized, sounded nice, and it was great fun.

About December first the battalion moved to Chard. This was a nice camp on the outskirts of the town, and it was within walking distance of a good dance hall and handy pubs. One of those large balloons that we thought was supposed to keep England afloat hung in the air near Chard.

My most vivid memory about Chard was the wonderful New Year's Eve dance we attended. We officers became acquainted with an older bar tender at one of the pubs, and he insisted that we accompany him and his wife to a village about twelve miles from Chard. We rode on a bus that burned coke for gasoline. The coke burner was on the back of the bus. It got us to our dance hall. We celebrated our entry into 1944 by everyone grasping the hands of our neighbors and singing, "Auld Lang Sine." That was the first time I welcomed the New Year in such a manner. I loved it. We danced a bit more, boarded our coke burner, and arrived safely home. 'Twas a grand way to celebrate the New Year.

We left for N. Ireland in the middle of January. I'm trying to remember how we got there. I believe we took a train to Stranraer, Scotland and boarded a ferry to Larne, N. Ireland, then proceeded by truck to the ruins of Lissanoure Castle, which is between two large towns: Ballymena and Ballymoney. A small town, Cloughmills, is about four miles from Lissanoure.

"The earliest record of a castle at Loughguile was in the year 1210. At an earlier date the shape was that of a Norman Keep, but that has escaped from estate maps when the present outline took shape. The castle, or fortified house, was demolished by an accidental explosion in 1847 and is now a ruin." The courtyard is still standing, and that's where our troops slept and ate. Battalion headquarters occupies a modern mansion by the lake, and that's where we officers slept and ate. Quite hoity toity living: bedrooms, pretty O's mess, and even bathtubs.

You're in the Army now!
Morgan signs up at age 21.

A big promotion.

Looking sharp.

CHAPTER 7

Louisa

THE 118TH WAS SENT TO N. IRELAND to start training troops for the 6960 Replacement Depot, we just called it the Repl. Depot. In order to start training troops we had to build a thousand inch rifle range and an obstacle course. In the evenings we would go to Ballymoney to dances. They were good with live musicians, so now we got a chance to compare the lovely colleens of Ireland to the lovely stulkas of Iceland. They compared very favorably. All are beautiful!

We officers had an orderly, Patrick Brennan, a good Irish name, who was always the first one in the outfit to find the good pubs. A week after we arrived in Ireland, Brennan informed us that there was fine pub in Cloughmills, so the following Saturday three of us O's commandeered a jeep and driver (we O's were not allowed to drive jeeps) and made our way to Maddy Patton's Pub.

The pub was just a house on the main street, and the bar was in the kitchen; however we were led straight into the parlor and plied with good Irish whiskey. As the drinks flowed we sang Irish songs, Gilbert and Sullivan songs, and some good old American songs. During this singing session, Maddy's niece, Jean Patton, walked in and announced that the Young Farmers were having a dance at the tennis hall. That brought us to immediate attention. We three O's, Maddy, and Jean, walked out of the pub and marched down the street to the tennis hall.

We were greeted by the host of the evening, David Weir, who had been in the British Merchant Marines and knew San Francisco. He welcomed us warmly and led us to the cloakroom to hang up our coats and caps. As we came back out, I looked down to my left and sitting there was one of the most beautiful girls I had ever seen. She was a blond, blue eyed, five foot three Irish wander. As the song goes, "Zing Went the Strings of My Heart."

I immediately asked her to dance, but she said, "I have to dance with this wee lad now," so I danced with Maddy Patton; she was a large, sturdy lady and easily swung me off my feet any time. There was no leading her; you went where she wanted to go. I caught sight of the Irish beauty's partner, and the wee lad turned out to be a handsome six-footer. I was not to be denied, though, for I got the next dance and every one for the rest of the night. She was an excellent dancer and thank goodness led me through "St. Bernard's Waltz, " and some tricky Irish reels. I learned her name was Louisa Adams, but I didn't get her address, so I went back to camp feeling a bit stupid.

I remembered that Dave Weir told us that he lived next to the Tennis Hall and invited us to come and see him sometime. Since the next day was Sunday, I got the jeep and driver and went to see Dave. Luckily, he knew where Louisa lived and gave me rather complicated directions, so we set off. I made it across the Main River, then I was supposed to drive along it until I came to a flax mill. Her house was across the road from the mill. Not knowing what a flax mill looked like, I missed it a couple of times.

Finally, I saw an elderly woman walking along carrying a milk can; we stopped and asked her where Louisa lived. She jumped to attention, nearly clicked her heels, and gave us a big smile with few teeth and said, "Ach aye, is it Louisa you're wantin'?" I assured her it was, and she continued, pointing to a pretty white farmhouse with a blue trim, "She lives right over there in the Kilcreen Mills house." I thanked her; she waved, clapped her hands, and laughed as though she were cheering me on.

We drove up a short lane to the house; I got out, walked nervously to the door and knocked. Louisa opened it and there she stood, looking just as pretty with her rosy Irish complexion as she did the night before. From that time on we were together as often as I could get away, going to movies in Ballymena, and country dances. I brought her to the officer's dining room a couple of times. I didn't want to bring her too often as any number of those officers would try to steal her from me. Later in our courtship I watched her milking a cow. Best looking milkmaid I ever saw.

There's always interesting things happening when one is in a different location. Across the lake from our living quarters was Shadow Camp where members of the Repl. Depot lived. Men from the 118th provided guard duty for that camp as well as our own. One night I was officer of the guard and as such inspected the guard once before midnight and once after. About ten p.m. I walked from checking the guard at the Castle and heard a noise coming toward me on the road. It sounded like puffing and slapping of feet; I immediately turned my flashlight on and saw two large badgers running very fast straight at me. I was a bit startled and feared they might run into me. I wanted to get out of their way, but they came so fast I didn't have time. They got to me and thank goodness split and ran around me and kept on going.

An occurrence on the after midnight checking of the guard requires a little explanation. Just down the road from our mansion are church ruins and, naturally, there are tombstones in the churchyard. One time during daylight I wandered into the ruins and checked the dates on some of tombstones. They were from the 1600s and on up. I had gone by the church at night and sometimes my imagination played tricks on me. This night the setting was perfect; the moon shone through the dark scudding clouds, and I started to feel the tingling hair on my neck along with a slight shiver. Suddenly there was a flapping noise, a loud squawk, and a large bird tore out of a tree by the church. Jumpin' Jasus! That really shook me; my heart beat frantically, chills up and down me spine. I walked on to Shadow Camp and talked to the guard, which helped me regain my composure.

After all our work constructing the rifle range and the obstacle course, we didn't train a single soldier. The ways of the military are sometimes unfathomable.

February, 1944 we were sent to Coleraine, which was about 20 miles from Lissanoure, to build another training facility, which we did, and furthermore, we actually trained some replacement troops on it. This move certainly made it more difficult to see Louisa, but I would get a jeep and sneak off to visit her as often as I could. By now I had met all the family, except for her father who had died before I met her. Her mother was the leader of the family. There were four brothers: Jim, Bob, Norman, and Fred, and two sisters: Sissy, and Elizabeth, always known as Lizzie. I'll try to get Sissy's real name later.

The boys all worked the farm and helped with the flax mill. The girls did the milking by hand and took food and tea during the tea breaks to the lads working in the fields. Another thing I thought was quite amazing, the girls served breakfast in bed to the brothers on Sunday mornings. Can you imagine American girls doing this for their brothers?

Eventually the brothers, except Fred, moved on to other jobs. Jim worked in the Department of Agriculture, Bob was a manager of a flax factory in Belfast, and Norman worked in construction. Fred stayed on the farm and ran it for the rest of his life. Fred and Louisa and their mother were the only ones living on the farm when I met her. The older sisters were married and lived nearby. They all visited the home, usually on weekends, and I got to know them fairly well and enjoyed them very much.

Louisa and I spent most of our time in the front room with a peat fire in the fireplace and kind of just hanging on to each other. The others in the house were very kind and left us alone. By the time April came around we took walks along the road and up a lane back of the Adam's house. There were the remains of a few cottages where some of the hired hands had lived.

Louisa found a couple of bicycles, so we rode around the neighborhood. One time, as we were pumping along, Louisa said, "Ach me lags are tired." I replied, "What did you say?" and she repeated, "Me lags are tired." (The sound was the same as the a in hat). I said, "You mean legs, not lags, don't you?" She reared back and said. "Don't you make fun of my accent," and pedaled swiftly away. I caught up with her and apologized most profusely. Never again did I say anything about the N.I. pronunciation of words. In fact I love the North Ireland lilt.

One time when Louisa came to dinner at the officer's mess she sat next to Jimmy Martin who was a nice looking small officer. Naturally, she conversed with him as well as the other officers. However the next time I went to her house she started talking about how nice Jimmy was and how good looking. Wait a minute now; jealousy raised its head. I don't need her telling me things like that, so I mentioned that Jimmy was married with five children, which was true. She didn't carry on about him anymore. I skewered him by damn!

Too soon the battalion was ordered to return to England. After a tearful goodbye and promises to write often, Louisa and I parted company. We took the ferry back to Scotland, boarded a train and journeyed to Warminster, and moved into a very nice British military compound. Shortly after we arrived there, a few officers and men were sent to Lady Sybil Phipps' cow pasture where we set up pup tents and a pyramidal for the O's.

This camp was near the village of Dilton Marsh, which is about twenty miles from Bath. Once again, we built a thousand inch range and were ready to train troops for combat.

Lady Sybil was lady in waiting to the queen, and she most generously invited us to her house. Her husband, Colonel Phipps (I never did get his first name), was retired from the British army. He was the absolute picture of a British Colonel: tall, gray hair, and a neatly trimmed moustache. We used to ask, "Colonel, you must have had a wonderful time in the army traveling to India and other exciting places." He would hastily reply, "Ah, yes, I served 27 years in the army and hated every minute of it!" He loved boxing and must have been an amateur. I had a good lieutenant friend who never boxed in his life, but I told the colonel that Benny was a good boxer. Every time we visited the Phipps, the colonel would approach Benny, take the boxing stance and say, "Come on, Benny, let's spar a bit." Then, of course, he would dance around and make a couple of jabs. Benny would cover his face and dance around a bit. That's all the colonel needed; he would stop and haul us over to the table and pour us a very good drink.

We had some wonderful parties in their lovely, large house. When the news came that a party would be held on a certain night, usually the weekend, one of the officers contacted the doctor and he brought excellent alcohol from his medical supplies. Then we persuaded the mess sergeant to give us a large can of mixed fruit to mix with the alcohol and, voila, a very good drink.

Luckily, an officer from the Repl. Depot was an outstanding piano player, so we made sure that he attended the parties. The event started quietly with everyone standing around the piano singing away and quietly sipping drinks. The piano man was playing some songs that we in the 118th had never heard, and I asked him where they came from. He told us from the musical

"Oklahoma." Well, of course, that musical opened after we left the US; we enjoyed hearing it for the first time. The colonel had dragged Benny away from the piano to go through the boxing routine.

By now the party was getting a bit noisier, and the piano man decided he wanted to join in conversations. The Phipps had two daughters, one in her twenties and a younger one fourteen. We left the living room and went out into the entryway where we could dance or talk or whatever. A large stairway ascended to the second floor, and some of us sat on the stairs watching the activities. Now there happened to be a parachute officer among us, and he climbed the stairs until he was about 12 feet off the floor then in a loud voice yelled "Geronimo!" and jumped, landing perfectly on the hardwood floor. Of course, some of the other O's tried it, though not any at twelve feet—a lot of Geronimos yelled. I'm pleased to report no broken bones. It was a good time to go home, and that was so easy; we walked down the driveway, across the road, and right into our tent for a good night's sleep.

At another party we were all gathered around the piano singing away, and Lady Sybil took my hand and gently held it while we sang. I thought oh, oh, what's going on here? A bit later a colonel that I didn't know came up, jostled me aside, returned my hand to me, and placed his in the Lady's hand. Ah well, as they say, "Rank has it's privileges." Of course, Benny and Colonel Phipps were off doing their imitation of a boxing match.

We were busy training a few replacement troops and sending them on to other units in England. There was quite a nice pub in Dilton Marsh, so we walked down the hill to the main street and slipped into the pub for a beer or ale. I was surprised to see Italian prisoners of war on the road to the village. They were never in the pub, but they were free to walk around in the evening. They were probably on a curfew. One of our GIs of Italian decent said to me that, "We Italians are better lovers than fighters." That sounds good.

There was a good movie theatre in Warminster, and we attended it. At that time in England when the film ended, everyone had to stand up while a recording played, "God save our gracious Queen," to the tune of, "My Country 'tis of Thee." Obviously, we stole the music from England.

The military compound at Warminster was a good place to be stationed. The officers had comfortable quarters, maybe five or six in a decent sized room along with toilets and showers, and slept on steel beds with good mattresses. Our place at Phipps was not as comfortable, but with the good weather and long daylight hours, I enjoyed it.

There were two activities at Warminster that lured us there. One was the Saturday night dance; girls from Warminster and Bath beautifully filled the hall. The other was the Sunday dinner (dinner at noon like in Ahia). These two activities were the idea of a new mess officer, Lt. Ed Bliss, and the best mess sergeant in the 118th, Bill Hoffman. These two created a wonderful Officer's club with an attractive bar and pleasantly lit dance hall, which was also the mess hall.

Ed and I both live in Monterey now and we had lunch the other day and he told me a story about his work as mess officer. It seems he was having a hard time getting liquor for the club, so he persuaded the motor pool to loan him a jeep. He, Bill Hoffman, the driver, and another officer drove to Scotland. They tried a couple of distilleries and managed to get cases of Johnny Walker; however, they were looking for a barrel of Scotch, so on to Glasgow.

They arrived, went to a hotel and were told there was no room. Ed is one who does not take no for an answer, so he said to the desk clerk, "I realize with the war going on things are certainly difficult; by the way do you have any problem getting whiskey?" The man replied, "We certainly do." Ed jumped right in and said, "We have a bit of whiskey and would be pleased to supply the liquor and have you join us in a party for some of your help." The desk clerk replied, "Oh, aye, that would be great." Ed and his mates got rooms.

The next day Lt. Ed told the others on the liquor quest to relax in the hotel, since he wanted to take taxi and look for whiskey alone. He gave the taxi driver a generous tip of five pounds, and said, "I'm looking for a barrel of good whiskey. Would you know anyplace where I could get that amount?" The taxi replied, "Well, noo, let me think aboot it a moment. If I go doon this street, I ken there's a mawn in a buildin' that could maybe be helpin' yez find what ye want." Ed said, "Good, show me the building, and I'll do the rest."

The driver took him to the proper building, and Ed went into the building and saw a sign that gave a man's name as a liquor broker on the second floor. Ed went up, entered the room, and was met by a man in a long black coat, a string tie, black hat, and a wooden leg. Ed immediately thought, "My God, Long John Silver, where's his eye patch?" The Scotsman told Ed to have a seat and he would be with him shortly. At that point another Scotsman with a peg leg walked in and Long John took care of him. It turned out that the liquor broker was also an administrator for the Disabled Veterans Association.

In a few minutes he turned to Ed and asked what he could do for him. Ed explained what he wanted and the gentleman said he could certainly procure the whiskey. He took him where the whiskey was located. Then he explained that the whiskey had to be diluted with water, and since, in its present state, it was colorless, he gave Ed some burnt sugar to add color. Ed then grabbed a cab back to the hotel, picked up his buddies and the jeep, returned to the whiskey storage building, loaded the barrel on the trailer and began the return journey to Warminster. It was indeed a very successful trip; all of us who drank the whiskey can add our voice of appreciation.

To return to Lady Sybil's cow pasture, life continued in the same way. My tent mates were Lt. Robert Lee, Lt. Kenny Comstock, and our orderly who was good ole Private Brennan, still searching for good pubs and letting us in on the locations of them. By this time we were receiving a ration of a bottle of whiskey once a month or so, and one time Brennan evidently couldn't get to one of his pubs, so he drank my ration of Three Feathers. I came in from an evening at the lady's house and found Brennan sprawled out on my cot quite drunk. I finally got him out and back to his tent. I didn't mind him drinking most of my Three Feathers; it certainly wasn't as good as the booze Lt. Bliss brought back from Scotland.

We began hearing rumors about the second front and were hopeful it would be soon. Every night we heard bombers on their way to Germany and other locations in Europe. Once in a while we took the train to London and saw some very good plays and saw the buskers who entertained outside the theatres. They don't have them anymore.

The English named a ballroom in one of the ritzy hotels the "American Palace," or something like that, and it was a good place to go dance with the English ladies. I remember one night I went there and had a pleasant dancing time and came outside to walk back to the YMCA where we were staying, and I couldn't see anything. One of those London fogs descended on the city. Luckily, I walked to the dance with a Norwegian officer, and he knew London, so he said, "Get back of me and grab hold of my belt and I'll lead you back." He was wearing a wide Sam Brown belt, so I obeyed his order and he got us back to the Y.

When we were stationed in Iceland, an officer received

permission to travel to England on R&R and when he returned, he told us he stayed at the Hotel Terminus in London. Can you imagine a name like that for a hotel? I think it fit that name, since it seemed to be approaching its end. However it was a cheap place to stay, so we made use of it a couple of times.

Mentioning the Terminus reminds me of the two or three times we went to London while the Germans were dropping buzz bombs all over the place. A taxi driver told us that when the buzzing stopped, to count ten seconds for the explosion. He was right on. During those ten seconds one was a bit apprehensive. I believe the buzz bomb looked down at the Terminus and said, "I'm not going to drop there; that place is done already." Thank goodness we were never near any explosions.

Things went along apace; training and visiting different interesting places. Lt. Shepherd and I went to Stonehenge, Bath (those Romans were pretty clean folks weren't they). In the meantime I was getting letters from my two lady friends, Arlee and Louisa, and replying to them. It was a bit tough making a decision.

June 5, 1944. We all felt the time was getting close for the landing in France; the number of bombers flying over had increased immeasurably. By the afternoon of June 6 we heard the Yanks had gone ashore in France. I know that we all prayed for success.

From that time on the number of troops going through our training increased rapidly, and when American casualties increased, recruits from the states arrived. We took them to the short range, zeroed them in and sent them to the front. Sometimes they were in and out in three days.

In September, John Shepherd and I got a three-day leave and flew to Belfast in a military plane. We took a train to Glarryford Station where Louisa's brother, Norman, picked us up. We dropped John off at Clough Mills, as he planned to stay there, and we drove on over to the Adams' house. We had a great time the rest of the day, a fine supper, and Norman and his girlfriend, Cissie McNeil, drove us to a dance one evening. As we came out of the dance, we noticed a crowd gathered around two Irish men, and it looked as though they were about to fight. One of them said in a loud voice, "Youse hat me!" The other replied, "I dinna hat yez." The first one said, "Yez did to hat me." Same reply, "I dinna hat yez." They did look to have been in a bit of a tussle, but with the dialogue going on it seemed they didn't wish to continue the scrap. Norman said, "Let's get out of here." I agreed, but Louisa wanted to stay on. We convinced her there would probably be no more fisticuffs that night, and we all went back to Kilcreen. There was a nice extra bedroom for me, so I had a good nights sleep.

The next day we went over to Clough Mills and picked up Shepherd. He seemed a bit shaken, and we finally got the story out of him. It seems that the folks were just getting over a death in the family, and they talked quite a bit about it to Shepherd. When they took him upstairs to his room, one of them said in a mournful tone, "Ach, he was such a dear ould mawn; he loved this room, so this is where we hawd the wake. Now I'm sure, Lieutenant, you'll have a good nights sleep, so we'll just leave you here with his pleasant memories.' Shep said, "Pleasant memories, hell. Here I'm tryin' to sleep in the bed where the ould mawn was laid out for his wake, and besides that, there were some spooky pictures on the walls. My imagination ran away with me; I didn't sleep a damn wink last night." Louisa said, "You must come and stay at our house tonight." I wondered where I was supposed to stay.

There were no empty bedrooms at Kilcreen, so I was relegated to the Adair Arms, a nice hotel in Ballymena. How come Shep wasn't sent to Ballymena? I'm sure Louisa felt sorry for him and felt being with her family would cheer him up, which was no doubt true. It worked out; we spent the days together.

On the last night in Ireland we all went to a dance in the Orange Hall. I had made a final decision: I planned to ask Louisa to marry me. I was nervous and scared, but I felt, by God, now was the time. We all went into the Hall: Norman, Cissie, Shep, and Morgan and Lou. Louisa and I danced a few times, then retreated to the car. We hugged and kissed maybe even more passionately then ever. I must have mentioned my plan to Shep, for I would just be ready to pop the question when Shep would come out of the hall and knock on the window. I'd wave him away. He did that two or three times while I was trying to get my nerve worked up to ask her. Finally, after more kissing, I said, "Louisa, darling, will you marry me?" She replied in the most lovely Irish lilt, "Oh, aye, Morgan, I certainly will." Oh, be Jasus, I was so happy; we jumped out of the car and ran into the Hall and told Norman and Cissie and knot head Shep. I'm sure the word got around to some of the dancers who knew the Adams group, for they congratulated us as we left for home. That night I slept with the Adams, and Shep slept at the Adair Arms.

The next morning I girded my loins again and sat down with Louisa's mother. We chatted about mundane things for a bit; then I said, "Mrs. Adams, I want to ask your permission to marry Louisa." She answered, "Yes, well, that's fine, if that's her wish." I replied, "Oh yes, it is; both of us want very much to get married." That was that. I arranged with Louisa's jeweler friend to get her an engagement ring; we said our tearful farewells, and departed for Warminster.

Now I had several decisions to make: first, I must write Arlee a Dear Mary letter. GI's were getting Dear John letters, and I suppose ladies at home got their share of Dear Mary's. It was a bit sad to write the letter, but I got through it. I never saw or heard from her again. Next I had to tell the Chaplain and senior officers that I planned to marry an Irish lady. The Chaplain then informed me that he needed a letter from Louisa agreeing to marry me.

Louisa sent the following letter.

```
                                          Kilcreen, Clanyford Co
                                          Antrim, North Ireland

                                          16 Oct 44

TO WHOM THIS MAY CONCERN:

                Lt. MORGAN STOCK has asked me to marry him. I have
consented and want to marry him.  Please accept this application for permission
for us to be married.

                Yours Truly


                                          /s/ (Miss) Louisa Adams
                                          /t/ (Miss) Louisa Adams

A TRUE COPY:


        Robert E. Van Houten
        ROBERT E. Van HOUTAN
        Major, Infantry
        Executive Officer
```

A Major and my company commander, Captain Corcoran, approved our request. Their recommendation was sent on to a higher authority. However, by the time General Matchett wrote his 4th endorsement in December '44, I was in France, so I had to resubmit to get back to the UK. General Matchett didn't "match it" up for Louisa and me for a while.

We continued training troops for another two months at the good Lady's cow pasture. I still went in to the noon meal and the dances at Warminster, but no more searching for a special girl. I had already found her. We received orders to proceed to France. We left England November 15, 1944, and arrived in France the next day, according to my army papers. Then we proceeded on to Compiegne in 40 by 8 boxcars left over from WWI. We were packed in like sardines, but that was all right, for it was cold as hell. We all had our overcoats on and I lay very close to Sgt. Knox. At one point the train was shunted onto a siding for a time, and before very long we saw some of the GI's running along with canteen cups in their hands. No doubt Brennan had found some wine barrels and got one opened, so there was wine for the taking. We all happily joined in. It improved our temperature and shortened the trip somewhat.

We arrived in Compiegne and were bussed to our quarters, which had been an apartment house, a good living place. We stayed in Compiegne about three days, long enough to go to the museum where the railroad car in which Hitler and a French General signed the peace treaty between France and Germany was located. There were several pictures of everyone involved; I believe I remember seeing a newsreel of Hitler doing his little jig after the signing. A day or two later, another lieutenant and I were assigned to take over an old hotel in Vieux Moulin, which means Old Mill. The village was about ten miles from Compiegne.

A few days later a lieutenant who had been wounded in combat joined us. His right arm and hand were all there, but he couldn't use them well. He had a terrible time buttoning his clothes; however he had worked out a system and got along, plus he had a great sense of humor, so he was a good addition.

Guess what our first job was. BUILD ANOTHER THOUSAND INCH RANGE! We were getting to be experts: level the firing line, set up thirty or forty targets at the base of a hill, no butts needed, and "Ready on the Left; Ready on the right; Commence firing."

There were a number of hunting lodges in our area where the wealthy and members of royalty from other European states came before the war to enjoy the hunting. Wouldn't you know that some of our Southern boys and Wyoming lads decided they should enjoy the hunting as well. The first buck they brought in was hung up, skinned, butchered, and cooked to perfection. I was very proud of them. However, they got carried away and brought in female deer and some barely beyond fawns. I said to some of the men, "Come on you guys, hell, you could practically walk up and club these young ones. From now on only bring in bucks with three or four points." They agreed.

Wild pigs also roamed the forest. Once, while on a hike, we heard grunting and pounding feet and 10 or 15 half grown hogs rushed on by us. I felt as though I were back on the farm. Of course, one of the GI's shot a boar a couple of days later. We loaded it in a jeep trailer and took it to Compiegne for Bill Hoffman to cook.

About that time another lieutenant and I went to Paris. That was great. We, of course, went to the Follies Bergere. We stayed at a hotel with a group of professional baseball players from the major leagues. They were doing USO shows for the troops. We spent an evening talking with them; they were so down home—great time. I'll try to get some of the names.

We were in Vieux Moulin when the Battle of the Bulge took place. As I recall, the battle started in late December and the Germans did well for a couple of weeks because the dense fog kept our planes grounded. However when the fog lifted, the Air force helped stop the big battle. I believe we were about forty miles from the fighting, but I got a battle star. I didn't deserve it, but if it gets me home earlier. I was right happy about it.

According to my army records, I was assistant S-3 with the Hq. 6978 Reinforcement Company of the 6960 Repl. Depot from January 31,'45 to June 3,'45. A lot happened during those months. We left Vieux Moulin shortly after the Battle of the Bulge and went to another camp. We lived in barracks there, which were fine. Many German prisoners also occupied the camp, but we had nothing to do with them. Our main duty at that camp was to train railroad officers who had been transferred from the Red Ball railroad battalion to the infantry as punishment for some kind of activity against military laws, maybe taking bribes. I don't know, I never discussed it with them. Probably some were completely innocent. We just trained them on infantry tactics.

One day the captain said, "Lieutenant, show these men how to throw a grenade," as he handed me a box of grenades. I said, "Yes sir, alright men, let's walk away from the buildings and we'll throw some grenades." Then I demonstrated how to pull the pin and throw the grenade. I walked about five yards away from the men, faced them and said " Now this time I am going to actually throw the grenade over to your right. It's ok, you'll be safe." I pulled the pin and dropped the grenade. You should have seen those men dive for the ground. I immediately picked up the grenade and threw it. It exploded with a wee pop, since it was just an aluminum grenade. This was done to show the men that if they dropped a real grenade they had about 4 seconds before it exploded, so they should pick it up and fling quickly. I felt badly about making the men hit the ground the way they did. Maybe I should have told them the grenade was a fake. On the other hand, perhaps the lesson stuck in their memory. I hope and trust they never needed it.

At this camp there was a nice mess hall, which included some French girls as kitchen help. One time I was standing in line and heard this large rawboned girl say rather angrily, "Pour quoi vous zig zig un American?" I couldn't translate the reply, but I suppose it was because she and the American desired it. There were a number of mademoiselles around the area with short hair caused by Frenchman shaving the heads of those who zig ziged Germans,

Next to the mess hall was a large recreation area where we could sit and sip a beer and mull over the days' activities, or just gossip about anything. This particular night I had decided to open a fifth of Bushmills Irish whiskey that Norman, Louisa's brother, sent me. Three or four of us had a drink, then I put the top back on the bottle so we could enjoy a drink another time. I was about to head back to my quarters when I saw a bedraggled looking lieutenant walk in. He was unshaven with dirty clothes, and his whole body was sagging. I watched him and thought that the guy looked vaguely familiar. About then, he made a body movement and straightened up a bit and I knew him. I stood up; Jumpin' Jasus, that's Norman Brooks. I yelled, "Norman, Norman Brooks, get over here!" Norman looked over toward me with a puzzled expression, then he yelled, "My God a Mighty, that's Morgan Stock, I'm a commin' to you," and we danced around hugging each other.

I reopened the Bushmills, poured us stiff drinks and asked, "Where in the hell have you been? You look like somethin' the cat drug in." He replied, "I feel like somepm the cat drug in." I said, "Let's sit down here and get caught up on our lives." He answered, "A big slug of this Bushmills and I'll get on a talkin' jag," and we certainly did.

Norman was with the 169th division that had not been in much combat before and it was one of the divisions the German hit first in the Battle of the Bulge. The division sustained a large number of casualties, and retreated quickly. That accounted for Norman's appearance. We talked on and on and finally were the last ones in the building. Then one of us said, "Here's one for mother." And threw a glass at what looked like a fireplace. We kept on with "Here's one for Roosevelt," "here's one for Eisenhower," etc., until all the glasses including the empty whiskey bottle lay shattered on the floor. Then we arose unsteadily and staggered to our quarters. I didn't see him after that; I guess he moved on with his company the next day.

We moved to another camp near the city of Soissons about the middle of April. Once again out in the boondocks, living in tents. Can you imagine, though, we did not build a thousand inch range. There was a 200-yard range on which the troops had a chance to fire their weapons at a better distance. This camp was about 70 miles from Rheims, and rumors were starting that the Allies and Germans may be meeting there to discuss surrender terms.

We hoped fervently that was the case; in the meantime we diligently worked at our job. Then Holy Moly Jesus, God, St. Peter, Mathew, Mark Mohammed, whoever else you want to thank, a peace agreement was signed on May 8, 1945. Oh my, we were a wildly happy group; probably not as happy as the brave men on the front line. I wonder if any of the Germans and Americans greeted each other on the battlefield that day. Maybe some old vet could answer that question. Anyway, it was a very joyous day throughout Europe, and I'm sure the States, even though there was still Japan to contend with.

I don't recall much celebrating in camp; I'm sure we drank quite a bit of champagne out of our canteen cups, and I remember we planned to go into Soissons the next day and maybe get some kisses from some of the French mademoiselles.

CHAPTER 8

Will It Be a Weddin' or a Wake?

HOWEVER, THIS OBNOXIOUS NEW colonel ordered us to keep right on with the training. I guess he thought if we were not working, we would run amok and Loot, Pillage, and Rape. Therefore, on May 9th, the day after VE Day, I was out in the butts, marking the targets while the soldats were firing the Bar (Browning Automatic Rifle). The butts in this makeshift range were not as well made as the permanent ones in the US. Here the engineers bulldozed a mound of dirt about eight feet high, and the targets stuck up above that.

The usual organization in the butts is to have privates marking the targets, a non-com in charge of ten targets, and an officer in charge of maybe twenty-five targets. This range had one hundred targets. Each non-com had a telephone man with him connected to the firing line, so instructions could be rapidly passed back and forth.

In order to see my targets and my men better, I had moved my ammunition box seat about fifteen feet back of the butts. It was quite safe; the bullets passed through the targets about ten feet above me. I did notice, though, that there were quite a few ricochets. I could hear them zipping and whining all day. It made me want to climb way down into my boots and way up into my helmet.

So there I was, about 2:00 p.m., May 9, 1945. The war was finished, peace was all over the land. My head was filled with thoughts of getting back to Ireland and marrying Louisa, when suddenly I felt this sharp sting in the front of my thigh about ten inches above my knee. I looked down and saw blood spurting up from a jagged hole in my fatigues. It didn't take a genius to tell me that I had been hit; I figured it out all by myself. The next step was to tell the phone man to notify the one in charge of the firing line to cease firing as this poor old Lt. sustained an injury in the butt—no, no, in the leg in the butts. Oh, to hell with it.

The problem was that I couldn't get the phone man's attention with all the racket of the firing and bullets snapping through targets. I felt I was quite calm. I said in a calm voice, "Hey, you on the phone, tell 'em to stop firing." He answered, " Whaj ya say lootenant?" I repeated quite a bit louder, "Tell em I been hit; stop firing." He answered the same way, "Whaj..." Jasus, shit! I was gonna sit here and bleed to death before I could get help. Thank God, a sharp old non-com who had just returned from combat took in the situation in a minute and told the phone man, "Get on the phone and stop the firing, the lieutenant has been hit." He then rushed over to me, cut my pants leg off above the wound, took my first aid packet from my belt, sprinkled sulfa powder on the wound, and finally slapped a bandage on it. During this whole procedure you don't for one instant think I watched the leg, do you? Not at all. I was looking everywhere but the leg. I tell you, I shall be grateful to that old sergeant for as long as I live.

The firing stopped and several of the men were standing around, and someone said, "Just like combat, the officer is usually the first one to get hit." A non-com I know and had drunk a few beers with came up to me with a very concerned look. He dug a pack of cigarettes out of his pocket, pulled one out, handed it to me and said, "Here lieutenant, have a smoke." And I replied, callously without thinking, "Thanks, Sarge, but I don't smoke." He looked a bit hurt and mumbled something and kind of stared off into the French horizon.

To my dieing day I will regret that stupid, thoughtless answer to the proffered smoke. I could just as easily have said, "Oh, God, thanks, Sarge. That's just what I need." and taken a few hungry drags on it. We have all observed that scene in countless movies. The sarge would have felt all warm and good inside; I wouldn't have this guilt trip laid on me; and the men standing around would have seen a marvelously acted scene with a beginning, middle, and end right out of a Hollywood war movie.

In a few moments, the sarge who had been acting as a medic handed me a couple of sulfa pills and someone handed me a canteen so I could wash them down. I thought I remained relatively calm throughout the ordeal, but when I raised the canteen to my lips, I noticed my hand shaking like mad and then the canteen rattled against my teeth. After a couple of quick swallows, I lowered the canteen and tried to regain my composure.

While all this is going on, I'm still sitting on the ammo box; about ten minutes had elapsed since the great event, about the time it took for an ambulance to arrive in the butts. The medics jumped out and rushed over to me with a stretcher. Now, I know how badly I was hurt, but I decided if I could stand, then there were no broken bones; so, as they say in the Bible, I girded my loins and stood. I would like miracle background music here, mostly strings and woodwinds, for Lo and Behold, I remained standing. What a feeling of relief swept over me; I felt pretty sure it was just a flesh wound. The medics insisted that I lie down on the stretcher, but I wouldn't do it. I agreed to sit on the stretcher, for I felt if I sat, I would be alright, whereas I wasn't sure what the result would be had I laid down. We made it to the ambulance in good shape, and I was driven to the hospital.

When we arrived there, an orderly greeted me and said,

"Go in that room and take off your clothes." I guess it was clear to everyone that I was an uninteresting walking wounded. I went into the room by myself, no help offered, and started taking off my boots. I removed the right one, and when I got the left one off, I noticed a lot of blood on my sock and in the boot. This had me buffaloed, for I was hit on the right leg. I thought perhaps by some strange quirk the blood from the right leg had traveled up the leg, across the body and descended into the left boot. It seemed a peculiar way to travel, but what did I know. Then I noticed the blood was oozing from a wee hole in my left calf. Obviously, I had been hit there as well, but it was such a minor wound that I never noticed it.

I speeded up the disrobing process, trusting I would not find any more leaks, and reported to the orderly. He nonchalantly directed me to a bed and asked me numerous questions, such as what outfit, name, rank, serial number, what happened, etc. I was then wheeled into the operating room and given a local anesthetic in both legs, and they spent a half hour probing for whatever was in there, without success. I was returned to my bed, and informed by the doctor that I was to remain flat on my back until the body grew a protective covering around the bullet fragments. Evidently if one walks around the fragments could move and cut an artery. This bit of information kept me flat on my back for three weeks. No argument!

While in the hospital, a couple of my buddies had cut up a little matchbox, and painted it purple. At the presentation they pinned the heart on with great dignity and kissed me on both cheeks. Well, when in France! So I got my fake purple heart.

My three weeks were up and the Doc walked in and said, "Okay, you can go now; you're discharged." I hadn't even set foot on the floor in three weeks and he says, "Go back to your unit." I can still feel the needles in my feet when I first stepped onto the floor. The hospital I was leaving was the 49th Field

Hospital, the same number as the one in Iceland. I didn't recognize anyone from Iceland in this hospital.

Before leaving this compelling story about my big wound, I will include reports from me, officers on the range, and a report from Headquarters of the 6960th Reinforcement depot.

C-O-N-F-I-D-E-N-T-I-A-L

15 May 1945

On 10 May 1945 at approximately 1515 hours 1st Lt Morgan E Stock, O-1284421, was brought by 6930th Reinforcement Battalion Dispensary in the 7th Regiment emergency ambulance. While on the D&R Range he had received a bullet wound in his right thigh. Emergency medical treatment had been administered on the range and no further treatment was necessary at the time. A blank Medical Department Form # 52-B was given the ambulance driver to be filled in for admission of the Lieutenant to the 49th Field Hospital, and he was immediately evacuated to this hospital.

He did not appear to be under the influence of either alcohol or narcotics.

W. S. Graf
Capt MC
6930 Bn Surgeon

```
                    1ST HOSPITALIZATION UNIT
                       49th FIELD HOSPITAL
                            APO 513
                                                    GGL/wjs
                                                    17 May 1945

SUBJECT:  Medical Statement on Stock, Morgan E. 1st/Lt.

TO      :  Commanding General, 6960th Reinforcement Depot (Prov) APO 269, US Army.


     1.  NBI wound, sharpnel, puncture, moderately severe, anterior surface,
middle third right thigh.

          NBI wound, sharpnel, puncture, moderately severe, upper third, left
leg.

     2.  AI about 1600 hours 9 May 1945, at Camp De Mailly, France, on range
KD72, target 31, while in setting position in target pit, bullet fragments
richouneted off target butts.

     3.  Sobority:  Sober.

     4.  Recovery from injury should not result in any permanent partial dis-
ability.



                                          GEORGE G. LENK,
                                          Capt, MC.
                                          Unit Surgeon.
```

```
                                                    18 May 1945


                        C E R T I F I C A T E


     I certify that I, was Pit Officer on 9 May 1945 on KD range 72 for 6975
Reinforcement Co (Prov) at about 1515 hours while controling the Pits from a
position about seven (7) feet in rear of target thirty one (31).  I was wound-
ed in the right thigh and left calf.

     I was not in a restricted area at the time I was wounded.


                                          MORGAN E. STOCK,
                                          1st Lt, Inf.
```

CERTIFICATE

15 May 1945.

Statement of 2nd Lt. Silas R. Stone, O-1825075
6976 Reinforcement Company (Prov)

On or about 1515 hours, 9 May 1945, I was conducting B.A.R. firing from the tower on known Distance Range #72. The particular exercise being fired was five rounds in short bursts. One of the telephone operators ran to the tower and informed me that there had been an accident in the pits.

I immediately gave orders to cease firing, clear pieces and move back of firing line. Requested Captain Morrison, 6975 Reinforcement Company Comdr. to send aid man to pits. Capt. Morrison agreed to investigate while I contacted transportation.

Upon the return of Capt. Morrison with details of the accident, I made report in full to Regimental Range officer by telephone.

Results of a personal investigation indicated that the embankment in front of pits was not of sufficient height to provide proper protection for pit personnel.

SILAS R. STONE O-1825075
2nd Lieutenant, Infantry

CERTIFICATE

15 May 1945

Statement of Captain Herman H. Morrison, O-1031580, 6970th Reinforcement Company (Provisional).

My Company fired the BAR, 9 May 1945 on the KD Range #72, Camp Mailly, France, at or about 1515 hours. While the men were firing bursts of two and three rounds, Lt. Silas Stone, the Officer in Charge of the range, gave the order to cease firing that there had been an accident in the pits and directed me to send my aid man to the pits. I followed immediately while Lt. Stone made arrangements for emergency transportation.

Upon arriving at the pits I learned that Lt. Stock, the Officer in charge of the pits, had been wounded in the right thigh by some sort of a missile. First Aid was administered and he was removed to the hospital at about 1530 hours.

I made a hasty investigation of such facts and circumstances as may have contributed to the accident. In reconstructing the chain of events both by questioning witnesses and by my own observation it appeared to me that a bullet had struck the crossbar of windmill target #31 from which it ricocheted downward in such a manner as to strike Lt. Stock in the right thigh. Lt. Stock's position was such that he could direct the entire pit detail. He was well within the zone of safety. It is my impression that the embankment in front of the targets of aforementioned KD Range #72 is not of sufficient height to prevent the occurence of accidents such as the one described in this report.

HERMAN H. MORRISON O-1031580
Captain, Infantry.

HEADQUARTERS (S)
6960TH REINFORCEMENT DEPOT (PROV)
APO 269   U S ARMY

C O N F I D E N T I A L   22 May 1945

REPORT OF INVESTIGATION ON ACCIDENT
INVOLVING 1ST LT. MORGAN E. STOCK

In compliance with instructions given in Par 1, SO 103, Hq 6960 RD, APO 269, 14 May 1945, and in conformance to AR 420-5 the following report is made:

1. Purpose: To investigate facts and circumstances connected with injuries received by 1st Lt. Morgan E. Stock, 01284421, AUS, AU 6930, GFRC, 6978 Reinf Co, (Prov), on 9 May 1945.

2. Brief on Accident: On 9 May 1945, at or about 1515 hours 1st Lt. Morgan E. Stock received wounds in the right thigh and left leg. At the time he was pit officer on KD range #72, sitting about seven feet in rear of target #31. The only witnesses in a position to see Lt. Stock at the time of the accident were Sgt. George E. Pett and Pfc. Ellis H. Fields. Full details are given by them in their included affidavits. I visited the scene of the accident with the Company Commander and witnesses.

3. Analysis: That Lt. Stock was sitting on a bench approximately 7 feet in rear of target #31. That he was hit by missiles after a bullet had ricocheted from the base 2" x 4" of the upper windmill target, as stated in the affidavit of Pfc Ellis H. Fields.

Major Keller, 2nd Bn., 1313th CE, certificate proves that it was possible for a bullet to hit the base 2" x 4" of the upper windmill target. That the center swivel is 7' - 5 1/8" from the ground. That the base 2" x 4" on the upper windmill target is 1' higher than the swivel or 8' - 5 1/8" inches from the level of the ground. The parapit in front of target #31 is 7' - 5 3/4" from the level of the ground.

Captain Zegolis certifies that the minimum safety height on this target is the height of the spindle or 7' - 5 1/8". That the height of the bullet impact in question was 8' - 5 1/8" from the ground. This height was well over any height of minimum requirements of the butts on any KD ranges at this depot.

1st Lt Stock certifies he was not in a restricted area at the time the injury occured.

All applicable regulations in AR 750-10 and TM #18 6960 Reinf Depot (Prov), were observed.

4. Findings:

a. All normal safety precautions were being followed.

b. There was no negligence shown on the part of anyone.

c. The subject individual was not in a restricted area at the time of injury.

C O N F I D E N T I A L
-1-

5. Recommendations:

    a. That all persons concerned be relieved of responsibility concerning this accident.

    b. That orders be issued prohibiting all personnel to be in rear of the line of targets while firing is in progress.

                                        Marsden P Earle
                                        MARSDEN P. EARLE,
                                        Lt Col., Infantry,
                                        Investigating Officer.

Exhibits "A" to "J"

APO 129, US Army
23 October 1944

SUBJECT: Permission to Marry.

TO   : Commanding General, Ground Force Replacement System, APO 413, US Army
          (Thru Channels)

    1. I hereby request permission to marry Miss Louisa Adams, Kilcreen, Glenyford,
Co. Antrim, Northern Ireland.

    2. The provisions of Circular #41, ETOUSA, 17 April 1944, and Letter WD,
24 November 1943, File AG 291.1 (11 Sept 43) OB-S-SFGAL-M, subject: "Overseas
Marriage of Military Personnel", are thoroughly understood by both parties.

                                        Morgan E. Stock
                                        MORGAN E. STOCK, O-1284421,
1 Incl.   1st Lt, 118th Infantry.
    Letter of Acquiescence – Miss Adams

201 – Stock, Morgan E. (0)   1st Ind.
Hq Co, 3d Bn, 118th Inf, APO 129, US Army, 23 October 1944.

To: Commanding General, GFRS, APO 413, US Army, (Thru Channels)

    1. Approved.

    2. I certify that from the official records in my custody and the information
available, it does not appear that the applicant is married.

                                        George T. Corcoran
                                        GEORGE T. CORCORAN,
                                        Capt, 118th Inf,
                                        Commanding.

201 – Stock, Morgan E. (0)   2d Ind.
Hq 3d Bn, 118th Inf, APO 129, U S Army, 21 Dec 44.

To: Commanding General, GFRS, APO 887, U S Army (Thru Channels)

    Approved.

            For the Commanding Officer: *George T. Corcoran*
                                        GEORGE T. CORCORAN,
                                        Capt, 118th Inf,
                                        Adj
2 Incls: 22 DEC 1944
    Added Incl 2   1030
    Incl 2 – Ltr of Recommendation – Chaplain Darkey

CHAPTER 9

The Wedding

ICALLED MY OUTFIT AND ARRANGED for transportation and staggered weakly out of the hospital to my lovely tent. The following day I went to the command officer and requested leave to return to N. Ireland and get married. By now I had gone through all the permissions from the Commanding General to our regimental chaplain, so approval came through in a week.

I sent a telegram to Louisa informing her to expect me any day, so by train, boat, and taxi, I arrived at Louisa's home on June 12, and the wedding date was set for June 14. Of course, when Louisa received my telegram, she sprang into action. First she went to .... But let's have her tell us in her own words.

We were supposed to be married at Christmas, but Morgan was a no show and for a long time I didn't hear from him. All of this gave great gossip to the locals, "He's been shot; he's off with a French woman." "Louie," they'd say, "You'd better start looking for another chap, an Irish one you can trust." I found out later Morgan had been shipped to France.

Just after I got engaged, my mother and I went to Belfast and bought my wedding dress, which we left in the shop until it was needed, as my mother said, "Sure and it's bad luck to have that dress in the house."

On June 11, I received the telegram that Morgan would be arriving on the 12th. That meant that I had to get the church and minister as quickly as possible, for Morgan only had a week's leave. I went to my own minister to arrange for the wedding, but he said he couldn't do it that fast, since no banns had been posted. When I returned home and told my family, my brother, Norman, told me to go to the car right now and we would drive to Cullybacky where the Presbytery is located. Once there we explained that there was no time for the posting of banns. Now, there was great doubt on this man's face, so finally my brother said in no uncertain terms, 'Be God, there's goin' to be a weddin' so back date those papers three weeks and let's get on with it." After a lot of talk about how unusual this was, he finally backdated the papers and the date was set for June 14.

Next, I had to go to Belfast and pick up the dress and make arrangements for the reception at the Carlton Hotel—plus get an appointment for a photo session before the reception. I then rushed back home and made arrangements for the bridesmaid and the best man (luckily that was my brother, Bob). Besides all this, I had to get new clothes for the honeymoon, make arrangements for flowers, get gloves for Morgan, and pick up the wedding ring, which I nearly forgot. And last, no time for invitations by mail, so I had to bicycle a mile down to the dispensary to phone relatives and friends to come to the wedding. By the morning of the 14th, I was a blitherin' idiot and just wished the whole thing would go away. I can say thank goodness it didn't go away.

The day before the wedding I said, "Louisa, when do we have the rehearsal?" She asked, "What rehearsal." I replied "The rehearsal for the wedding." She looked at me with disbelief and stated emphatically, "We don't have rehearsals; we just go down there and do it." Okay, I thought, we'll just by God do it.

The day of the wedding was bright and sunny, unusual for Northern Ireland. I figured this was a great way to start the marriage. I rode to the church with Bob, my best man, and finally understood why Louisa had to buy gloves for me. They are part of the marriage ritual. When I reached the door of the church, this pleasant looking lady stepped forward and extended her hand; I thought how nice of her she is welcoming this Yank to her church. I grabbed her hand and enthusiastically shook it. Then I heard Bob muttering, "The gloves, Morgan, give her the gloves." I still don't understand what this has to do with anything, but I complied quickly and we went into the church.

Those were the only words Bob uttered during the ceremony. He was a shy person, so I guess being best man was quite an ordeal for him. I must say his not talking was a bit rough on me, for when we entered the church, I whispered to Bob, "Which way do we go." No answer, but there was a slight pressure on my shoulder, so I headed down the center aisle. As we walked down the aisle I noticed a fenced enclosure at the front of the church. I believe the choir sits in there during regular services. Again I didn't know where to go; I whispered to Bob, "Where, Bob, where?" Again, no answer, but there was a nudging on my right arm, which I knew meant a sharp left turn into the fenced-in section where we stood waiting patiently.

By now the church was filling up, and I was hoping the ceremony would start soon, for I am also the nervous sort under the best of circumstances, and all things seem to conspire against you at your very own wedding. Bob's chattering teeth beside me didn't help either. I was afraid he was going to faint. I'd heard of brides fainting, but never a best man.

After what seemed a long time, although it was probably just a few minutes, the Reverend McDermot appeared from behind the organ and stood in front of us. Very soon the strains of the wedding march echoed through the church. It soon became obvious that Bob and I were not the only nervous ones at this function, for when I turned to see Louisa coming down the aisle, her bouquet was shaking like a quaking aspen. But, my God, was she beautiful. I couldn't believe my eyes or my luck. Here this dumb Yank comes over and snaps up the most gorgeous girl in all of N. Ireland. When she got beside me we calmed down a little and listened to the reverend do his part.

The ceremony proceeded in the standard manner until the reverend departed from the regular script and lectured us on some matters I don't recall. However, there was one statement I shall never forget. He said very slowly and very clearly, "Wives be in subjection to your husbands." I swear he said it. Ask Louisa. And, of course, Louisa has followed that rule religiously ever since. If you believe that, you know that pigs fly and rain falls up. Eventually we said our "I do's" and headed out of the church. When we reached the outside porch, the lady handed me back my gloves

Many of the people had gathered outside the church, and it was that sort of embarrassing moment before the congratulations start, so in order to get something going I told Louisa to throw her bouquet. She looked puzzled and hesitated a bit, so I said again, "Go ahead, throw the bouquet toward the crowd," and no doubt remembering the Reverend's admonition, she flung the flowers in the direction of some of the girls. I guess this custom isn't done at Killeymurris Church, maybe not in N. Ireland, because the girls looked absolutely stunned. They probably thought Louisa was going to rescind the whole thing right there. Finally, one of the girls picked up the bouquet and handed it back to Louisa: Faux pas number two, Morg. Now everyone congratulated us and wished us happiness. Maddy and Jean Patton, the two well-wishers who started this romance, were among them. Maddy gave me such a hug I had to gasp for breath. It was a good thing the girl gave the bouquet back to Louisa for it was needed for the wedding pictures at the next stop in Belfast.

That was a bit of a trying time; not the posing for pictures, but because of the crowd we drew when we arrived at the studio. It was on a busy street, and as soon as they saw Louisa in her wedding dress the crowd gathered, mostly women, of course. We got out of the car, and the crowd formed two lines between which we walked and nodded to the folks. I felt as though I were going to the Oscars. I heard a few words, "Oh, isn't she lovely, that's a beautiful dress, she's marrying an American." Not a word about the handsome Yank. Ah, well, cest la vie.

When we emerged from the studio they were still there and more had joined them. We managed to get in the car and close the door. Then the car would not start. Now they really oooed and aaaahed and practically flattened their noses against the window. I'm trying to smile and look anywhere but at them. Louisa is blushing a deep purple by now, and we both are wishing we were any place but here. I know now how celebrities must feel. The car finally started and we went to the reception. From the reception we sped to the Marine Hotel in Ballycastle for our honeymoon.

That was a wild month after VE day. Thank the Lord there was no Wake in France, but there sure was a darlin' Weddin' in Ireland.

Our first night together in bed was delayed a bit, for Norman had short sheeted us and folded the bedclothes in a number of ways. Finally we climbed into bed pretty well exhausted, but not too exhausted to enjoy one another's' naked bodies. The night was well worth the wait.

We spent three days at the Marine. We walked all around Ballycastle, went to the Giants Causeway, a formation of rocks sticking up like organ pipes, and took a taxi to Portrush. We just thoroughly enjoyed being together. I had never been happier. We then took the train to Belfast, and moved back into society.

We stayed with friends of the Adams family. We saw a play there, and visited many interesting places, but all too quickly my week leave was over. After a tearful farewell, brother Fred

Mr. and Mrs. Morgan and Louisa Stock.

drove me to the airport; I caught a plane to London, a train to Dover, a boat to France, and a train to Chateau Thierry.

The city has an interesting history. Attila the Hun captured it in the fifth century. In the fifteenth century, England captured it and ruled for eight years. In 1429, Jeanne d'Arc defeated the English. The city has been captured and recaptured so many times, why bother about it. The final battle was in WWI when the Americans and French held off the Germans in the battle of the Marne. There is a large monument honoring those soldiers in that battle. That's enough history.

After the accident on the range, the colonel ordered it closed—good move. Shortly thereafter, the company went different ways. I was in the group sent to Chateau Thierry. After that move, we no longer trained infantry soldiers. I suppose we were to think of ways to entertain troops there, or entertain each other, until we received orders to go home.

I was assigned to form a jazz band, so I went through the soldiers' numbers and found three saxophone players, two trumpet players, a drummer, a good guitar player, and an excellent piano player. Once again I got lucky, because the trumpet man and sax man were very good, and the drummer kept fairly decent time. That was my orchestra. While we were rehearsing, a clever carpenter built and painted very nice music stands. We finally got our first job, playing for the troops in a large tent. After the gig, we sat around and talked about it. We needed to do better. One of the sax men said he felt the band needed a leader to kick off the beat. Someone else said, "Lieutenant, you be the leader." I answered, "If it will help any, I'll give it a try." At our next gig I led the band. At one point I counted off one, two, three, four, and no one started to play. I felt right stupid, since we had a large crowd of GIs for an audience. From then on I had Vinnie Gravino, the pianist, secretly give me the proper time. He just kept his hand down by the keys and snapped his fingers. Then I started them off with the correct beat.

We had a good library of the popular songs of the day. With the war over in Europe we had a lot of requests for "I'll be home for Christmas." The audience would sing along with us. From then on I sang a few songs. My favorite was "Sentimental Journey." Having the orchestra was a good outlet for all of us.

With the war continuing in Japan, we all felt a bit concerned that we may be sent over there, but, thank the Lord, Harry Truman had the courage to drop the atom bomb and finish the war. I know it was horrible that so many innocent Japanese had to die, but think how many American lives were saved.

We had a chance to really celebrate, so we got a couple of jeeps and rode through the streets, yelling, "La Guere Finis," and drank some champagne. That was it, a very simple celebration. Maybe now we really would be home for Christmas.

We lived in a house downtown near the town square. The officer's mess was halfway up a very high hill. It was on that hill where royalty held forth for centuries, and where Jeanne d'Arc was commissioned by King Charles the second.

The Red Cross had taken over a large building on one side of the square; that's where we played most Saturday nights unless we had an order to play for this or that general's party. One night at the Red Cross, a fellow came up to me and said, "Are you Morgan Stock?" I answered, "Yeah, I'm that very fella." He replied, " I knew you in Granville High School." And he told me his name; of course, I recognized him then. Now I have forgotten his name.

We kept pretty busy with rehearsals and gigs. The rest of the time, we helped USO shows find locations to stay in for a few days; I played softball, read, and wrote letters to Louisa and home, anything to keep busy and make time go faster. I went to a few dances but my heart wasn't in it. Except one time, a French lady, maybe in her forties, danced with me, pressing very close and making sexual movements. I nearly had a heart attack. Whew! I got out of that situation quickly. I'm a firm believer in one of the commandments, "Thou Shalt Not Commit Adultery."

CHAPTER 10

Back to Louisa
and Real Eggs

IN LATE OCTOBER I RECEIVED ORDERS to pack up and report to a camp in Belgium. However, I found out I had signed for some equipment and couldn't find it; a large water bag and some other things. I don't think I was an S-3 in supply, but maybe I was. If I couldn't find the equipment, I would be charged for it. I didn't want that. Luckily, there was a corporal there who knew his way around and retrieved, some way or another, all the things I signed for. Believe me, I was very grateful to that corporal.

A driver was assigned to take me to Belgium, and we were on our way. I reported in at that camp. The day we arrived I went to dinner, and who should be there but Lt. Ponik, my best buddy in Iceland. We had a lot to talk about while we hung out for two or three days at the camp. In a short time, I was sent to camp Lucky Strike, a tent city near Antwerp. I was assigned as the leader of a group of about twenty-five enlisted men bound for Fort MacArthur near Los Angeles. The Army returned us to the post at which we were inducted. We all boarded a Liberty ship on November 5th, 1945, bound for the good old USA. According to my Army records, we arrived at Boston on November 14th. Them there Liberty ships was kinda slow!

At the Boston Harbor we left the ship, boarded Army trucks, and went to a fort outside the city. There was no one to greet us, no big parade. I suppose they had the big celebration after Japan surrendered. Anyway, we celebrated—I almost stooped down and kissed the ground.

We remained in Boston for a couple of days, had good food, and real eggs. There were German prisoners of war on the kitchen staff; that kind of surprised me; I thought they would have sent them home by now.

We finally got on the train and made an uneventful trip cross-country to Los Angeles. While sitting in the train station waiting for transportation to San Pedro where Fort MacArthur is located, one of the first people I saw was an old sergeant from Camp Roberts. We chatted a bit, then I had to leave and get on down to the Fort so I could get my honorable discharge on November 23, 1945, three months severance pay, and a promotion to captain in the reserves. Thus endeth four years and four months in the United States Army.

I called Francie and Jack and they picked me up and drove me to their home at Dorcas Place in Hollywood. I was home at last, home at last, Thank God I was Home at last! And I did make it home for Christmas.

I didn't do much for a week or so, just sat around and ate four or five real eggs for breakfast every morning, and drove old 81 all over LA looking at familiar places. What was strange, I loved driving in traffic. I never did before, but I guess the fact that I seldom drove in the Army made driving pleasurable now. I called Jack Joly and learned that he now had a restaurant on Western Avenue near Beverly called "Joly's Grill"—rather original, I thought. I drove down and found Jack swabbing out the floor. I told him it looked as though he had been in the Navy instead of the Army.

We chatted a while and caught up with one another's experiences. I talked about my marriage to Louisa, and he told me he was married to Dolly Hancock. I then asked how life in the Army treated him, and he informed me of his experiences. He went to OCS in the Quartermaster Corp. He became depressed and spent some time in the Army hospital in Pasadena, and was eventually discharged. Knowing Jack, I suspect that his having to take orders from anyone other than his wives must have really bothered him; that was not his cup of tea.

In January, I heard from Louisa; she had decided to fly to the US rather than come by ship, which was fine with me; I hoped she would get here faster that way. However, I felt it necessary to get busy with something, so I spent time at Joly's Grill. Jack and Doll were the waiters, along with another lady. I greeted people and seated them, still in my Army uniform, as my old civi clothes did not fit me at all. This was all volunteer work, but it gave me something to do.

During my pleasant work greeting folks, I noticed that an older gentleman came in nearly every night for dinner. I asked Jack who he was, and he told me he was the night editor for the LA Times newspaper. Obviously, in his position he knew a lot of what was going on around LA. One evening, he told Jack that the City was going to help finance a housing project in Griffith Park for returning veterans, and he mentioned they needed someone to run a food stand nearby for the construction workers. Jack said, "Morgan and I shall do it." I responded, "Okay, Jack, but gimme nae orders."

Jack got in touch with the boss at the construction site and scheduled a meeting for us. The boss showed us a room off of a larger building where we could open one side, install a counter, and serve the men. Thank goodness Jack had learned construction from his dad. In a week's time, we had the side hinged so we could prop it up, which gave us a good serving space, and had coffee ready to go. On a Monday morning I went out early and started the coffees; Jack went to Safeway and picked up 30 sandwiches and some soft drinks, and at noon we opened the side, ready for business. That first day we sold maybe twenty sandwiches and quite a few cups of coffee. Word got around quickly, and within a week we increased our sandwich sales to 100. After a week, the headman of the construction company asked us when we would put in a cash register, because they wanted a percentage from our business. We told him we would have the register very soon. Business improved rapidly; it kept us jumping. Again we were told to put in a cash register. We said we would. After a month, though, we both got tired of the work and sold it to a young man for $1000.00. Pretty good investment, uh?

Doll and Jack loved to go to the Santa Anita races and dine out occasionally, so I went along. I bought a jacket and a pair of pants and was stunned by the price; no more Desmond suits for $27.00. I also became a dishwasher at the grill. That lasted a week. Why in the world would an Army Captain be doing KP? I should mention that Dad was so proud of my captain's rank that he always introduced me to his friends as my son, Captain Morgan.

It was by now March, and I received the good news that Louisa was booked on a flight the next week. I immediately called a Chateau Thierry officer friend who lives in New Jersey and asked him to meet her plane in New York to make sure she made the transfer to the flight for LA.

He did his job very well, and Louisa landed in Burbank on March 26, 1946. I went to meet her, and when I saw her again, she was just as lovely as I remembered; I felt my life was now complete. We hugged and kissed, and probably embarrassing people around us, but what did we care; we were once again with one another, and looking forward to a full wonderful life together.

I took her to Francie and Jack's house and introduced her to them. We stayed one night and left the next day on our second honeymoon in good old 81. As we drove out Wilshire Blvd on the way to Highway 101, Louisa kept mentioning the large cars in the US. Of course, N. Ireland was still on gas rationing, so they didn't even see many small cars there. Incidentally, we were still on gas rationing in the US, but I guess some folks were able to get gas for their guzzlers. Anyway, we had a wonderful drive to Ventura, where we had a wonderful dinner with excellent live music and we danced the evening away.

The next day we drove on to Santa Barbara and remained there for three days. I showed Louisa the state college, which was in the town of Santa Barbara then, the Mission, and other interesting places I remembered from my time there five years ago. I introduced Louisa to the Hancocks (you recall, I took care of their children).

We then drove leisurely to Monterey (one is obliged to drive leisurely with Ole 81) and visited Jake, Grace, and by now, four children. After greetings and hugs and kisses, and introductions, Louisa and I drove around searching for a place to spend a few nights. We found a pleasant group of stucco cottages on David Avenue in Pacific Grove, so we stayed three or four nights. Amazingly, those cottages are still in use, looking exactly the same as they did in '46, and I now drive by them two or three times a week; I'm talking 60 years later.

We spent the days with the other Stocks. Jake had become a mason by day and was still a musician at night. In fact, he and Grace were playing in an orchestra, so we would go to the nightclub, enjoy the music, and dance the evening away—shades of Ireland.

Enough visiting, it was time to get back to LA and start playing the young married couple, looking for a place to live and think about making a living. We stayed with Francie and Jack for about a week. It was pleasant, however, we felt we shouldn't upset their lives; besides, we wanted to be alone in a house of our own. It took some time to find a place, and as I was still helping out a bit at Joly's restaurant, they invited us to move in with them, which we did. Thank goodness sister Kay came to our rescue; she found out that a house she and Kenny had lived in was again for rent. We immediately applied for it and were successful. It was a small house: one bedroom, a living room, small kitchen, and bathroom. There was a large front yard, so we took up residence on 220 Poppy Ave. Monrovia, California. Now we were the Young Married Couple, ready to get on with our lives; the world simply had to be our oyster!

We were not broke financially; I had bought a $25.00 savings bond every month for the three and one half years I was an officer. Plus, Louisa came over with three thousand dollars, which her mother explained was to be her inheritance had she remained in N. Ireland. However we had both been through some very poor days and it seemed right for me to look for a job immediately. Therefore, I turned to Kenny and went to work for him pumping gas in his station on Wilshire Blvd, located about a block from the 4 star movie theatre. The only problem was the twenty-five mile commute, but it was good to be busy until I found out what I really wanted to do.

Louisa knew she had a cousin living in Southern California and, through writing her mother in Ireland, finally got the address of the cousin who lived in El Monte not far from Monrovia. She called her and later we visited. She was married to David Sloan. They had left N. Ireland maybe twenty years before Louisa, so she had someone from an older generation who still knew some of the same people. Moreover, Dave and Lizzie kept their Irish lilt and helped introduce Louisa into a similar, but slightly different, culture. Thus it was that we spent quite a bit of time with Dave and Lizzie Sloan.

They had a dairy farm practically within the town of El Monte. I couldn't believe they had a dairy farm in such a small area. It was probably not more than an acre. They had a large barn in which to milk their eighty cows twice a day. They appeared to let them out in the small barnyard while they shoveled shyster the rest of the day. Dave told me he arose at 4:00 a.m. to start the milking. I'm not sure when they did the afternoon milking; I would guess no later than three o'clock. They certainly worked hard.

They also engaged in some playtime. One thing they loved to do was go to Los Angeles to a Scottish club that met once a month. We went with them several times. A piper outside the club would play Scotland the Brave, Loch Lomond, and many other Scot tunes. Eats and drinks could be purchased inside the club. Several acts entertained us; I remember one lady sang something along the lines of, "I tell ye my hearts me ain and I'll keep it that way say I." I thought to myself: I don't want hers; I have someone else's heart to cherish. After that, we all enjoyed a bit of dancing. These evenings out with the Sloans were pleasant.

The Sloans introduced us to friends of theirs who had a 1940 Packard car for sale. The price, $1000.00, seemed reasonable, so we bought it. Now we had two cars, but not for long; A friend of mine from the Playhouse was desperate for a car, so I loaned him 81 for a time. I must say that driving the Packard was very comfortable and made the trip to LA easier.

Easier yes, but still too long to be away from my bride. Consequently, I started checking around to locate a job closer to Monrovia and found one at the Davis Lumber Company on Foothill Blvd. in Pasadena. It was an eight to four job and the commute was only fifteen minutes. Much better.

Ah, yes, better for the hours, but the work was considerably tougher. I handled two by fours, two by sixes, four by fours, any size, you name it. I grabbed the wood from the saw and stacked it, loaded trucks and unloaded freight cars. The worst job was unloading fake shingles made of cement. Each package

must have weighed about 70 lbs. That labor alone took about
three days. The older, more experienced workers shoved the
wood through the saw; that was never my job. I did deliver
a load of lumber to someone in Altadena, but that was the
only time. I probably dallied too long on that endeavor. Quite
often I came home in the evening and soaked in the bathtub to
recover from aching muscles.

Things were going along well at home; we visited my
family often. Louisa got along very well with Kay and Francie
and Jack and Kenny. However, there was one small problem;
at least I thought it was small. Louisa was not pregnant yet,
and she would tell me how her sisters all had babies about nine
months after they married. Actually, we both wanted children,
so I was doing my part as well as I could. This was no huge
problem; Louisa would be disappointed for a few days after her
period arrived, but she would get her spirits up and hope for
the next time. We did go through the information that stated
the best time for intercourse to become pregnant was so many
days after her period, about a week's time. We followed that
information carefully, but no pregnancy yet.

While working at the lumberyard, I persuaded Louisa to
allow me to try out for a play at the Playhouse. I went to the
audition and landed a part. When I told Lou, she said, "Good,
how much do they pay you?" I explained that, as an amateur, I
would not get paid. She thought that was a lot of hours to work
and not get paid.

The production was a Chinese play called "Lady Precious
Stream." The part was Wey the Tiger General. I was made up
with black streaks down my face and the proper costume. I had
to stomp around stage, raising the feet very high, turn them
out and slam the feet down on the floor. It was a lot of fun; we
had a great cast, and it was wonderful to be on stage again.

One night after the performance, as I walked out to my

car, someone stopped me, and asked, "Pardon me, are you Morgan Stock?" I replied, "Yeah, you got the name right." He continued, "I'm Al Trescony, talent scout for MGM." I thought: Holy Jesus, yeah Jesus, give me a hand here. I've desired this for years. Mr. Trescony went on, "We are casting a show with June Allyson and Peter Lawford in the leads, and we need someone to play June's brother, a college football player. The way you stomped on the stage makes me think you can do it." I quickly replied, "Yes, well, I agree with you, I believe I can handle it." He then said, "There's one problem; I see you are losing your hair." I said, "Just put a toupee on me like Bing Crosby or Charles Boyer." He answered, "Well, of course, they are stars, but anyway, I'll speak to William Brady about you. In the meantime, if you do any more plays, give me a call at MGM." I said, "I certainly will, and thank you for this interview; it was a pleasure to talk with you." Jumpin' Jeemany, how about that? I could bend Shakespeare here; instead of "For the want of a horse..." I say, "For want of some hair...," a part was lost. I did a play later on and called him, left a message, and never heard from him.

In the meantime, Mr. Davis, the owner of the lumber company, knew that I had been an officer in the Army and was trying to figure out what I wanted to do. One day he called me in his office and asked me if I wanted to be a policeman. I was a bit startled with this question, and he told me he was a friend of the chief in San Marino, and they needed a desk officer. I thought, why not try it, I might like it, so I said yes. Mr. Davis called the chief and secured an appointment. The Chief interviewed me and I landed the job.

There was one slight problem; the desk officer job I would be working was an eight-hour shift from midnight to eight a.m.. Louisa and I talked it over and we decided to give it a try. I would, at least, spend some of the day and evening with her.

San Marino is a small, upscale town just south of Pasadena. I suppose it could be compare to Bell Aire, or any other place where the wealthy live. One difference was that the Big Red Car tracks still ran right down the main street of San Marino, on out to the Santa Anita race track and beyond. There were not many stores in the town. I believe there was one small clothing store on Huntington Drive. The two main places the police guarded were the Bank of America just across the street from the police station and the Huntington Museum, a national treasure.

Maybe another reason Louisa agreed that I should work at this job was because she was gloriously happy. Louisa became PREGNANT! Ah, now we could look forward to other wonderful things. We told Lizzie Sloan about our good news; her daughter was about to have a baby, so she suggested we use the same doctor. We were all set, ready to go forward with wonderful high hopes for the future.

I spent the first week with the other desk officer who instructed me on my duties: I learned how to book prisoners; if they were to go into the cells, I took there personal items: neckties, shoe laces, belts, anything they might have that could injure them, and typed a receipt for all items. I also learned how to receive and forward calls to the police officers out on the street, and, finally, how to scrub and mop the floor and the latrine. There was a lot of idle time, so I practiced my typing.

Activity on the streets was minimal during the hours I worked. However, the daytime was usually quite busy, mainly keeping traffic going along the main street. This was particularly true during the racing season at Santa Ana. I believe San Marino ran the city on fines the folks paid for speeding through town.

I had two or three incidents while I worked as desk officer: First, an officer brought in a drunk who was driving down the center railway tracks, bumping over the ties. As I took his personal effects, he kept joking with me, saying, "Oh, man, you're not taking my shoelaces away, how will I ever keep my shoes on? You want my belt? Now my pants 'll fall down. Here take my shirt, too; I'll probably strangle myself with the sleeves." Then, when I started to type the list, he turned to the arresting officer and, pointing at me, said, "Look at him. Is that guy the best you could find for this job? Here, let me back in there and I'll show what a real typist can do." He probably would have climbed right over the counter to help me, but the officer said, "Okay, mister, let's get on back to the cell," and led him away. I must certainly practice my typing.

Another time, the youngest and newest officer caught a man robbing a clothing store on Huntington Drive and brought him in, handcuffed. I went through the routine with him and the sergeant conducted him back to the cell. The young officer and I talked for a time. It was his first arrest and he needed to calm down. Just before going back on the street, he grabbed a piece of paper, wrote something, and handed it to me. He had written, "I was scared shitless!" I would have been too.

The last incident I remember was when a gentleman called me on the phone and said in a calm voice, "I wish to report that my son has committed suicide. Would you please send an officer to my home." He then gave me his address and I broadcasted the message to the officers. That was a very sad phone call. I probably mumbled how sorry I was for him.

At home, life proceeded very well. We borrowed a crib from sister Kay and bought diapers and other baby clothes. By now we could feel the little soul kicking, and we looked forward to becoming a family of three. The months flew, and in April 1947 Louisa felt the first labor pains. I called the doctor, and we went to the hospital in El Monte. She was in labor almost two days and the delivery was difficult; the doctor had to use forceps to assist with the birth, but, finally, the eight-pound baby boy arrived. We had chosen the name, Michael Patrick, weeks ago. I looked in the window at him, and he looked great, like a dark haired blue-eyed Irishman; Louisa had the blue eyes and I had the dark hair. I sat with Louisa for a time and she said I should go on home and catch up on my sleep, and be sure to send a telegram to her folks in Ireland. I went home and sent the message, "Package arrived, tassels attached." Then I added his name. That's what Lou instructed me to write.

Three days later the doctor told us Michael was not normal, that there could be some brain damage. He called in another doctor and they said the damage was severe and he may not live. This news was devastating, but one stumbles on. I don't want to get maudlin over this scene. Louisa was still in the hospital; I had a difficult time telling her, but I felt I should. We clung to each other for a time, then I went home and got rid of the crib and the rest of the baby things. Michael died two days later and I buried him in the El Monte cemetery. The next day Louisa came back to Monrovia, and we slowly put our lives back together.

I had loaned ole 81 to Jim Bandy who was living In Whittier, and at that time he and I chatted about going back to college. Whittier College had a good drama department, so for a while I considered it. However other things kept me busy, and when our tragedy occurred, Louisa and I decided to move away from the area and check out Monterey. I said goodbye to my fellow officers, we bid farewell to Dad, sisters, friends, and neighbors, and moved to Monterey in July 1947.

We lived for a short time with Jake and Grace and their five children: yeah, every year one more. I understand Grace wanted ten: Well, she was halfway there. Fortunately, Jake had just finished adding on a large bedroom and bath adobe, so we slept in that room with the three boys: Jay, Phillip, and Jackson. When nine of us sat down for meals, the table was a bit crowded, but we managed.

I planned to work with Jake and see if I was attracted to the masonry trade. I learned how to mix the cement and carry it and bricks to Jake—I was a plain old hod carrier. The first job I worked, we built a fireplace, the next one a brick wall. On the last job, Jake was working on a scaffold about ten or twelve feet high, so I climbed the ladder with bricks and mortar. I decided then that I preferred working with my head more and less with my back. Not that masons don't work with their heads; they have to solve all kinds of problems, and some of the work Jake did with stone and bricks were absolutely beautiful works of art. It just wasn't for me.

Louisa and I still had some money saved, but I felt we should keep that for a rainy day. Therefore, I joined the 52/20 Club. Translated in real terms, that meant veterans could apply for twenty dollars a week for one year. Then I looked for other jobs.

One day I walked by a local radio station in Monterey and thought I should see if there was any need for an announcer or any other job for which I could apply. I went in and talked to someone in charge and he told me there were no jobs at the moment, then he asked me if I could sing. I said yes, and we arranged for an audition time. I went home, talked it over with Grace, we worked up three or four numbers, and gave the audition. When we finished, the man listening to us ran in and said, "You are wonderful. We will put you on at five o'clock five days a week and call the program 'Monterey Melodies.' Can you start next Monday?" I said, "Certainly," and "Thank you very much." We drove home riding on a cloud.

Grace and I worked on four tunes and decided we would use a few bars of " In my adobe hacienda there's a touch of Mexico" as our theme song. While Grace and I spent our time at the station, Louisa got the fun of babysitting the Stock children. Performing was interesting; I even got a few fan letters. I sang the popular songs of the day recorded by the likes of Bing and Perry, although I don't believe they ever recorded one I sang: "Six tall slim slick sycamore saplings opossum up a tree..." etc.

The second week, I inquired how much I would be paid; the boss said, "Well yes, you should go out to some of the businesses in town and persuade them to use the show as advertisement for their products." I mumbled, " Oh, I see yes, well, I'll give it a try." Here I am, trying to sell myself, which I have never been good at. Okay, try it for a while, Morg. I did, and didn't get a nibble. Grace and I gave up our radio show in a month.

I looked for another job, and read in the paper that the roller skating rink needed someone to clean the place every day. Moreover, the best part of the job was living in a small house next door to the rink, for which we paid no rent. I made about twenty dollars a week plus a place where Louisa and I could be by ourselves. We loved it. Jake and Grace were so kind to let us live with them, but if you have ever lived with another family I'm sure you understand our joy at finding our own place. The job wasn't at all hard; I swept the floor with a large broom, cleaned the restrooms, and kept the place nice and tidy. I developed a nice steady rhythm while sweeping, almost dancing.

One day I read in the paper that Monterey was starting a Jr. college; the classes would be held from five to ten at night at the Monterey High School. Jumpin' Jasus, the light went on over my head and I said to myself, this is it, this is what I've been waiting for; I'll go one year in Monterey then transfer to the state college in San Jose and get my teaching credential. Louisa agreed, and it felt so wonderful to work for a permanent goal.

Another good thing happened in a very short time. I found another job running two mimeograph machines at the Naval

Post Graduate School from eight to four. Furthermore, it was just a short walk from our little house and I could still clean the rink. In September, I registered at the Jr. College, and life was on the fast track. The best news of all, though, was that Louisa was pregnant again.

I enrolled in three classes: US History, Zoology, and Psychology. The faculty was excellent, as was the young forty-two year old president, Cal Flint. Since there were only about seventy students, everyone knew each other, and it was most enjoyable—but hard work.

Bill Smith taught History, and Ferd Ruth Zoology. I can't remember the Psychology teacher's name. However, I certainly remember one incident in Zoology class. Mr. Ruth brought in a non-poisonous gopher snake and a lizard in separate cages. When we all arrived in class, he placed the cages on a table and told us to gather around. He then picked up the gopher snake and put it in the same cage as the lizard. The two eyed each other a while, then the lizard made a move to climb up in the cage. The snake grabbed him with his mouth and wrapped his body around the lizard. The lizard clamped his jaws on the snake just behind his/her head, and they remained in that position quite a while. Every once in a while the snake wrapped a little tighter, but the lizard hung on. Eventually, the lizard let go and the snake opened his mouth very wide and shoved the lizard's head in. The snake moved his head from side to side and, little by little, the lizard disappeared, but you could still see his outline inside the snake. I was surprised how long this took. It must have been a half hour. A most interesting demonstration although I don't think the lizard thought so.

The high school held adult classes the same time as ours; consequently, Louisa enrolled in a sewing class so she didn't have to stay home alone so much. She met Cal Flint's wife in the class and the two became friends.

With my constant work and school, we certainly enjoyed the weekends; After cleaning the rink, Louisa and I would jump into the Packard and head for the Santa Cruz Board Walk, Big Sur, San Juan Baptista, or any other interesting place, for a little R&R. We were both movie buffs, and Monterey, Pacific Grove, and Carmel had very good single auditorium movie houses. Throw in some homework, and we had busy weekends. Best of all, though, we were very happy looking forward to a new arrival in the family.

CHAPTER 11

Stanford

ICONTINUED ON WITH THE SECOND semester, and about April, Cal Flint told us that Dean Winbigler would be on campus with entry exams for Stanford University. In a day or two, I met Cal in the hallway, and he asked, "Are you going to take the exam?" I answered, "Oh, I don't know, Cal, with my high school grades and Santa Barbara, I'd be lucky to get into Podunk College." Cal said, "Do me a favor, Morgan, take the exam. It can't hurt, and, who knows, you may pass it." I said, "Okay, I'll give it a try, what have I got to lose."

The following Saturday the good Dean arrived, and four of us took the exam. As I recall, it covered many subjects; of course, the one I felt the weakest in was math, but I did the best I could. A couple of weeks later, I received a letter saying I had qualified to enroll at Stanford. I was absolutely stunned. I couldn't believe it. But, by golly, Miss Molly, this fella was jolly.

A week later Louisa gave birth to a healthy boy, David Kent Stock. Hallelujah, two wonderful happenings in one week. Louisa and David came home in a couple of days; we stuck him in his crib and were ready to become happy, caring, loving parents.

In the middle of May, I left my job at the Navy School and we drove up to Stanford to check on housing. We bought the Palo Alto Times and looked for rentals, checked out a couple of them, but didn't think they were right for us. A real estate agent suggested we try the housing office at Stanford, so we did. We got a few addresses and tried them. Sometimes the rent was too high, or the neighborhood was not right. We made a couple more trips, to no avail. I said I would try one more time, and if we didn't find anything, I would put in my application to become a regular US Army Captain under the Tomlinson Act.

The next time we tried a place on 17th Ave, just east of Middlefield Road, near Atherton. Dr. Vollert, his wife, and five children lived there in the summer time, and San Francisco the rest of the year. In back of their house was a small one-bedroom abode, and, as we went in to check it, the student who was moving out spoke to us. I asked how much it cost to rent the place. He told me twenty dollars a month, including any work the Vollerts required. Later, when I discussed the financial arrangement with the doctor, he wanted forty dollars a month. I said we could only afford twenty, and, surprisingly, he agreed. I was so glad I talked to the student before I spoke with Doctor Vollert.

With the arrangement satisfactory to us, we moved from Monterey in a week, and I registered for summer school. I took two classes, Spanish and English. I wanted to get used to the campus, students, and teachers. Our Spanish teacher was a wee lovely Latino lady, which naturally made the course more interesting. Maybe I shouldn't say such things, but it is sort of true isn't it? A pretty woman gets immediate attention, whereas, one not so pretty takes a bit longer to discover her wonderful qualities. Anyway the summer was good, and I was happy to see quite a few GIs around my age, twenty-eight or so, enrolled at Stanford. In the Spanish class, I met Russ Pomeroy, an ex-GI, and Louisa and I became friends with him and his wife, Bea.

I was required to take bonehead English, so I enrolled in the extreme calcification class, which was taught by a lady from Bakersfield Jr. College. I suspect she was working on her masters. She was a good teacher, and certainly marked up my papers with comments: comma fault, tense changes, not a complete sentence, wrong subjunctive, and many more. After one very heavily marked up paper, I wrote in the next theme that I would go up in the Hoover tower, jump off, perform a half gainer, and crash into her classroom. She must have believed me, for she gave me a B on the paper. That didn't last long. I got a D in the class, so I took a few more English lessons. I also began typing my themes. I believe that helped raise my grades a bit. Finally, I achieved the glory of receiving an A in my last English class.

A brief word about the work for the Vollert family: There was a nice pool near our house; I vacuumed the pool once a week by moving the vacuum cleaner, which sucked up the dirt on the bottom of the pool, and depositing it in a storage tank. I also put chlorine in the pool twice a week. In the evening we washed the dinner dishes. I also did other jobs around the place as the need arose.

A loaded fig tree stood in the garden, and one day Mrs. Vollert said to me, " Now Morgan, are you any good at pig ficking?" I replied, "No, Mrs. Vollert, I am not any good at pig ficking; however I am quite good at fig picking." She kinda smirked and said, "Please pick me some figs." And walked into her house.

There were five Vollert children: three boys, two girls. We got along with them well, except some times the oldest son, John, about seventeen, would imitate David if he were crying, or just be obstreperous in general. One time Russ Pomeroy was out with us and witnessed one of these incidents, and said to me, "I'd deck him." I hastily replied, "Oh, no, Russ, I couldn't do that. This place is too reasonable to live in." The last sentence reminds me of a story about Winston Churchill. He wrote in a document the sentence, " This is the sort of nonsense which I cannot put up with." Someone noticed he ended the sentence with a preposition and mentioned it to him. Churchill replied,

"This is the sort of nonsense up with which I cannot put. Is that better?" Ah, yes, to get on with my Stanford days.

I heard there was a rehearsal of a play to be produced that summer, so I went to the Memorial Auditorium ("Mem Aud") and discovered they were having a first reading with everyone present. I listened for a time; the actors were very good. In fact, the three or four years before I arrived at Stanford were called the Golden Years for the drama department because of the excellent plays and operas they produced. We may not have been as good as the Golden Years group, but we certainly had fun, and I met some of the finest folks I've ever known. More about that later.

Summer school was over and we had a month before the fall term began. Stanford was on the quarter system, which accounted for the long free time after summer school. The Vollerts kept us very busy; I tended the many camellias they planted in a large greenhouse, and did other work spading, hoeing, gardening—plus the housework. I'm not complaining, mind you, for the living expenses were so reasonable. Married veterans received $90.00 a month, and we still had a bit of savings left, so we managed alright.

The summer work ended when the Vollerts returned to San Francisco. What a pleasant feeling that was, no more washing dishes. I continued cleaning the pool because I swam in it regularly, and the owners occasionally came down on weekends.

I majored in Speech and Drama for my BA degree, and minored in History. I was lucky that Stanford gave me credit for the courses I took at Santa Barbara and MPC; that excused me from taking science and math courses. In the fall quarter of '48, all Freshmen were required to enroll in The History of Western Civilization class, which pleased me. The lectures were held in the Mem Aud to seat the large number of students.

Different lecturers spoke to us, and we observed films. We also met in smaller groups during the week. All in all I enjoyed the class very much.

It's unnecessary to discuss each class I took: that would be boring. I'll end this paragraph by saying all the professors and graduate students that taught me were good. Some, of course, better than others, but that's life. Obviously Professor Atkinson, who gave me that "A" in my last English class, was the very best.

I received a transcript of my grades, and I saw my D+ in very plain view. Would you believe that the transcript was written, not typed? Considering the transcript is about 55 years old, there was no computer back then to make the task easier.

I think what I shall do is mention some incidents that occurred in some of the classes. I didn't cut classes; these courses were not easy for me. I took notes every day and worked like hell to keep my grade average on the proper level. I was in an American History class together with a friend of mine in the drama department, Frank Wolf.. Frank was one who lived life to the fullest; he ran for student body president and just missed being elected. He was a good actor; he and I did a scene from "Death Of A Salesman" in our acting class and received compliments from the teacher and from our mates.

Frank would cut classes at times and, when a midterm came up, he borrowed my notes, perhaps even for the final exam. He would get them back to me in time for me to do some last minute work. Well, you know what happens; he gets a B in the course and I get a C, with History as my minor. I really enjoyed Frank.

Another course that was interesting was Speech Correction. We had a very good teacher who had written books on the subject. One of the rather strange exercises he had us do was pronounce our names backwards, so my name was pronounced

Nagrom Kots, a friend of mine, John Clark, was pronounced Noj Kralk. We wrote the sound of the word Phonetically: Kots was spelled Kats, the a having the ah sound as in father. The same phonetic symbol was used for Naj. We called each other Naj and Nagrom for a time. Speaking of different ways of saying things, I grew up sometimes speaking Pig Latin. Can you speak Pig Latin? was written Anca ouya peaksa igpa atinla. My name is Organma Tocksa. Oh, forget it!

Back to things of more interest at Stanford. I tried out for my first play and got a good part. I played a ghost of some famous American actor of the early 1900's in the big theatre in Mem Aud. There was also a little theatre in the building, and I acted there as well. Some other parts I played were Gaev in the Cherry Orchard, Tybalt in Romeo and Juliet (the San Francisco papers called me, "The tame Tybalt," and "The not so fiery Tybalt" —isn't it remarkable how one remembers the bad reviews?), Rodrigo in Othello (Richard Egan played Othello; he became a movie star later), Judge Brack in Hedda Gabler, A Connect Yankee in King Arthur's Court, and The Madwoman of Chaillot. There are more; I was quite busy in the theatre at Stanford.

I was an assistant stage manager for the "Oresteia," The Tale Of The House of Atreus, the one remaining complete trilogy by the first Greek playwright, Aeschylus. The play was performed in the Mem Aud and directed by F. Cowles Strickland, who taught the acting and directing classes. There were some excellent actors in the production, and after a long rehearsal period, the play or plays were ready. Opening night came and there were probably 500 in the audience, no doubt mostly history majors and drama students. The performance started at eight and ended after eleven. By the end of the play there were maybe 50 people in the audience: a long, long evening! However it was a very good experience for the actors, crew, costumer, and Strick, as we called him. He was the first director I ever saw that remained back stage during the performance. Most of us sat out in the audience in the last row to get the feel of the reactions and made notes for improvement during the run of the production.

Every fall the Stanford students put on a musical around Big Game time. That's the game between Cal and Stanford. The format is similar to a vaudeville show: skits, singles, chorus. Every one connected to the production—actors, musicians, dancers, choreographers, set designers, lighting designers, and technicians—were all students. The shows were produced by the Rams Head student club and were called The Gaieties. I was in two of them. In the first one, I played guitar and sang a song, with lyrics I barely remember, something like this, "Let me go down to Stanford, let me go down today, let me sing, let me cheer, let me drink Rosotti's beer, no other life is finer, no other life with the charm. There's no other life, like life on the farm." Another verse ended, "Send your daughter to Stanford, send her down today, because, I say, it's the only way she'll ever get a man." That refers to the fact that women were 1/3 of the student body. I don't know if it is still that way.

In the other Gaieties I played a professor who rode in on a bicycle and had a stand up comic routine. The act did well—a lot of laughs. I should have taken it on the road. I coulda been a contenduh!

I met many wonderful folks at Stanford. Shortly after we arrived at the Vollerts, we met a couple across the street, Nick Neklason and his wife whom we all called Auntie Nick. At the moment, I can't remember her first name. Nick migrated from Sweden to Minnesota. When he and his brother were in their twenties, they went to Alaska and lived in the Matanuska Valley where they started a saw mill. Eventually they returned to the states, and Nick married and settled down in California and worked as a carpenter and builder. They had a nice large house, but one thing I thought was rather amazing; Uncle Nick didn't have a refrigerator in the house. He simply built a large cupboard and left it exposed to the elements on the outside. He must have had something to prevent the rain from coming in. We spent many hours with them, particularly listening to his stories about Alaska.

The folks we were close to were married, about our age, and three of them had a child. Consequently, we were not very involved in activities that interested the younger students. Our three best friends had been in the Army.

One of the couples was Russ and Bea Pomeroy whom I have already mentioned. Russ went out for the varsity team in his second year, and David and I would go to watch spring training at one of the practice fields. When the season started, Louisa and David and I went to the games in Stanford stadium. I would get very worked up at the games. David probably slept through them. Russ was a safety and, in his final year, won the prestigious Pop Warner award. One summer Russ was working near Reno, and when Louisa and I had our month off we went up and stayed with them for a couple of days. Russ and Bea took us to a gambling casino, and I had my first experience gambling at a casino. Russ stood by me at the crap table and told me what to do and, would you believe, I won seventy-five dollars! I have never won that much again. Hell, what am I talking about, I usually lose, but never that much. By now, Russ and Bea had a baby. Speaking of babies, when David was a year old, Russ and I would sometimes toss him back and forth to each other. He seemed to love it, but Louisa saw us doing it and said never again. She was right. How horrible Russ or I would have felt had we dropped him.

I was busy practice teaching at Mountain View High School and asked Russ to come down and show the film of a game, which he did. You should have seen the girls almost swoon over Russ, and of course, the boys considered him their hero whom they would love to emulate. At the end of our four years, Russ and Bea and Louisa and I celebrated our graduation by going to a classy restaurant in San Francisco. Russ was a geologist and went to work in Colorado. They bought a home on the outskirts of Denver, and we continued to visit them, as they did us. Age makes it rougher to take the trip these days.

John Clark and his wife Darlene are another couple we enjoyed very much. John and I were in the drama department where we landed parts in "The Madwoman of Chaillot." The Madwoman sent John and me into a bottomless pit because we wanted to tear up Paris and get to the oil that was supposed to be under the city.

One of the most enjoyable activities the Clarks and the Stocks had was performing at the Bracebridge dinner in Yosemite. Ansel Adams, the great photographer, took a bit from Dickens and created the dinner at the Yosemite Lodge. There was a men's chorus from San Francisco. In the afternoon the Yule log was brought in and placed in a large fireplace. The drama students played the aristocratic family and sat on a stage above the rest of the diners. I was the clown or fool and ran around the dining room doing anything to make them laugh. John, Darlene, and Louisa were seated on the stage, politely eating the dinner. The second year, I was on the stage playing the parson and had to memorize some lines, such as blessing the Baron of beef as it comes into the dining room. At one point I forgot some lines, but, luckily, the piano player was sitting right below me and straightened me out. John finished his doctorate and became a teacher in the drama department at San Francisco State. Then he moved on to Sonoma state, and finally ended his teaching career in Illinois. We kept in touch and visited them when they were in the west, but visited less when they moved east.

Fred and Ginny Forsman were another couple we enjoyed at Stanford. Fred was in the drama department and also in the Gaieties. He did a wonderful job coming on stage in drag as a big busted dietitian advising the audience to, "Eat all your spinach and pea on your plate." Ok, I know, but that's the way of Gaieties. Fred and I were also in "Billy Budd," a very sad play based on Herman Mellville's, book. We played small parts; Fred was the Swede and I was the Irishman O'Brien.

Another good friend, Ross Durfee, played Claggart, the very mean Master-at-Arms that Billy Budd killed. The play was a real tear jerker. Our friendship with the Forsmans continued after Stanford.

I enjoyed my chance to do quite a bit of acting while at Stanford. Probably the one performance I liked the most was "Juno and the Paycock" by Sean O'Casy. The director was Hal Todd who was working on his masters. We performed it in the round on the Mem Aud stage. The audience sat on folding chairs surrounding the actors. I loved the cast and Hal's directing. He was quite firm and knew what he wanted. Occasionally, he got angry and broke his pencil. Then I would be very careful not to make that mistake again. Similar to all our friendships, we continued the one with Hal and his wife, Jo, after leaving Stanford.

I must return to the living conditions of Morgan and Louisa. When the Vollerts told us they would be down for the weekend, it was our duty to make sure the place was clean and dusted. We examined the house and found the kitchen and bedrooms to be all in order. Then we walked into the living room and it discovered that it was a mess. The fireplace was very dusty, papers were strewn around on the floor, and lampshades were askew. We looked around, thinking someone must have broken into the house. Finally we spotted the culprit. It was a small owl, sitting on a lampshade. He no doubt came down the chimney and then made the mess trying to make his escape. I finally caught him and we took him back to our place.

We tried to make a pet of him/her, but we couldn't get it to eat anything. The owl no doubt only eats what it has killed. One evening we went out, opened the box, and watched her/him fly happily into the sky.

At the end of the first year with the Vollerts, we were told we could move into Stanford Village in Menlo Park. This was the Old Dibble Hospital that had been made into apartments for married Stanford students. Staying with the Vollerts was fine, but the village was closer to Stanford, and it was pleasant to have students nearby. Sometimes they seemed almost too close, for I believe there was only one sheet of plywood between apartments. We would sit in our tiny kitchen and hear the neighbor's radio. Also, our small bathroom was next to the other neighbor's kitchen, so I learned right quick to pee sitting down. Then, too, the sex act was performed very, very quietly. With a baby aboard, we had already learned to reduce the noise. The bedroom was large enough for a double bed. The kitchen stove burned kerosene; practice made the cooking perfect. The rent was forty dollars a month. Shortly, Louisa got a job taking care of a two-year old baby girl whose parents lived in the village. The father was a student and his wife was working, so she dropped off Audrey every weekday morning. The extra money helped us get through very well.

Bob Hoops and his wife lived just a few doors from us in the village. He was an English professor at Stanford—a brilliant young man; we were good friends. He taught a Shakespeare class one quarter, and I decided to enroll. I remember getting a D on my first paper on a play we were reading. My God, that was embarrassing! I was determined not to let him see how dumb I was, so I worked like hell for the rest of the time and received a B in the course. He certainly did not let our friendship get in the way of making me work for my grade. I was right proud of him.

A community theatre in Menlo Park produced their plays at a little theatre in the village. The theater was most likely a movie theatre when the place was a hospital. I directed a couple of plays there: "The Cat and the Canary," and "The Hasty Heart." I was happy with them; I don't recall the reviews, if there were any. I certainly would have remembered bad ones.

Toward the end of my final year at Stanford, life became a bit more hectic. During spring break, I came to Carmel to write my thesis on the Carmel Theatre from 1910-1935. I decided to end it in 1935, for the first Golden Bough theatre burned down then. That made a nice ending for a thesis. I spent a week in the basement of the Carmel library reading every issue of the Pine Cone or any other paper that had material concerning the theatre. I wrote the theatre news on 5x7 cards and stuffed them in a shoebox. After spring break, I returned to the village and typed my thesis. I would hand in parts to Strickland, who was my supervisor. He would make suggestions; then I would pass the corrected part to Hilma Bowers, an A1 typist who lived in the village with husband Tom, another good friend who was working on his Doctorate in Speech and Drama. Finally, the thesis was completed and accepted.

In March of '52, Louisa gave birth to Kevin, our second son. He was delivered at the hospital in Redwood City. A couple of weeks later, Dad wrote to us from Glendora that he was coming up to live with us. Wheeeoo! Where to put Dad. We finally asked him to hold off on the move until we knew where we would be located.

Early in June I was called in to professor Heffner's office, hoping for the news that I had earned my Master's degree. Chester Barker, Doc Heffner's secretary, greeted me, and the expression on his face told me...Nothing. Did I pass or did I fail? I sat a little while and was then told to go in. Prof Heffner greeted me casually and then said, "Well, Morgan, I." He then stopped talking and looked down at my records. I thought: Oh, Jasus, I must have to take some course over again, or something else is amiss. He looked for a little while longer, then stood up and said, "Congratulations, Morgan, you now have the Masters Degree in Speech and Drama from Stanford University." Oh man, I wanted to kiss him. Instead, I thanked him heartily, retreated, and gave a thumbs up to Chester; he congratulated me and I left the office. I have often wondered if that is a routine Doc Heffner and Chester worked out for fun. If so, it sure as hell worked with me.

A short time after the meeting with Prof Heffner, I was interviewed by members of the education department and awarded the General Secondary teaching certificate. I started interviewing for jobs, and had a meeting with the Superintendent of Schools in Santa Rosa, Lloyd K. Wood. He offered me a job teaching English and drama at Santa Rosa High, and I gladly took it. My salary was $3400 a year with an extra $200 for producing a play a semester. Another friend of mine, Hap Habberman at Stanford, got a job at the University of Buffalo at $3300 a year. Teaching high school wasn't so bad.

What can I write to explain my feelings upon graduation from Stanford? Well, let's give it a try. First, I want to impress on you children the terrific feeling of accomplishment and useful learning derived from pursuing and completing a formal education. It often helps one decide on a career. Second, please be prepared for a lot of hard work, however, the wonderful new things learned and the new friends made eases the strain of the labor. Please encourage your children and anyone else on whom you have influence to continue their education. Third, there will always be down times. The best I can say about that is, "pick yourself up, dust yourself off, and start all over again."

Last, I want to say how much I enjoyed all the schools I attended. Particularly Stanford. The friends I made, the things I learned, and the fact that I could do it gave me a bit more confidence to get on with life. I know that many people never complete their formal education, but are highly successful in life. I am sure they gain the same things I mentioned with fellow workers, friends, CEO'S. Whatever your choice is, either a formal education or work right after high school, make the most of it.

The Cherry Orchard, the Stanford Little Theatre, 1950.

Hedda Gabler, the Stanford Little Theatre, 1950.

The Return of Peter Grimm, Stanford Memorial Auditorium, 1950.

Billy Budd, the Stanford Memorial Auditorium (Mem-Aud), 1952.

Mad Woman, the Stanford Memorial Auditorium (Mem-Aud), 1950s.

CHAPTER 12

Teaching

DURING THE SUMMER OF '52, Louisa, David, and I made a few trips to Santa Rosa to find a place to live. We found a new development being built near Sonoma County fairgrounds and scrounged the $700 down payment for the $5000 three bedroom home. We rented a trailer and took our bits of furniture to Santa Rosa, and stored it for a time, since our house was not yet finished. Consequently, we had to live in a motel for about a month.

Shortly thereafter, Francie and Jack brought Dad up to our motel. Almost immediately the father and mother of little Audrey announced that we should keep little Audrey for a month while they went to Alaska for an interview to work with the fisheries, which was sensible since the Audrey's father was an ichthyologist. There were now five of us at the motel instead of the original three. Life went on.

We received a call from sister Kay that they had a good couch and an easy chair we could have if we came down for them, so Dad and I rented another trailer and headed for Arcadia. That drive was the best I ever experienced with him. We talked nonstop about his life, and I'm sure much of his history I have already written came from that ride. Therefore, kids, take a long ride with your dad, or your mom, just the two of you. We arrived back in Santa Rosa with our nice gifts from Kay.

The superintendent called a meeting of the teachers a week before the start of the fall semester. He gave a good speech and the principal, Fred Dewey, spoke, along with the financial officer of the district. Everyone was enthusiastic, and this helped me feel more relaxed. Lucy Spaulding, the chairwoman of the English department, was very gracious, kind, and helpful to me during my time at Santa Rosa, as were all the teachers. I loved that group from the day I started. Three or four other new teachers were interesting and we became friends.

The first day of school, I'm sure you can believe how nervous and excited I was. At 7:30 we signed in on a time sheet at the principal's office. There were three levels of English: regular, intermediate and academic. At 8:00 I met my first class, which was a freshman regular English. I thought, yeah, this is something I can teach. I introduced myself and told a few stories and asked the students to say a word or two. Then I gave them an assignment to write a paper about what they had done in the summer.

The next hour was another English class, so I ran the same routine. Thank goodness, the students seemed happy to be back and behaved well. I had study hall at ten o'clock. This would give me some time to grade papers. However, after the first week, I was seated in study hall and the Principal came in and said, "Come out in the hall, Morgan." I arose immediately and followed him. In the hall he said, "Morgan, I want you to teach the basic math class." I replied, "Mr. Dewey, I am not very good at math; I'm not positive that 6 plus 5 is 11. I don't think I should teach the class." Mr. Dewey looked at me and said, "You have a General Secondary don't you?" I said, "Yes." He stated very firmly, "You will teach the math class starting tomorrow." "Yes sir," I said, snapped to attention, and almost saluted.

After another English class it was time for lunch. For the first week I ate lunch at my desk. A little later, Doug Campbell, an English teacher, told me that some of the men ate lunch in the basement furnace room. That was very good, for conversation flowed and humor was rampant.

Doug Campbell came through for me in a big way. I kept trying to think of some book that would get the students interested in reading. If they discovered the fun of reading one book, they just might decide to read another, and hopefully continue reading on through life. One day I asked Doug if he had any suggestions, and he said he found that the book "Gold" caught the attention of the students best. There were several copies in the library, so we used that book. I read to the students; the students read to me. I assigned pages to read and quizzed them on it. Happily, the kids enjoyed the book.

Lucy Spaulding told me to save Friday for the students to read magazines. Several of them were available: Saturday Evening Post, Colliers, sport magazines, nationally published high school magazines, magazines for the girls. All thirty students retrieved a magazine and returned to their seats, and I expected silence supreme, but what I got was the rustle of turning pages; they wanted to look at pictures. Of course, some spent the time reading. I occasionally asked them to write a theme on what they read and perhaps that made magazine day a modicum winner.

Let us now return to math, or mathz, as the Irish say. I passed out the textbooks and certainly kept one for the math professor. The first lessons reviewed the simple things that I remembered: add, subtract, multiply, divide, simple fractions. Oh-oh, what's this? Improper fractions? I needed to see a real math teacher, so I contacted Potia Patchett who taught math. She straightened me out, at least enough to help my students.

Another problem I had was the lack of an answer book. I had the text, but I had to work out the problems in order to get the answers. Finally, in a couple of weeks I did get an answer book. I would work out a problem and check the book. If my answer was correct, I could explain the procedure to the students. I hoped. Several of the students were faster than I at adding and subtracting.

Toward the end of the semester we got into simple algebra; Harvey Williams, where are you now when I need you? I trudged back to Miss Patchett. She graciously worked with me several afternoons until I got the rudiments under control.

The afternoon was devoted to drama. Glen Guymon, who was the drama teacher before I was hired, didn't produce many plays. His main interest was training students to go to competitions under the National Forensic League. There were several categories to enter: humorous interpretations, dramatic interpretations, duo interpretations, original poetry or prose, original oratory, and different kinds of debates. In fact, the year before I came, his prize student won the State championship in dramatic interpretation. However the powers that be at school thought there was too much emphasis on this activity. They wanted students to be in more plays. I was happy to oblige, but didn't get a three act play produced until the spring semester.

We kept very busy in Room 200 with the tiny stage. The students acted in scenes, did monologues, improvisations, anything to free them. Occasionally, students put on assemblies for the entire student body in the auditorium, so one way or another my drama students were getting experience.

During my first semester, we teachers put on an assembly. Glen Guyman directed us, put it together, and the cast was from different departments: music, drama-me, and two women coaches from PE. I sang a male duet with a young first year music teacher and there were comedy skits. The assembly was a real hit. The students and teachers loved it.

Spring semester I put on my first play entitled "Our Hearts Were Young and Gay," by Cornelia Otis Skinner. Lloyd Wasmuth, the art teacher, designed the set and the maintenance men built it. We rehearsed for six weeks and played one weekend. It was reasonably successful and several of the drama students had a chance to be on stage. Also, some of the students had a chance to do some technical work, such as hanging lights and running the light board. There was a stage manager and assistant, along with a prompter. We had twelve students in the cast and crew who gained theatrical experience. I was very pleased.

In the past, Playhouse actors had difficulty exiting the stage. I instructed the set builders to make sure all doors opened properly. During the performance one door did not open, so, instead of going out the front door, a couple of the actors had to exit into the bathroom. Bless Winnie McCune for taking a bobby pin and jimmying the lock so the actors could again use the door.

At the end of the run on Sunday afternoon, I suggested to Louisa that we have a dinner for the cast and crew, and, thank goodness, she agreed. This Irish lady, who never cooked spaghetti in her life, prepared the Italian dish. She learned a little about cooking the dish when we lived with Jake and Grace in Monterey and realized how great the dinners were for large gatherings, Thus began a ritual that lasted 30 years, for every show I directed until I retired. We did some large cast shows, but she just threw in more ingredients, and made a spaghetti dinner as good as any high class Italian cook.

When I retired, the Monterey Herald theatre critique, Steve Hauk, interviewed Louisa. She said to him, "Thank God I don't have to cook any more spaghetti dinners. Morgan never knew how many people would attend." True, true, all true, especially with large cast shows.

Back to the classroom in Santa Rosa: I didn't have much trouble from the kids in my classes. If you would like to read about troubles in the classroom, you should read Frank McCourt's book, "Teacher Man" There was one lad, Dan, who was rather obstreperous. I had to leave the room one time, and

I returned to notice that Dan had disappeared. The students didn't look at me; they were in on the act also. I looked around the room and on the stage, where there was a curtain open a bit, I saw a pair of feet sticking out under the curtain. I left the room for a moment and got word to Jim Dardis, the dean of boys. He came into the room and said, "It seems there is a student missing; did anyone see him jump out the window or go anywhere?" Jim then walked to the stage and said, "Maybe he decided to become an actor." With that remark, he pulled aside the curtain and there stood Dan, with a most amazed expression on his face. Jim took him down to his office and told him to return to the room and sit quietly for the rest of the class, which he did. He wasn't a bad kid, he just got carried away once in a while.

The English classes went along fine. Early on, after handing papers back that I had graded, I corrected one that Jim wrote: He was a farm boy, and when he read the corrections, he raised his hand and I called on him. He said, "Mr. Stock, I'm a farmer, and I'll always be a farmer. Now them cows and horses and pigs don't give a damn whether I say, 'we was goin' to town' or 'we were goin' to town.' You hear what I'm sayin', Mr Stock?" "I certainly do, Jim, and I know a lot of you in this class probably have the same question. Let's just stop and think a minute. You are now freshmen and I'm sure most of you will probably graduate from high school. You may decide that you might want to be something else that you hadn't even thought of in your freshman year. That's part of the reason I want you to learn the basics of English.

"There are also other reasons. Does someone care to suggest any?" A few hands went up, "Yes, Dorothy." "Well, uh, you might want to show some people you can talk right." "Good, what about you, Harald?" "I gotta talk correctly or mom gives me a slap across my face. Oh, shoot, I should have said, 'I have to speak correctly.'" "Good to hear, Harald. Yes, Phyllis." "I'm just thinking I don't want to appear stupid writing to a friend, so I better learn some punctuation, too." "Hey, we'll get right on it. Ok, Dale." "You see I might have to write a, uh, what do you say when you want to get a job?" Three or four responded, "Application." "Yeah, that's it, an application for a job. We don't own no farm, so I'm gonna have to get work some way. I might have to write sumpin' about my background. I want to do it right." "Ok, gang, I think that's enough good reasons why we should work on grammar, punctuation, conjugation, all of those basic parts that make for reasonably good English."

A high school teacher does other duties besides meeting the students in the classroom. I was advisor to the California Junior Statesmen Club. Once each semester we went to another town and met with other Statesmen Clubs. The club members played the role of the lawmakers in Sacramento. Consequently, they had to stay abreast of politics in the state. It was a good extracurricular activity.

I took three girls and three boys from the Club to Bakersfield one time. All the clubs debated different laws that the senate and assembly had before them, and I was fascinated by the knowledge of the members.

Our location in the hotel was the only bad thing about the meeting in Bakersfield. There was some kind of a conference going on at the same time, and those in attendance had rooms next to ours. Liquor must have flowed freely at their meeting, for they spent the night yelling, laughing, and using rough language. I called the hotel desk a couple of times and they tried to make them be quiet, but it was no use. Finally, around 2:00 a.m., the place got quiet, and this senior and the Junior Statesmen got a bit of sleep.

Some of the men faculty had to attend home football games, to be available if any eruptions occurred in the stands. A more pleasant activity was taking the drama club to see three one-act plays that my Stanford friend Bud Irving had directed at San Francisco State. First, we were late in arriving, but they had held the curtain for us. We saw two one-acts, which were very good, and we were watching the third one when the actress feinted so gracefully and the curtain came down. I said to the students, "Did you see how that actress feinted. It was so beautiful and relaxed; if you are ever called on to feint, remember how she did it." A minute of so after I spoke, Bud came out through the curtains and apologized to the audience, saying that the actress had actually feinted so the play could not be completed. I thought the play ended a bit abruptly. Ah, well, I told the students, remember how she feinted, but don't really do it.

I should have mentioned that we had moved into our new house the middle of September. How wonderful it was; Dave and Kevin had a bedroom, Dad had a small one, and Lou and I had nice large one. After the motel, this was heaven. Dad and I put in a lawn, a screen door, and a fence across the back yard. Farm work had taught us how to build the fence, but neither one of us was talented for the other tasks. However, we persevered and completed the job. Louisa planted flowers and a beautiful Cecil Bruner Rosebush.

That was a very happy time for us; Dad could smoke his cigars in his room or outside. Often we visited different interesting places on the weekend. One early morning in November, I was sitting on the throne and heard a loud cry from Dad. Louisa came rushing in from the kitchen, yelling at me. I rushed in where he was lying on his bed, grabbed his hand, and heard the death rattle—the involuntary last breathing. His eyes were closed. I didn't know how to do CPR, so I just kept rubbing his arm. Obviously, he was gone; so we called the mortuary, and they picked him up. I called school and told them I wouldn't be in that day. Why did I have to be sitting on the toilet when that happened; I know it would have made no difference. It just seems more appropriate to have been at the table with Louisa.

The next day I had to go to the mortuary and pick out a casket. I have a thing about horribly expensive funerals, so I picked out the cheapest one I could get. Then we sent my father's remains down to Forest Lawn near LA, where mother is buried. Everyone was very nice to us concerning our loss, so we picked ourselves up and got on with life.

I have to tell a story about lunches at the school. There was a teacher's lounge where most of us ate lunch, but there was also another place where the smokers gathered—the furnace room in the basement of the school. I didn't smoke, but I joined the smokers a few times to hear their stories.

There were some rickety folding chairs there, and it was relaxing to hear gossip and nonsense. One story told was about a group of guys sitting around bragging on their sex equipment. One said he had six inches; others gave different sizes, another one bragged how far his testicles dropped. Finally, one older member said his was so long that twelve sparrows could stand on it. The others said, "Aw, come on now, that's not true; you're really bragging." He replies, "Well, yeah, I am, that last sparrow is standing on one leg." Will you tell me why in the hell I remember that story heard fifty-four years ago? That's why I went to the furnace room.

The end of the first year was upon us. I didn't have to go to the prom, but I did have to go to the graduation and, after the ceremony, we were on an anti-kiss detail. We prowled the halls and watched the students to make sure the hormones didn't boil over.

During summer vacation, I went to the labor office in Santa Rosa and got a job cleaning out a henhouse, among a few other things. I overheard the owner of the farm saying to someone, "That fellow in the henhouse doesn't look like a farm worker;

MORGAN STOCK

I wonder what he does." I didn't say a word. The next job I
had on a different farm was lifting hay bales onto a wagon. My
muscles hurt so much I took a hot bath when I got home. My
last job that summer was hoeing weeds in a hop field. Guess
who was working along side of me? It was Dan, the kid who hid
behind the curtain. The expression on his face when he saw me
was wonderful. He said, "Mr. Stock, what are you doing here?"
I said, "The same as you, Dan, weedin' these here hops."

One other very important and exciting event occurred that
summer. July 25, 1953, son Brian Evans Stock was born. By
this time we knew what to do. We waited until the labor pains
came often and then took Louisa to the Santa Rosa Hospital.
In a few hours we had an eight-pound healthy boy.

Life was going along well then; we bought an automatic
shift car and Louisa learned to drive. She took David to
kindergarten. School started after Labor Day, and that year I
had all English and drama, no more math.

I had seen a wonderful variety show at SF State, written
by students and directed by Bud Irving, and I asked Bud if
I could perform it in Santa Rosa. He said sure, and gave me
the script. I held auditions and we performed the show for the
fall semester. Our school mascot was a panther, so we called it
"The Pantherieties." It was one of those lucky times when we
got the best actors, best singers, and best musicians. We played
it three nights and a matinee, and filled the auditorium.

During the semester, Glen Guymon talked me into taking
students to the National Forensic League Competition. We
worked on comedy, drama, and debate, and went to Burlingame
High for the meeting. Nobody walked off with any honors, but
it was good experience for me as well as the students.

One of the coaches came up with the idea that the faculty
should have a basketball game with the senior students.
Thirteen of the faculty joined in, including the good singing

lady coaches. We practiced a bit and had our game. There was a fine crowd, and we all had fun. One time we lifted the lightest lady coach up so she could drop the ball in the basket. Another time one of the seniors, Harold Taylor, was dribbling the ball and running toward the basket. I stuck my arm out and caught him on his chest. His feet flew up and he hit the floor; oh dear, I did a bad. I was afraid I had hurt him, but he scrambled up, at which time the audience booed me, and I got a foul. They gave him three shots for my behavior. The students won the game.

During the spring semester, Glen Guymon went to San Francisco to see "New Faces of 1954," which had come from New York. He thought it was such a good show, he went backstage and talked with the actors and director and persuaded them to come to Santa Rosa and perform on our stage. Eartha Kitt, a Frenchman, another good actor, and a couple of chorus girls made the trip. They did numbers from the show, and it was great fun. Later on, Glen brought Frankie Lane, a very popular singer in that day. I believe he did the theme song for the TV show Rawhide. He was a bit raunchy for the high school crowd; otherwise, he was very entertaining.

The play for the semester was, "Heaven Can Wait." I had a perfect cast, so the production was probably the high point of my career at Santa Rosa. One incident that occurred during rehearsal of the play was fun for all of us. Marvin Shapiro played the part of the boxer's manager, and for some reason I felt he should be bald. I asked Marvin if he would agree to that, and he assented quickly. Consequently, several of the cast members and I gathered in the barbershop to watch Marvin lose his black hair. Darrel Martin said, "Hey guys, he's looking more like Mr. Stock, isn't he?" The barber left a little fringe, and we all agreed he now looked perfect for the part.

The play was a huge hit. We filled the theater all three performances and received an excellent review from the Santa

Rosa Press Democrat.

April of 1954 while in my English class, I was notified there was a phone call for me. Someone took over the class, and I hurried down to the office; I was getting more worried, and I prayed that nothing was wrong with the kids. The call was from Cal Flint, offering me a job at MPC. I jumped for joy, clicked my heels, and accepted. I couldn't believe it, but, by God, it was true. I had run into him during the summer quarter at Stanford, for he was working on his doctorate at the time, and he remembered me. The rest of the time at Santa Rosa High was a blast. I didn't worry about anything.

We attended a few farewell parties, and I was again on the anti-kiss detail at commencement. I walked the halls, and if I found anyone kissing, I quickly turned and walked away.

I must say a few words about our two years in Santa Rosa. Except for Dad's death, the rest of the time was very pleasant. We owned a home; we had three lovely children, very nice helpful neighbors and we met some wonderful people. Santa Rosa is a beautiful town, and there are many interesting places to see nearby; Luther Burbank's gardens, the Russian River, a petrified forest, the ruins of Jack London's Wolf House, and many more.

A final word about the faculty as I have already mentioned how helpful they were. I keep wanting to say, "I can't believe how helpful they were." Why should I say, I can't believe? That's an insult to the faculty. They knew that this thirty three year old feller could use some help, and they gladly provided it, not only in my teaching, but in social activities as well. They were such a friendly group; they included the Irish lady, Louisa, and she loved and enjoyed them. Let's not forget the administrators, and the classified help; they all were very capable. In fact, if I stayed another year at Santa Rosa High, I'm sure I would have remained there for the rest of my teaching years.

CHAPTER 13

Monterey Peninsula College

AND NOW LET'S GET ON WITH A different phase of our lives: We bid farewell to friends and neighbors and sold our tract house to the Agriculture teacher, Don Lehman, for $700 more than we paid. Don offered to help us move, so he and I loaded our furniture on a rental truck and headed for Monterey, with Louisa and the kids following close by in the car. We arrived safely, stored the furniture, and moved in with Jacob and Grace until we could find a place to rent. We thanked Don profusely, and he drove back to Santa Rosa.

We quickly found a rental; thank goodness we didn't impose on Jake and Grace very long, for by now they had six children and, with our three thrown in, we had to eat in shifts and sleep on the floor. Our house was located just off Fremont on Palos Verde, kitty corner from Sambo's restaurant. Actually, the house was well located for us, since it was close to MPC and Del Monte Elementary School, where David would be a student. The house consisted of three bedrooms, one bath, a living room, a kitchen, and a good back yard. I built a sand box in the back yard for the boys.

Once we were settled in, it was necessary for me to find a job for a regular supply of money. I found work at Pierce-Rudolph Furniture Moving Company. I thought throwing bales of hay up on a wagon or the Pasadena lumber company work was tough, but it didn't compare with moving furniture. You can imagine moving refrigerators, pianos, dressers, any number of heavy objects, down two flights of stairs, then loading them on a truck. Such heavy lifts. That phrase reminds me of an Irish saying. I asked brother-in-law, Fred, "What do you do in the winter when there isn't much work to do outside?" He answered, "Heavy lifts around the dresser."

Fort Ord was in operation those days, and the houses were mostly one story so we were very happy to move the soldiers around. The train also ran at the time, and we often loaded furniture on and off the freight cars. I stayed on that job through July and part of August, when I got a call from brother-in-law Jack Rock.

He was writing scripts for the TV show, "I Led Three Lives", and said he secured a part for me in one segment, and he sent me the script. I was to report to the Ziv Production Studios in about a week, so I learned lines and took a Greyhound bus to LA. A lady in the seat next to me didn't mind cueing me, and I got the script down perfectly. We shot it in two days, and the experience permitted me to join The Screen Actors Guild.

After I left Monterey in 1948, the school district bought land along Fremont street just a short distance from downtown Monterey. They also bought some buildings from an abandoned army camp in Watsonville. These buildings formed the administration building, the library, a student union, and classrooms.

Labor Day arrived, and thirty-five faculty members met in a small room in the student union. Cal Flint greeted me warmly and I told him how happy I was returning to MPC, as a teacher no less. I knew some of the teachers from my year as a student at MPC: Bill Smith, Gus Armanasco, Joe Blacow, and Marge Landon. Oh, it was wonderful to see these folks and meet the others. Cal gave a good enthusiastic welcome speech, and all members were ready for a banner year.

I was assigned an office in the home economics building with Tor Spindler, a P. E. teacher and assistant football coach. We were both so busy teaching our classes that we seldom saw each other in our office. He was a good office mate.

My classes were English, remedial English, Public Speaking, and Drama. I had two English classes at 9 and ten o'clock Monday, Wednesday, and Friday, and the public speaking class at 11. On Tuesday and Thursday, I had the acting class at 10, and 2 in the afternoon the same group met to rehearse scenes. The acting class was taught in room L six, which had a little stage. The entire room was small, but we managed. What else is one to do when that is the only space available?

There were wonderful benefits teaching at MPC such as having the opportunity for an office away from the classroom. It was so great to have a place to go when solitude was needed, or to prepare lessons. The students who were there to learn worked hard, no playing around in class. The faculty was helpful, and the afternoons were free. I didn't leave campus; that was a time to get things accomplished, free time to work on other college activities, such as auditioning the cheer leading girls, or advising the Hogan's Club. See what I mean, wonderful benefits.

Just as Doug Campbell was my mentor at Santa Rosa High, Max Tadlock, Dean of Instruction, was my mentor at MPC. He occasionally visited my classes and gave me good suggestions on my presentations, especially in the public speaking class and English classes. I think it was only right that he was my mentor, since we were a couple of Buckeyes from Ohio. Max hailed from the large city of Toledo. I'm sure Max pronounced it, Tuhleduh, Ahia.

The classes progressed along satisfactorily. I graded many papers for the English classes, listened to many speeches in the public speaking class, and worked with actors in the acting class. There were two very good speakers in the public speaking class: Harkjoon Paik and Dwain Fullerton. Harkjoon won an American Legion speech contest in high school, and went on to Stanford to receive his law degree and later became a superior court judge in Monterey. Dwain went to Stanford and, last I heard, was working there in some capacity. Have I mentioned that teachers learn as much from students as students learn from teachers? I firmly believed that. MPC was a wonderful place to work.

The home front was in good shape as well; Louisa was with the children during the day. David was in second grade at Del Monte School. I was home in the evenings and weekends to help with the kids and housework. At Christmas we went to Los Angeles, with the kids asking the proverbial question, "Are we there yet?" And the whole family gathered at Francie and Jack's house at Dorcas Place up near the HOLLYWOOD sign. Francie and Jack did their old vaudeville routine. Dad, when he waa alive, recited some of his own poetry, we all sang songs, told stories, and had a great time.

January was exam time and the end of the fall semester. Consequently, much work had to be done: grading papers, averaging the semester grades and getting them to the office on time. I graded on the bell curve, but gave no F's. That's probably why I won the Red Hot Professor award one semester.

Fall semester 1955, I was hired to put on plays, and the acting students were anxious to be in a play before an audience. Come on, Morgan, think of some way to do this: Ok, we will do three one-acts in the student union. There was a large room where students ate lunch, so we used that room for the theatre and put the plays on during the weekend.

I had to do a few things before I could get the play on stage, such as borrowing the band risers from the music department for the audience to sit on, renting a small dimmer board, and borrowing some theatre lights from the local theatres. I rehearsed the actors in the evening.

I wanted to get as much publicity as I could for the production, so I contacted Irene Alexander, the theatre critic for the local newspaper, and asked her to please review the plays. To my surprise and dismay, she said she wouldn't. I asked her why, and she told me that she reviewed a play that the high school had staged, and got all sorts of flack from parents, teachers, and others, for telling the truth as she saw it. Consequently, the local paper would not review any production put on by educational groups. Well, maybe the school paper might.

I chose three one-act plays: "If Men Played Cards As Women Do", "The Marriage Proposal", and "Suppressed Desires". The actors and their plays included: Allen Knight, Don Martine, Floyd Adams, Bruce Langshaw, in "If Men Played Cards"; Dick Grielick, Walt Bailey, and Sandra Six in "The Marriage Proposal"; and Sandy Wright and Gene Norton in "Suppressed Desires".

In 1955 Erv Harlacher joined the faculty as the journalism teacher, and Louisa and I became very friendly with him and his lovely wife, Norma Joe. They came to see the production, and about a week later we were discussing it and Erv said, "I didn't see any review of the plays." I replied, "*The Herald* won't review them." He said firmly, "Well, we are going right down there and speak to them." I called for an appointment. With Irene and Erv and I walked in and pleaded our case, and *The Herald* agreed to review our plays in the future. Erv is quite persuasive!

"The Hasty Heart" was my first choice for a three-act play in the student union. I had directed it in Menlo Park, and knew what kind of audience pleaser it was, and what fun if was for the actors. Furthermore, I had the right men, and a lovely nurse for the play. Irene Alexander gave us a very good review. I quote from her opening paragraph, "An outstanding play, fine casting and direction, and youthful spirits linked in many cases with undoubted acting talent, combine to make the current offering of MPC'S drama department very worthwhile indeed." Maybe we will measure up to the other amateur theatres in the area. Again, thank you, Erv!

"Brother Rat" was the next production. It was a play about students in the Virginia Military Institute. Luckily, there was an older gentleman in the community who was a graduate of VMI, and he instructed us how the cadets acted in real life at the military school, which was most helpful. We rented costumes from the Western Costume Company in Hollywood. I was pleased with the performance, and we even received another good review from Irene.

The next play in the union was "The Time of Your Life" by William Saroyan. The play was set in a San Francisco barroom. The set was very simple: we built a bar and brought in a marble machine and placed some of the student union tables around and rehearsed. During the other plays the students realized we were rehearsing and sat away from us, but now the students would wander in and sit down with the actors and drink coffee. This was pretty disconcerting to the actors and the students— mainly the students, for they couldn't fathom what was going on. Finally, they would rise and walk away, looking back in amazement until they realized that it was a rehearsal.

It became too much trouble to continue producing our plays at the Student Union, what with night students coming in from 7 to 10, board meetings, and other interruptions, so we went back to our little L six, borrowed band risers and put on four more full length plays. This was damn tough, too, for we had to paint the sets on the lawn. When up on the tiny stage, in order to exit, the actors had to climb through a window and wait outside, then climb back through the window if he made an entrance. We needed a stepladder for that maneuver. There was a classroom next door; luckily they didn't have any night classes in it so we used it for a dressing and makeup room. We did the Madwoman of Chaillot and had the action take place on a sidewalk café. With all these problems and my worrying about the audience falling off the band risers, the actors and I decided to make another change.

The Wharf Theatre, on the wharf in Monterey, was an amateur group that produced plays year round on the weekends. I had acted in a few plays for the producers, Bob Carson and Tom Brock, so I asked them if we could put on plays during the weeknights. They agreed, and we moved our activities there.

We did three one-acts to get the feel of the place. Then I directed "Stage Door". The cast was large, and we couldn't completely remove the set that the Wharf was using on the weekends. Furthermore, a seal cage was right next door to the theatre, and one wall didn't prevent the seal noise from being heard by everyone in the theatre. A line would go something like this, "Oh, my dearest, I love you so. I know sweetheart and I..." Honk, Honk, Honk! Those seals knew when to break into a conversation. We all decided to move again.

The Defense Language School is located at the Presidio in Monterey, and has a large tin barn among the buildings. The students did plays in the barn occasionally, so I asked the lady in charge if we could possibly use it for the MPC productions. She said yes and we were set.

The barn was large and had room enough for an audience of 200 on folding chairs. The elevated stage made viewing perfect, there was an area for building sets, the lighting was adequate, and there were dressing rooms. This turned out to be the best place for us to produce our plays since coming to Monterey.

In the spring we did the same musical I did at Santa Rosa High. This time we called it "The Loborieties", since the school was known as the Lobos. It was a tremendous hit. The actors did well and the artistically inclined students made some beautiful props for the show.

At this point I must say that I had become convinced that Murphy's Law operates as readily in drama or maybe even more so than in other disciplines. We all remember Murphy's Law, don't we? "What can go wrong, will go wrong."

The second production took place during the rainy season. It was "The Petrified Forest", a play set in Arizona during the summer. On opening night we had one of those wind and rainstorms that occasionally lash this area. The tin barn is just that – corrugated tin on the sides and roof. Consequently, the rain on the roof drowned out all dialogue. We wrote LOUDER on pieces of cardboard and held them up in the wings for the actors to see. Not only was the rain drowning out the actors, so was the wind, for some of the siding was loose and when a particularly strong gust hit, it sounded like Duke Mantee's Tommy gun firing. Duke was the gangster in the play, and that part brought fame to Humphrey Bogart in the movie.

On top of all that, we found out the tin barn was not leak proof either; in a very short time a sturdy stream was running right down through the audience. All things considered, I would rather have been in Philadelphia that night.

Shortly after this disaster, the college built a new library and gave us the old one. It had no stage, no fly space, no wing space, and, thank goodness, no tin anywhere. The best part about it was that it was all ours—with room to build our sets, plus a costume room. What more could anyone ask for? Well, we did ask the maintenance men to build a stage, and a gradual rising seat arrangement for the audience. Old seats from a movie theatre were cleaned up and screwed down securely. The college purchased a couple of large army surplus trailers and gave the theatre one of them. We solved the lack of wing space by knocking a hole in the wall, and jamming the trailer against it. Whenever I wanted to clear the actors off stage fast, I'd yell, "Ok everybody, into the trailer."

We painted the walls of the theatre black, which improved the lighting effects on the stage. I mean if the Shakespeare Theatre in Stratford had a black box theatre, certainly we could have one as well.

We opened the theatre with Arthur Miller's "The Crucible" in 1960, and continued producing our plays there for the next ten years. By now I no longer taught English, and the public speaking classes moved to the English department, so we had all drama classes in our theatre. I rewrote the class requirements so it matched the lower division theatre courses in the four-year colleges.

In the early years at MPC, I hired Ig Heniford as the technical teacher, and to do some directing; he did well with the plays he directed, but somehow the president of the college didn't think he was right for the position, and I didn't stand up for him well enough, so he left after a couple of years for a teaching job in Salinas. Bill Bogess then joined the department and taught radio and did some tech work for us at the tin barn. He left shortly to teach at the Navy School where I once worked. Then, along in the late sixties, I convinced the administration to hire Ross Durphy, who was in the Billy Bud cast with me at Stanford. Again, two of us ran the drama department; part-timers were hired as tech directors. The very best one was Ruth Jordan Allan.

October 1956 was a very important date for Louisa and me. We bought a new tract house on Toyon Drive in Monterey. Several MPC teachers helped me move, and I reciprocated many times. I borrowed $700 from my old Stanford friend, Fred Forsman, for the down payment. We received a GI real estate loan at 4 percent, so payments were about $105 month. We were very happy with everything about the place.

The house had three bedrooms, two baths, a living room with a large high ceiling, and a nice kitchen. A couple of years later, Uncle Nick came down and put another bedroom over the garage. The boys all moved there and it gave us room for a study. Our house was the last house in the tract, so we had no neighbors on one side, but as the years rolled on, we gained neighbors all over the place. None in back of us, though; for there was a deep gorge that drained water in the winter. There was also a nice forest to the rear of the house. It was a wonderful place for the kids to play in as they grew up. That house has lots of memories in it.

Pasadena Playhouse acting class, 1939.

The Lesson,
The Old Wharf
Theater.

Separate Tables,
The Golden
Bough Circle
Theater, late
1950's.

The Diary of Anne Frank, The Old Wharf Theater, 1956.

Bench In the Sun, Morgan, Edie Karas aand Mike Robins.

As Kit Carson from
The Time of Your Life, 1993.

*The Bells
are Ringing,*
The Old Wharf
Theater, 1960,
Edie Karas and
Morgan.

The Cocktail Hour, Kevin Stock, Mindy Stock, Morgan
and Janice O'Brian.

The Stock Family at home in Monterey, California.
Left to right: Kevin, Maggie, Louisa, Morgan, Brian and David.

CHAPTER 14

Ireland and England

IT'S TIME TO GET AWAY FROM THE college and describe a trip that the family took in the summer of 1957. Louisa had arrived in the states in March 1946; she hadn't seen her Irish family in eleven years, so she lined up the American family and spoke in no uncertain terms, "We are going to Northern Ireland this summer!" We answered, "Oh yes, absolutely, yes, of course, Louisa!" The boys were 9, 5, and 3 years old. Perhaps that helps you understand a little more about this trip. Lou and I contacted a travel agent and found out it was much cheaper to go by boat than air, so we figured we would take a train to New York, catch a boat, and land in England. I told sister Francie our plans, and she insisted that we take money from her and fly to New York. I did not argue and thanked her profusely.

My nephew Jay Stock drove us to San Francisco to catch the plane. Of course we missed it, and had to wait around for another one. Finally we were all aboard and settled in. By the time we flew over Reno, five year old Kevin piped up and asked, "Are we in Ireland yet?" The flight was perfect. We landed in New York and took a taxi to a small hotel where we spent the night.

The next morning we arose and grabbed a taxi to the pier and boarded the Scythia, probably the oldest boat in the Cunard line. Our stateroom was on D deck, the lowest passenger deck, but it was clean and slept the five of us. That was if we could sleep. Every night the porters rolled barrels out from either above us or below us, I didn't know which. The room was very warm and Louisa kept wiping the kids faces with wet washcloths. We mentioned the heat to the help and they said don't worry, in a couple of days we'd be in the Gulf Stream and it would cool off. It never happened.

The day, however, was wonderful. We had three deck chairs for David, the nine year old, and Louisa and I. Brian, the three year old, and Kevin played continually, running around our chairs and the deck, but always where we could watch them. The first day on the boat I noticed there was room for the boys to plunge into the ocean between the lifeboats and the railing, so we were very alert to that possibility.

One evening close to sunset, we were relaxing on deck and two of the stewards were talking when suddenly they sprang to life, yelled, "Man overboard!" They grabbed a couple of life preservers and threw them overboard, then rushed down the stairs and disappeared. Oh, my God, where were Kevin and Brian? Thank goodness they were just a few steps away from us, but it was such a startling incident that we momentarily forgot they were right by us.

We then hurried to the back rail and saw the man in the water getting farther and farther away as the ship started turning around. Passengers gathered along the port side of the ship on every deck, for we heard that the deck hands would lower a boat to pick up the man. Everyone gathered except Louisa; she said that if too many people gathered on one side, the ship would tip over. She remained on the other side, which must have been right, for the ship did not go over. She could claim that she saved the ship. The rest of us watched the crew lower a boat from inside the ship, just above the water line, and go after the man. We couldn't see them save the man as the ship and the fading light blocked our view, but save him they did.

We heard later that the man was being deported and was a prisoner in a room above the deck where we were sitting. Evidently someone guarding him left the room for a moment and he managed to get out and make his grand jump. That was quite an exciting event and provided us with a good story.

That experience made us even tenser with the children, particularly Brian. He was nearly four and never sat still a minute, always active. If we saw him just sitting there, we thought there was something wrong with him. Of course, you can see it coming; we were comfortable in our chairs, Kevin and Brian were playing around us, and perhaps I dozed off. I looked over at David and Kevin and asked them where Brian was and neither one of them knew. Holy Jumpin' Jasus! Lou was reading a book and I said, "Brian isn't here; let's look for him." We all jumped up and looked around the deck and ran off in all directions, unconquerable fear mounting. I went to the steps leading down to the next deck, and as I did I saw a lady coming up the steps leading Brian by the hand. I grabbed him, hugged him very tightly, and thanked her. She said she met him coming down the stairs and thought he was a bit young to be walking alone; she had probably asked him where his family was and he somehow got the message to her, so she had taken him by the hand and brought him back up the stairs. I thanked her again and rejoined the family as we all breathed a sigh of relief.

There was no punishment, just a firm command that he never leave our chairs again without one of us accompanying him. We were even more vigilant from that day on.

The old Scythia showed it's age, for it took us ten days to make the trip to Ireland. However, there was entertainment for the children in the way of movies and other activities. The adults could enjoy bingo and other games, or listen to the entertainers. With our three children, though, we didn't want to leave them at night. Besides, we still had to try and keep them cool.

We finally landed in Cobh, Ireland, and took a train to Cork, then another one to Dublin, and a third one to Belfast.

During this trip we were introduced to the wild Irish drivers. The first one was a taxi driver in Dublin. He drove us from one train station to another and must have thought we would miss our train, since he drove fast and applied the brakes as well as the horn. Then Lou's brother, Norman, drove us from Belfast to the Adams farm. He exemplified the way I describe Irish drivers. They love to go sixty miles an hour on a two-lane highway up a hill and pass someone on the curve in the road. When I was there during the war, there was no wild driving seen as there were so few cars on the road.

Tears of joy and rapture greeted Louisa's homecoming. I believe that most of the family—Lou's mother four brothers, two sisters and husbands and wives—were in attendance. If some missed it, we saw them off and on during the summer. We stayed at Kilcreen with mother, brother Fred and his wife, Adeline.

I wonder if that is the usual Irish way; one son stays on as a farmer and brings a wife to live with him and his mother. That is how it happened at Kilcreen. Luckily, Jim, Bob, and Norman didn't care to be farmers and had already left the homestead. Fred was doing a great job, for the family was prosperous and happy with their lives. They raised flax, potatoes, oats, hay, pigs, milk cows, and worked like hell.

Mother Adams was a benevolent dictator. Louisa wore pants that were popular in those days; they were tight around the calves, came down to the ankles, and were very colorful. The name of the style was toreador, or harlequin. When Louisa appeared in those pants one morning, mother Adams led her into the pantry and very nicely told her not to wear those any more while in N. Ireland. Of course, Louisa refrained from wearing those pants for the rest of the visit.

The kids enjoyed everything about the farm: pigs being born, potatoes dug up, flax placed in the flax pond, riding on the tractor with uncle Fred, and playing with cousins their own age. Along with all that came July twelfth, the day the Orange Men marched with bagpipes and the huge Lambeg drums. There was an Orange Hall not far from the farm, and we heard the band rehearsing. One could hear those drums miles away on a pleasant summer evening.

Writing about the large drums reminds me when Max Tadlock, Dean of Instruction, was on a sabbatical, along with his wife, Marion, and daughters Maxa and Susan, when they visited at Louisa's farm. While they were visiting, we heard about a drumming contest in Clough Mills. We attended, and six drummers showed up. We could hear the drumming as we got out of the car. As we got closer, the drumbeats were in our ears, our chests, practically over our entire body. We listened for a time and then went back to the quiet of the home. The Tadlocks went on to Spain the next day.

On July 25, Brian celebrated his fourth birthday. Relatives came with their children. The children played around for a while, then came in and presented Brian with a red fire engine. He still remembers that occasion.

Mom and Pop visited all the relatives in their homes and experienced afternoon teas and dinners with scrumptious pastries. Naturally, Louisa did a lot of catching up concerning friends in the neighborhood, and was happy to know that all were among the land of the livin', as they say in Norn Iron. When one speaks quickly, Norn Iron is Northern Ireland, kind of like my Nerk Ahia. That expression is not mine; someone gave me a book with Norn Iron as the title. It is filled with wonderful, humorous Irish stories.

The Main River runs through the farm; one could walk from the house, across the road, through an opened gate, across the railroad tracks, then on down through the peat bog to the river. Fred and I would go fishing in the evening. The walk to the river was about a 1/2 mile and most it was on solid ground, but you did have to be careful not to step in the bog. I did once, and I was in to the top of my knee-high boot. I thought I would have to call Fred to help pull me out, but I managed to keep one foot on firm ground and get loose. Fred told a story of one of the cows getting in the bog; they searched for her and finally found just the horns sticking up. I didn't care to be found with just me ears sticking up.

We fly fished. I had done a bit of it at home, but wasn't any good at casting the flys. I was better at making the flys. Fred gathered some feathers from a Bard Rock rooster and tied them on the hook. He showed me how to do it, so I spent a few afternoons replenishing our fly supply. The first trout I caught was maybe eight inches long. Fred said, "He's no a brave Briton, but he's a troot all the same."

That brings me to a few more expressions I heard on the visit: Fred and I went to see a motorcycle race, and as they roared by, Fred said, "Talk about your Thack Eedgits," "No as bahd as a bahd marriage," and, after a riot, "There'll be wigs on the green and hats for the liftin'," "Only drops from the Boyne," "All roads and directions," "Sick, sore, and tired," and, speaking about the Lambeg drums, "Grand sound and a glorious noise," "Have to be thick to be a drummer."

In early August it was time to head on back to the states. After many farewells, Louisa's sister, Sissie, drove us to Dublin where we caught the train to Kobh. That evening we walked along an inlet bordered street. Kevin was kicking along when one of his shoes flew off into the inlet. The water was too deep for us to recover the shoe, and we had no extra pair. The stores were closing, but we finally found one just in time to slip in and buy shoes for Kevin. We returned to the room we rented for the night and found out it was over the pub: not much sleep that night

The next day we boarded the Sylvania, and had a much better stateroom than the Scythia. We ran into a pretty rough storm out of Kobh and Dave got seasick. The stewardess said "Ah, David, you'll feel much better when the moon comes up," to which David replied, "Oh gosh, did I swallow that, too?" We made it back to New York in good time. One of the first things we did was enter a restaurant and eat hamburgers. We missed that good old American fat making food.

We stayed overnight in New York and caught a plane the next day. We had read that if a family was traveling, it was wise to take two different planes, which we did. I can't remember who flew with whom, but we all arrived safely in San Francisco. One of the other Stocks picked us up, and we were home again.

By the fall of 1957, we were still in our little theatre, busily producing plays. It was hard to remember what year a certain play was performed, however, I could recall performances that were outstanding for some reason or another. I never saved reviews of plays, but Louisa did.

The following is a letter to the editor of our local paper from Marine Major Charles E. Thompson:

I presume that Irene Alexander's critique of "The Hostage" would be considered very good by those concerned with the performance; however, as a spectator who could stomach but the first act, this critique left something to be desired.

Had I written this critique the headline would have been something like, "Putrid Sore Bursts On The Peninsula," for, you see, that is exactly what the play really is. This play is in the same category as the Eros Magazine, which was recently banned from recent production.

I seriously question the motivation of Mr. Morgan Stock, director of the play, and the Monterey Peninsula College in presenting, under the guise of education, a portrayal of the lowest forms of humanity.

In the face of mounting evidence of gross immorality and the attendant increases of the crime rates in our country, it seems that an educator would want to major on the moral points of our Christian heritage which would serve to curb the very things portrayed in Hostage.

For those who would say that such curbing is an intended message of this play, I must retort that one doesn't have to see corruption to round out his education; it is impossible to avoid it in real life."

The Major went on to say that drama departments and parents and churches are responsible to educate young folks to recognize the base forms of life and turn their backs on them. He further stated there were many plays that accomplished this, and they were good entertainment as well. He made a few other points. I must say he writes a very good letter; perhaps if he had stayed for the final two acts, the putrid sore wouldn't have been so putrid.

The cast replied to the Major in the following letter to the editor:

Concerning the letter from Major Thompson criticizing the production of Brendan Behan's The Hostage being presented at MPC; we would like to state our opinion of this play as members of its cast, who have worked on it for six weeks and done varying amounts of research into background material about Behan and his countrymen.

Major Thompson calls the play putrid and immoral. He says he would like to see plays that educate youth to recognize the base forms of life and turn their backs on them.

The Hostage accomplishes this very purpose. Major Thompson turned his back on these forms of life when he left the play after the first act. Had he stayed for the rest of the play he might have had an opportunity to judge The Hostage. However, if he had seen the last two acts, he might have been shocked to realize that Behan's message is not to deplore criminals, prostitutes, or homosexuals.

Behan likes criminals, prostitutes; he even likes homosexuals. In fact, Behan likes everyone in the world. He deplores hypocrisy, cruelty, poverty, crime, prostitution, and homosexuality, but he loves humanity and respects the human spirit, despite the depths into which humanity is pulled. He hates the forces that pull men down, but he loves the men themselves." In another paragraph the students wrote,

The purpose of the play is to make the audience enjoy itself and leave the theatre happy. The last song in the play is called There's No Place On Earth Like The World. The author meant it, we mean it, and the audience knows it.

Major Thompson asks for plays that have no message but are good entertainment. The value of The Hostage is that it provides the best of both. The audience loves it, and we involved in the production love it. Behan's humor is in such a tone that even the bawdiest lines never fall below the level of good taste.

But the play has a message as well —the oldest message in the world, and anyone who sees the whole play could never mistake it or take offence at it. The message of The Hostage is simply this: Love your fellow man.

Ah, yes, this was an example of what could happen when one puts on a play. Some may enjoy it immensely and others may not like it at all. I was happy with this play and the reaction of the audience. Of course, in this business there are bound to be bad productions. One hopes there are more good results then bad ones. Hey, that's life, isn't it?

In the summer of 1959 I had a chance to go to England. Brother-in-law Jack Rock and an American film producer who lived in England had the idea of producing a TV show called River Patrol in which English police would patrol the Thames

River. Jack wrote the script and my old Stanford buddy, Fred Forsman, and I would take the script to London and see what we could accomplish. Jack got a bit upset with me since Fred hadn't given him a check for the script. I said "Okay Jack, I shall speak to Fred about it." I should explain: Fred had money: his mother was a Pillsbury and his father a successful manufacturer.

I said to my buddy, "Fred, Jack is concerned about payment for his script, and since you and I are going to London to get the project off the ground, perhaps you could present him a check for $1500." I sort of held my breath, and Fred said, "Why sure, Morg, no problem." He gave Jack the check the following day. We all breathed easier after that.

Fred and I met in San Francisco on the appointed day and the first thing he said to me was, "Don't look at the paper, Morg." Naturally, I looked immediately and saw in large headlines, "? Airline Crashed and Everyone On Board Was Killed." The reason for the question mark is that I cannot remember which airline it was. I did know, however, that it was the same airline we would be flying on. The airline booked us into a hotel that night and the next morning we boarded the plane and landed safely in London.

We found the American producer, Dick Thomas, and he invited us to stay with him for a couple of nights while we traveled to studios and met some minor executives and achieved nothing. About a year later we heard that an English company had a successful TV show called River Patrol. Did they steal ours? We did have good lunches in studio restaurants. Once Lawrence Olivier was enjoying lunch four tables away from us, so the trip wasn't a total loss.

We left the Thomas's and moved in with a sister of a lady I know in Monterey. Dick Thomas introduced us to a successful West end actor, and he insisted we drive down to Brighton to see a circus. In the meantime, Fred had spent an evening in Soho, where he picked up a floosie, and he brought her to Brighton. Why we went to see the circus I don't know, unless someone thought we would put some money in it.

A few days later, Fred and I left for Ireland. We arrived in Dublin and stayed at the Gresham Hotel. Talking with Fred the other day, I asked him if he remembered something about the trip, and he said no, but he did remember the time he was taking a bath and a maid came in and scrubbed his back for him. I remember when maids came into rooms and offered tea while you were still in bed.

During dinner one evening, I told Fred about the troubles that were just beginning in the North, and he raised his glass and said, "Up Ulster—possibly." I replied quickly, "No, no Fred, not so loud; we don't want any TROUBLES down here tonight."

From Dublin we went up north to see my in-laws, stayed a couple of days there, then on to London and back to Grass Valley where Louisa and the kids were staying with Fred's wife and children. It was a very interesting trip even though we didn't accomplish our mission.

Through 1959, 60, 61, I continued producing plays in our Little Theatre, some good, some bad. The main thing Louisa produced in October of 1960 was a baby girl, Maggie. Thank goodness Louisa now had a female companion. What a doll she was, and still is. What fun it is to have the two sexes in a family; pretty dresses for the girl and cowboy clothes for the boys, besides other differences

We hired another director, Richard Frazer. He was head of the speech and drama department for that year, since I was leaving for my first sabbatical in September.

The reason we didn't leave in June was that I had an opportunity to pick up some extra money by acting at the

Wharf Theatre and Opera House in the musical "Take Me Along," with Jack Carson in the lead. Sam Karas and I played a round of golf with him and his son. Jack was fun to be around; he told us of many interesting experiences while working on stage and movies, such as choosing which chorus girl to sleep with that night. In September the Stock family flew back to New York and boarded the Queen Mary. Surprise, surprise, there were Mary Rile and Lynne Bynum, teachers from MPC. The Queen Mary was much nicer than the other two ships we had traveled on. Of course with Maggie, our one-year old daughter, traveling was a bit different; perhaps I should say a lot different—just use your imagination.

We had two adjoining staterooms; the three boys stayed in one and Lou and I and Maggie occupied the other. We ate our good meals in shifts; the boys watched "The Guns of Navarrone" at the movie theatre all five days of the voyage. We landed in South Hampton and took a small craft to Cobh, Ireland; thence by train to Ballymena where Louisa's brother, Fred, picked us up.

After the hugs and kisses and tears of joy, we discovered a bit of a problem at Kilcreen: The Adams family was in the process of installing a new bathroom. We were very pleased that we didn't have to use the outhouse anymore, but distressed at the inconvenience we added to the family. Furthermore, the Stocks all had colds and worried about infecting Norman and Winifred, the young Adams children, Fred and Adeline, and grandma. I named everyone so you could remember them for future reference and to impress upon you the inconvenience of adding our six to the household.

Louisa and I talked about the problem, but couldn't come up with a solution. In the meantime, we installed Kevin and Brian in a two-room schoolhouse just down the road. Later, Fred and I were walking along the railroad track and I told him of our feelings. He agreed very nicely and suggested that perhaps the boys could stay with Louisa's sisters. Consequently, David went to live with Lizzie Weir and her two sons about David's age, and went to a school in Ballymena with them. A little later Kevin and Brian went to another sister, Sissy Gaston, who had several children about their age. Both of these families lived on farms and raised pigs, so the boys learned a bit about farming in N. Ireland. These moves relieved the congestion at Kilcreen.

Louisa and I helped on the farm. When we arrived, the potato harvest was in progress. Fred showed me how to sew the top of a burlap bag full of spuds, so that is what I did until the potato harvest was completed. We raised potatoes in Ohio, but just enough for our own use. Louisa, meanwhile, helped in the house, cooking, putting eggs in a crate for sale, and doing a number of other household chores.

I wish to explain that Fred Forsman, Sam Karas and I participated in another project. We paid for an option on a book written by a friend, Beaulah Powers, called "Keepers of the Bell," to make it into a film. The story was set in Ireland, and since I would be there, it seemed proper that I should write a rough draft screenplay. Therefore, when I wasn't busy on the farm, I took pen in hand and started the script.

We visited all the Adams family during our two-month stay in the area. In November I went to Dun Laoghaire in the Republic of Ireland and contacted a real estate agent, a very nice lady, and she suggested I look at a house in Dalkey, which I did. I decided that we would live there until January when I was to be admitted to the Shakespeare Institute in Stratford-on-Avon. I returned to Kilcreen, we bid farewell to the family, packed our belongings, and took the train and bus to Dalkey.

The house was satisfactory with one medium sized bedroom and two smaller ones, a small living room with a fireplace, a small kitchen, and a very small dining area. We all squeezed in for our meals.

Louisa and I felt the boys should be in school. One night I went to a pub and joined in the conversation with the locals. They were very pleased when I told them I was from California, and had good things to say about us Yanks. I thought this was a good chance to ask about schools, so I said, "Perhaps you could tell me how to get my boys enrolled in school." They replied, "Would you be a Catholic now?" I was afraid this question might come. Ah, dear, what should I say? Just tell them in a nice way you aren't a Catholic. I said, "Well no, I just want to get the boys in school." One of them answered, "Ah, well, you'll want to be talkin' to Reverend O'Brien of the Church of Ireland. That's the Protestant school." I thanked them and felt a definite cooling toward me. I left shortly after. I went to the pub again some time later and realized the boy from California was no longer very welcome.

The boys were enrolled and we continued our life on Tubbermore Street. Dalkey is a small town, but it had the green grocer, the butcher shop, and a place where one could buy a bundle of peat, which we certainly needed to keep our house reasonably warm. The area around was beautiful; there was a small mountain within walking distance and we used to climb up it and sit in the wishing chair near the top. Maggie was fine and happy; we bought a small harness for her and led her along like a dog. When we came to a curb, we lifted her up by the harness straps and carried her across the street. She loved that. I kept working on the script.

We had to watch our pennies, for during a year sabbatical, we got half a year's salary. I was making about $7,500 a year, so you understand why we played it close to the vest. However, we did take the kids to Dublin for a night out a couple of times. I also took the boys to a movie one evening in Dun Laoghaire

where we saw "One Eyed Jacks" with Marlon Brando. When
we came out of the movie, it was quite cold and while waiting
for the bus we saw a kid about ten years old in a ragged T
shirt talking loudly to himself and yelling at times. I couldn't
understand anything he said, but I felt so sorry for him. I don't
think we tried to talk to him. We weren't sure if he was a mental
case or what. Our bus came and we went on back to Dalkey.
I have never forgot that incident. Isn't it amazing what one
remembers?

I went into Dublin to the Volkswagen dealer and paid
$1400 for a new bus. We had saved that money before the
trip. They wouldn't have the vehicle until February, so I had
them ship it to Birmingham. I wish we could have driven it
home from Dublin because it's doubly hard to get around on
the busses with the children. We looked forward to getting it
in England.

I finished the script in December and found a lady in
Dalkey to type it for me. There was a film studio in Bray and
I went there and talked to some executives. They were very
kind, but said they were not interested at the moment since
they had several projects going. I thought I should get it to a
Dublin studio. I did, and got the same reaction. Ah well, we
had to try.

The boy's school put on a Christmas celebration. The
part one segment was a short one-act play. David played King
Herod; a pretty blonde David's age, thirteen, was the Virgin
Mary. Kevin and Brian were shepherds. Brian remembered a
line he spoke, "It's as if, it's as if we are waiting for something."
Sounds as if it may be for the wise men. As he spoke the lines,
he kept rocking back and forth in his chair. Irish children
played the rest of the characters. Then, later in the program he
sang a little song, "I'm a little Gollywog, black as any old dead
log." What that was about I have no idea. Anyway, it was great

fun to see the Irish and American children in a play.

A couple days before Christmas, we took the train back to Ballymena; it was so cold that the boys kept their pajamas on under their clothes. Brother Fred picked us up and took us to Kilcreen. How good it was to have the new bathroom.

They didn't bother with a Christmas tree, or lights, or much of anything of the outward expression of Christmas, but the spiritual feeling was there. We exchanged presents, enjoyed seeing all the relatives again, and returned to Dalkey. It was still cold and we all remembered Louisa washing the sheets in the bathtub and hanging them out to dry where in no time at all they were frozen hard—shades of an Ohio winter.

The next move was approaching, so we packed all our belongings and were ready to board the ship from Dun Laoghaire to Holyhead, Wales, on January 2nd, 1962. The ship was full; one was lucky to find a stair to sit on. The trip took close to three hours. We landed at night and had to find our way to the railway station for the train to Birmingham. The trip was pleasant; the kids slept most of the way, and we were all together in a cozy compartment

We carried our luggage to a hotel near the railway station and stopped at the registration desk. We were a sight to behold. I can still see us; Maggie standing there with a coat down to the floor, the two young boys sitting on our suitcases, thirteen year old David standing a bit aloof from us. Along with our reasonably neat suitcases, we had a couple of sloppy bags and a cardboard box tied together with twine. We could have been the Joads, heading for California. Well, I tell you, this much luggage was needed to keep body and soul together.

We stayed a couple of nights in Birmingham and then took the train to Stratford-on-Avon and found a hotel room opposite the Royal Shakespeare Theatre. A few days later we located a cheaper hotel called the Beeches on Warwick Road. The room had two double beds in it, so it was comfortable for us.

Miss Jelfs ran the hotel. I remember her very well, for she paid us a nice compliment. She said, "You have such a well behaved family, we are happy to have you staying with us," Sam and Edie Karas, our best friends in Monterey, visited us for a couple of days at the Beeches. Eventually we moved into an apartment just off the main hotel and remained there the rest of our stay in Stratford.

The apartment was small: one large room where we all slept, watched TV, warmed ourselves at an electric fireplace, and ate our meals; we lived in that room. Thank goodness the apartment had a small kitchen and a small bathroom. That was it, but it served our purpose and was reasonable.

I enrolled at the Shakespeare Institute and Kevin and Brian went to Broad Street School; David attended Hugh Clopton High School. We all walked to our classes, which was good for us. The boys were reasonably happy with their schools.

I was very happy with the Institute; Birmingham University controlled it, and once a week five or six of us piled into a large station wagon and traveled the twenty miles to Birmingham for lectures. The rest of the time we met with professors at the Institute; it was practically a one on one situation, which was fine.

My main project was to do a prompt script of, "Much Ado About Nothing." I went to the archives of the Shakespeare Theatre and looked at a script that one of the directors had used, to see how he marked movements, and for any other advice to give the actors. I did discover the way he wrote his blocking down, which I now use when I direct a play. Place the script in a three-ring notebook with a blank page opposite the playwright's words, then use numbers on the playwright's script and transfer those numbers to the blank page along with the actor's movements. Example: "2 Malvolio X L to Olivia." The

X L means cross left. One may also add a bit of characterization in his note, such as, "Malvolio haughtily X L to Olivia." I used to write directions in the script, and half the time I couldn't read what I had written. I really appreciated what I learned from that director.

I worked with professor Brown and he told me to write the characterization of each actor plus set design, lights, costumes, and sound. When I read something on costumes, the author said that a gown should be goose turd green. That's the first time I ever heard that term.

Life at the Beeches was good; we were just on the outskirts of Stratford and could walk into town. We located a restaurant, called the Hatches, that was very reasonable, and they didn't mind a very young girl running around the place. Of course, we didn't permit that if other patrons were at the restaurant. On the way to the Hatches we passed by a market and on a bar outside hung several rabbits. This gave the kids a chance to see nature in the raw.

We walked to the famous spots in the town, such as the house where Shakespeare was born, the church where he was buried, and the school which he attended. We also walked down Warwick Road a short distance to where we left the road and entered the beautiful countryside. There was a fairly high hill and we had a good view all around. We even overlooked the fancy Warwick Road Hotel. There was no golf course at the hotel when we lived nearby, but now there is a fine course.

The Royal Shakespeare Theatre opened their spring season and I wanted to see some rehearsals; consequently, I asked the professors at the Institute if they could get me in. I was quite surprised when they said I should do it myself. It sounded as though there wasn't much come hither with the theatre. I went there and found out to whom I should speak, and he said, "Sure, come on in any time." I thanked him and had the good fortune of watching rehearsals of "A Midsummer Night's Dream" with Judy Dench as the Fairy Queen and Ian Holms as Puck. Neither one of them could have been much over twenty. That was a most enjoyable experience. Later, Louisa, David and I saw the performance with an audience, and it was wonderful.

In early March I received a message that our Volkswagen had arrived in Liverpool. The next day David and I took a train to Liverpool, found our way to the harbor, jumped into the VW, and headed for Stratford. Thank goodness a man who worked for the company drove us through the city and left us on the highway heading for Stratford. That had been my first opportunity to drive on the left lane; it was a bit dicey at first, but after ten minutes, I had the hang of it. After turning a corner, one must be very careful to get back into the left lane. It also took a while to get used to the round-abouts. Anyway, we made it safely back to Stratford.

The arrival of the VW opened up a whole new life for us. Sort of like Martin Luther King, "Free At Last, Thank God We're Free At Last." We didn't have to walk the cold streets quite as much, but the real pleasure was going to places like Bath, Upper and Lower Slaughter, Stowe on the Wold (where we had a high tea), Burton on the Water, Blenheim Palace (where Churchill was born), Oxford, and Kenilworth Castle where the boys had a great time climbing the stairs, jumping and running around. Queen Elizabeth visited there a few times. David had a dream about the castle. He was back in the sixteenth century and he went to Kenilworth Knight School. One thing was rather strange when riding around Stratford in the VW; Brian would always duck down out of sight if he saw any of his classmates on the street. I guess maybe he didn't want to have his mates see him riding in a VW. It may have been the first VW bus in Stratford.

We had a couple experiences with doctors while at Stratford. David had a sore throat, we called a doctor, and he made a house call. Well, he began talking with us about California and forgot David. Finally, he realized his delay and said, "Oh the poor lad on his bed of pain. I didn't forget you. Open your mouth and say aaaah." David obeyed. The doctor looked in and said, "A bit of inflammation here. I'll write you a prescription and in a couple of days he'll be right as rain." I'm happy to report he was. Louisa had a tooth pulled. What I'm getting at is how inexpensive everything was. The doctors charged nothing and the prescriptions were maybe a shilling. Socialized medicine was great; the French women came to England to have their babies. I bet it doesn't happen now.

We were having a little trouble at the Beeches: as spring rolled in, the boys began playing soccer with a woolen ball in front of our apartment and the lady upstairs was quite upset with the noise they made. She often leaned out her window and told them to keep quiet or go play ball somewhere else. We tried to handle the noise level, but with four kids on a fine spring day it was a difficult task.

By the middle of May, we all decided it was time to go home. I had finished my requirements at the Institute, so we headed for the good old U. S. of A. We drove to Liverpool, boarded the Sylvania, and were on our way.

The ship was fairly new, our cabins were fine, and we arrived in New York in five days.

After going through customs, I went in search of the VW. Louisa told me she was a bit worried about me being so long, so she asked one of the customs officials if he had seen me. He said, "You mean that tall guy in the chino pants?" I wasn't that tall and I didn't know what Chino pants were, but Louisa said yes, and he replied, "He went to pick up the car and should be back here pretty soon."

I found the VW and picked up Louisa and the kids for a wild ride through New York City, searching for a route to get us to our cousins in Ohio. Finally, we left the city behind and drove on through Pennsylvania, to West Virginia to see our cousins, Charles and Frances Evans, who lived about a quarter of a mile from what used to be our house in Sharon Valley.

Thank goodness they had a large house, and Charles and Frances had their bedroom downstairs, since Charles was crippled with Polio. (I mentioned him in the story about threshing time.) We had the upstairs with plenty of bedrooms.

We had a great time visiting relatives and friends and driving the children around to see my old haunts: the gravel pit in Granville where I learned to swim; Shawnee where Dad worked in the mines; Millersberg, an Amish town; Newark on the square where the bands played on holidays. The boys and I enjoyed the big barn I helped build in 1933. It was empty, but we all ran around in the big haymow and up and down the stairs. After thirty years, the old barn was standing firmly.

My uncle Joe, Dad's brother, came out to the farm. I hadn't seen him in twenty years, and what surprised me was how much he looked like Dad. When we all lived in Ohio, I didn't see much likeness at all; I suppose ageing has a lot to do with it.

After a pleasant week with the Evans group, we left Ohio and took route 66 to California. The trip was fine; I kept thanking the powers that be for having the foresight to buy the VW bus. It was so nice and roomy for the six of us.

We arrived in Los Angeles and I visited my two sisters, Frances, and Kay. By now Kay and Kenny lived in Azusa and had five children: Malinda, Marsha, Debbie, Kent, and Kendra—all lovely children. We then drove up to Monterey to visit Brother Jake and Grace and their nine children—more lovely children: Jay, Phillip, Judy, Jackson, Susan, Pete, and

Mindy, and the baby, Sally Jane. Oh-oh came one more and her pretty name is Katie—Bar the door, put a lock on it, no more, no more! Repeat those names over and over and one can hear the rhythm. From the time she married, Grace always said she wanted ten children. Well, she nearly got her wish.

We had a problem; our house was rented for a year and here we were back in late May. The renter taught at Monterey High School, and I knew the school year would end in June, so I asked him if he could move out sooner then the time we had agreed upon. He said it would be hard to do, but they would try to find another place. I said we would live with friends in the valley until July, which would give him another month.

Beaulah and Bill Powers had a made over garage and that was our home for June. We were a bit crowded (shades of the Beeches) but the scenery was beautiful and Beaulah's horse woke us up every morning by bumping our door.

In early July I drove into Monterey intending to check on the renters, and the wife answered the door. She said they found a place and were in the process of moving and closed the door. I got in the car and as I was driving away, I saw her throwing stuff off the sun deck. "Okay, keep on going, Morg, you don't need to deal with an angry woman," I thought to myself.

A word about sabbaticals seems in order here. I wish everyone in any kind of work would have the opportunity to take a sabbatical. It is so great to be able to say, I don't have to be at a certain place at a certain time every day; I don't have to lay that pipe; I don't have to saw that wood; I don't have to put that radiator on that car; I don't have to be in the courtroom today. Well, you get the idea. Vacations are fine, but a sabbatical allows more time to recharge the batteries, and to do exactly what you want. One feels refreshed and happy to return to work after a sabbatical.

We moved back into our house in July and before we knew

it, September came and it was back to school for the boys and I. We looked forward to it, and I'm sure Louisa looked forward to just having Maggie to worry about.

The faculty gathered for the first meeting, and it was great fun seeing the whole group together again. On the first day of school, I remembered very well some of us youngish hard ankles sitting on the wall in front of the Student Union, eyeing the lovely young coeds, claiming a bumper crop was enrolling this year. Of course this happened every year, and as we grew older the young ladies looked more beautiful. What am I talking about? The whole student body was lovely. Watching and listening as the students in the classroom improved and learned was a wonderful experience.

I decided to produce a Shakespeare play. I hesitated during my first eight years at MPC, because I didn't think I knew enough to do a good job. But, by damn, now was the time to do it! I chose "Much Ado about Nothing," since that was the prompt script I worked on at Stratford, and I saw it in Coventry. I always cut Shakespeare; not much, mind you, but I feel the story goes along nicely without so many words. I once directed Hamlet and cut it; later, I read the script Maurice Evans used in his production and the cuts were close to the same. I felt even better about cutting Shakespeare. One must also realize that today's audience is much different from Shakespeare's.

Luckily, I had a good cast for "Much Ado", and I was very pleased with the production. In fact the football coach came up to me and said, "Hey Morg, I liked the show. It took me about five minutes listening to the dialogue, before I understood what they were saying. After that I went right along with it." I heartily thanked him.

We kept producing plays in our little theatre for the next eight years. We did Moliere, another Lorca, musicals, comedies, and another Shakespeare, "Othello." I had a wonderful, large black actor, John Hancock, who later played the same part in a professional production in San Francisco and later still, secured a regular part in a half hour TV series in Hollywood. He was in the show for several weeks, then he up and died, still a young man. Is that life? No, no, that's death! Whatever—it ain't good!

CHAPTER 15

The New Theatre

ROSS DURFEE, MY OLD FRIEND FROM Stanford, got the job to work with me in the speech and drama department. In the meantime, the president of MPC, Bob Faul, and the members of the board: Lou Fenton, Ralph Atkinson, Russ Hansen, Sherman Smith, and Lillian Eldred had worked hard and our district passed a bond issue to build a new art building, a new student union, and a new theatre.

The college hired the architect Edward Larrabee Barnes, and in 1969 the ground was leveled where the theatre would be built. After a good solid foundation was in place, two wood walls about a foot apart and twenty feet high were built on the foundation, forming the outline of the building. Then the area between the wood walls was filled with concrete. The wood was removed and the theatre was really beginning to take shape.

From then on I walked by the building nearly every day and supervised the job, telling the workmen how to do things. In a pig's eye I did. My only words were, "Hey, you're doin' great!"

When it came time for the inside work, I found a theatre consultant, Paul Landry, and he and I worked together on the interior of the theatre. I remember one thing on which we had a disagreement. He planned to have the scene shop under the stage, and I said, "Whoa there, you can't have the shop under the stage. The noise created building a set would certainly interfere with classes going on in the theatre. Let's put the shop on the other side of the hall that runs the length of the building." He finally agreed and we achieved a long roomy shop. Of course, in no time, it didn't seem so roomy, but that's

The Last Meeting of the Knights of
the White Magnolia

MPC Theatre - Morgan Stock Stage

Theatre under construction

Seating area ➤

Building the Morgan Stock stage

Monterey Peninsula College Productions

West Side Story - 1970

Arsenic and Old Lace -2001

Man Of La Mancha

The Last Meeting of the Knights of
the White Magnolia

That Championship Season

true of every shop ever built.

At the rear of the stage there was a costume room on the second floor, a dressing room on the ground floor, a good fly gallery above the stage, a counter weight system on the stage right wall, a light and sound booth at the rear of the auditorium, and an orchestra pit in front of the stage. I wanted a hydraulic lift for the pit, but didn't get it. There were two classrooms, one of which we made into a small studio theatre, and, the final crowning glory, a 350 seat auditorium, each row high enough for perfect vision. After sixteen years of laboring with several different theatres, this was my greatest wish come true.

The next question was what production would be perfect for opening the theatre. We all thought a flashy, good musical would be best. However there were problems doing a large production because we didn't have the light and sound system in place yet, and we needed more time to get drapes and curtains working properly. At least the counter weight system worked perfectly so we could raise and lower scenery and back drops. I was almost ready to cast a play and do the musical later, but with the help of the technical director Ruth Allan, and renting a dimmer board and a sound system, we made the final decision to produce "West Side Story."

Anyone who has directed a musical knows the amount of work that goes into the production, and "West Side Story," with its large cast, takes more work than any show I directed up to that time. Moreover, we didn't have a lot of time. As I recall, we only had five weeks to bring the show up to performance level. However with the marvelous work of Ruth Jordon Allan, technical director; Dale Lefler, choreographer; Jean Miller, costume director; Dick Sheere, choral director; and Dan Haerle, music director, the show quickly took shape.

On top of the good work of the people mentioned, I had an absolutely wonderful cast, from the leads on down to the last little walk on. How could I be so lucky?

During rehearsals, we would work with a piano player. Three or four days before opening we worked with the full orchestra. The first rehearsal with the orchestra was full of glitches and stumbles, but we got them worked out. Next, during the technical rehearsal, more stumbles and glitches, which were straightened out and, finally, the full dress rehearsal. There is a saying in the theatre, "Good dress rehearsal, bad opening night," and vice versa.

May 28, 1970, the President of the board, Ralph Atkinson, dedicated the new theatre. "Good evening ladies and gentlemen. It is my pleasure and privilege to welcome you to the new theater at M.P.C., designed by Edward Larrabee Barnes.

"We Americans are prone to think of the theater either as entertainment or as downright frivolity, and I'm sure some may ask why a college should put so much effort into the lighter side of life, especially in a community which has an ample supply of struggling theater groups.

Let me tell you why I think so, and as for everything else in western civilization, I must take you back to Greece. DIONYSOS was the Olympian god of vegetation, thence of the vine, thence of the grape harvest, and thence of the spring and fall celebrations famous for their gayety, their dancing and their singing. Human values all!

"Sometime in the middle of the sixth century B.C., by which time the rites of Dionysus had become stylized, a vigorous young member of the chorus – Thespis – broke ranks and jumped on the altar of Dionysus. No doubt he was only celebrating the grape harvest – but he talked back to the chorus and initiated the give and take between voices we still call by the same Greek word - dialogue

"So theater began, and in the hands of the great Greek dramatists it presents to us the human being in all its fearsome wonder. Love and hate, growth and decline, dreams and nightmares, truth and falsehood are all stripped bare of non-essentials and laid open for our pleasure, our vicarious satisfaction, and our knowledge of what many and marvelous things it is to be human.

"There was another Olympian- APOLLO – god of light, thence god of reason, and him we celebrate – I sometimes think too much – but almost every other building on this campus is in his honor. Language, history, mathematics, business, chemistry, philosophy – and on and on – all celebrate the intellect, pay tribute to our thinking in honor of Apollo.

"It seems clear to me that many of our troubles today do not result from man's inability to reason, but from his inability to understand the heart of his fellow man. If we are not to end by falling upon each other with stones, we must listen to our own hearts, and to those of our fellows. I think it highly appropriate that we celebrate Dionysus in this building in an attempt to do so. The "WEST SIDE STORY" must have been chosen for tonight's production to illustrate my point.

"We need the critical and rational Apollo, but we are all too human, and we must not forget Dionysus. In a College that honors Apollo at every turn, I am pleased that our tallest structure and one of our handsomest buildings honors creativity and imagination, the struggles of our all too human emotions to guide our lives.

"And now that I have paid tribute to the Olympian Dionysus, let me present to you a real one in flesh and blood – the Dionysus of Monterey, Director and producer of tonight's production, Head of the Drama Department at M. P. C., Mr. Morgan Stock!"

I walked on stage, thanked all the proper people including the audience, left the stage, joined Louisa, and we took our seats in the last row of the auditorium and nervously watched the performance. From here on, please read Irene Alexander's review of the performance.

Thrilling Production Opens MPC Theatre

Devoted friends of Monterey Peninsula College, not only an area wide representation, but a number from out of town, donned formal garb and thronged to last night's official opening of the impressive new theater on campus. The occasion was marked by the launching of "West Side Story with music by Leonard Bernstein, book by Arthur Laurents and lyrics by the composer and Stephen Sondheim. The cast of fifty young drama students under the direction of drama department chairman, Morgan Stock and accompanied by a 27-piece orchestra conducted by music director Dan Haerle, gave superb accounting of themselves.

The production reflected also the skill, originality and verve of choreographer, Dale Lefler, the artistry of set designer, Ruth Jordan Allan, the colorful stimulus of costuming by Jean Miller, and the masterly touch of Dick Sheere, choral director.

West Side Story" stems from Jerome Robbins' idea of translating the "Romeo and Juliet" theme in terms of 20th century New York with the feuding Capulets and Montagues represented by warring street gangs. The musical opened on Broadway in 1957.

To this reviewer, who was deeply moved by the original New York production, the musical seems more relevant today. The Monterey Peninsula College production has two factors that made last night's performance more thrilling and unforgettable than the first viewing.

The Jets and the Sharks by their very youth and exuberance, gave throughout a sense of greater immediacy and tragic reality to the spectacle. The direction of stage movement was flawless. The action flowed. The dancing bubbled with youth and spontaneity. The ballet sequence, one of the highlights of the second act, and enlivened by a solo by Linda Fierro, was excellently performed by Greg Stegeman, Rick Shoup, Steve Cronin, Mary Mabe, Sue Sewald, Betty Brown, Wanda Allen, Clarise Beene, Candy Davis, Granville J. S. Andrews, Kevin Huston, John Sewald, Debbie Berry, Cathryn Wynde True, and Nicolette Hariri.

A second factor which promoted the MPC "West Side Story" to top billing in this viewer's estimation was the creative artistry of the set designs by Ruth Jordan Allan, the enhanced stimulus to the imagination effected by replacement of a realistic creation of a West Side slum street. A certain universality was suggested, underscoring the theme, the ugliness of racial hates, of violence and killings.

Joseph Solomone's lighting effects contributed much to the evening's triumph.

High Voltage Cast

Every member of the large cast richly deserves an accolade, but space permits only a singling out of the leading performers. The story of "West Side" centers about Tony, outstandingly played by Dale Diggs, a reluctant recruit to the Jets in the violent feud between that gang and the Sharks, a persecuted minority group, and little Maria, sister of Bernardo, the militant leader of the sharks.

Kitty Hendrix most appealingly played the role of Maria. Her portrayal was greatly enhanced by her possession of a singularly clear and beautiful singing voice. With Dale Diggs, the ill-starred Romeo to her Juliet, also an accomplished vocalist, she gave delight in such songs as "Tonight" and "One Hand, One Heart," and both scored in solos as well as with the well-equipped and trained chorus.

Jason Cronin as Riff, leader of the Jets, and Orlando Bonner, as Bernardo, leader of the Sharks, gave frighteningly convincing characterizations. Each had his favorite henchman in his gang; Tony, devoted to Riff, Chino (played dauntlessly by Alfredo Valdez),

Pat Bryans as loyal Anita, a girl friend of Bernardo, and Greta Dansby, as Rosalita, also allied with the Sharks, both scored as songbirds.

One diminutive young gangster (the object of considerable mauling by bullies, but seemingly indestructible) stood out as a comedian. It would be good to identify him, but the program offers no certain clue.

Lively Action

The musical is full of lively action – never dull – and suspense mounts as a "rumble" is planned and eventually takes place, on the eve of the marriage planned by Tony and Maria. Tony avenges his friend and is forced with Maria to seek refuge from Bernardo's friend, Chino, when Riff, the Jets' leader, is killed by Bernardo. They are discovered and betrayed by Anita, and in their fight, Tony is slain.

The new theater offered a perfect setting for this action-packed musical with its series of lively confrontations among half a hundred participants.

Its story is engrossing and its music haunting from beginning to end and should attract full houses during its limited run. "West Side Story" plays again tonight, continuing next week on June 3, 4, 5 and 6. All performances are scheduled for 8:30 p.m. This notable achievement by the MPC Players, the staff and corps of assistants should be viewed by all who appreciate first-rate theater.

This successful opening of our beautiful, new theatre seems an ideal place to finish this part of my journal, but before I do, I must mention a few things that happened the following years. You recall the problem we had with water at the Tin Barn. There was no escaping it. In the fall of the year we opened, a heavy rainstorm flooded the dressing room, the tech shop, and the rear of the stage. Thank goodness it didn't warp the boards on the stage. The next disaster with water was man made, or rather woman made. We had a young lady as assistant tech director, and she was unloading some flys from the battens and forgot to unload weights from the counter weight system, resulting in the batten flying up and hitting the sprinkler system, and voila, a rainstorm descended on the stage. We got the water turned off, mopped the stage, fixed the sprinkler, and were back in business. The third time, I came to class one morning and water was rushing in a door on the left side of the auditorium down the steps and into the orchestra pit. This time someone had dropped a coke can inside a drain outside the theatre, which caused the flooding. The can was removed, the flooding stopped, and the maintenance men brought in large propeller wind machines and dried the rug in the pit. Water is such a wonderful necessity, but sometimes it does get out of control.

I received permission to hire an ex-student of mine, Peter DeBono. His job was a combination director and technical teacher. He and Ross Durfee ran the department when I went on my second sabbatical.

One more story must be told before I finish this journal. The greatest audience pleaser of my thirty years of directing productions was "America's Tribal Love-Rock Musical, Hair," which took Broadway by Storm in 1969. I saw a production in London in 1971 and another in Los Angeles a couple of years later, and I thought it would be a good musical to do at MPC. The amateur rights were released in 1974, so we immediately secured our permission to produce "Hair."

At least a hundred showed up for auditions and we cast fifty of them. We had perfect actors for all the parts. Not only did we have perfect actors, we also had a perfect tech crew, production crew, and Jim Bindi, a Vietnam vet, as stage manager. He was so happy to be in an anti-war show. Tom Fordham led the perfect orchestra, and Jean Miller did the perfect costumes. I should mention all the actor's names, but there are just too many. Yeah, Morg, another one of those wonderful times!

The first major question to come up was how to handle the nude scene. I thought maybe just have teeny bikinis, but that didn't seem right. I finally decided to do the scene behind a scrim, which is a cheesecloth like curtain easily seen through with proper lighting.

Rehearsals went very well; on the final Sunday before opening, I ordered all the theatre doors locked and we gathered the cast on stage. I said, "The time has come, tribe, for us all to strip down to the buff." In no time at all everyone was completely nude, including fifty-five year old Morg. Well, I figured if everyone else has to go nude, I should certainly do the same. The kids really enjoyed it as they ran up and down the stairs in the auditorium. Eventually nude Akemi Ito, choreographer, got them back on stage and put in some small movements while Claude sang his song. It was an excellent rehearsal. A few of the cast didn't care to do the nude scene, so during the show they sat on stage in front of the scrim.

We opened March 21st, 1974, and I quote from Steve Hauk's review:

The sensations of yesterday are often the duds of today. Not so with Hair. It has lost its urgency since it first surfaced six or seven years ago and was shut down in various theaters throughout the country for its infamous nude scene, but it has aged well, the mellowing of time not antiquating it, but adding to its entertainment value. It doesn't frighten as perhaps it once did.

The famous rock musical opened last night at the MPC Theater, and it is one of the college's finest, if not the finest, in several years." Then Steve talks about the large crowds, and we certainly did have them. Every night all seats were filled and people sat in the aisles. He also talked about the folks in the lobby wondering how the *nude scene would be handled. Would it be a cover up job or would it be nude? He then continues how the scene was done.*

Esthetically, chum. Very nicely, sex can be pretty, sex can be repulsive—it can also be asexual. Here the bodies are rose colored and sculpted. How? Why destroy the fun?

Later in his review, Steve writes:

The choreography by the talented Akemi Ito, and I don't think you can say anything nicer than in the way the dances so naturally mesh, crash into being and then suddenly subside, that you hardly think of the word choreography, or that what is going on is anything other than spontaneous celebration." He continues on, "The voices in Hair outweigh the action two to one in importance. The script is not all that literate, the spoken word secondary to the songs. And what voices Stock has going for him. It's rare, extremely rare, to find so many talented singers in an amateur production.

The actors he writes about with the voices are: Nancy Servies, Steve Barnes, Audrey Swanson, Sid Cato, Robert Scancarello, and Ben Leudke. As I keep saying, it was one of those times when everything came together. I know that I went to the opening night party thrilled as could be at our grand first night. I believe the cast members partied all night, for which I do not blame them in the least.

The nude scene was a distinct hit; as I mentioned we used the scrim, but about halfway through the song, the flyman raised the scrim. There stood the tribe in all its glory. Of course I didn't know this was going to happen, but it worked so beautifully I kept it in for the run of the show.

You may recall this was the time of flashing; you know, run naked from one place to another. Some of the cast members flashed from the student union to the theatre once. Another time, just before the nude scene, a girl who was not in the cast came out from behind the screen stark naked, ran across the stage, down the steps into the auditorium, and out a door. This led to another interesting problem.

Steve Barnes' wife was about six months pregnant, so she asked if she could be in the nude scene. As she said, it would be the baby's first appearance on stage. I said, "Go ahead!" Then I began to notice more people in the nude scene, and they weren't the ones who had decided to sit it out. Shortly after that, one of the actors said. "Mr. Stock, there are some people not in the cast doing the nude scene. After the scene is over we have a hell of a time finding our clothes." At different times there must have been half the students at MPC in the nude scene. We put in some guards to prevent that happening again.

One more story about the nude scene: Nancy Servies, one of the leads, initially sat out during the nude scene, but participated later. Afterward she came up to me all excited and exclaimed, "Mr. Stock, I did the nude scene! Did you see me?" I quickly answered, "Why of course I did; you looked beautiful." I really didn't see her; it's tough to pick out a new one in a group of nudes. I did however see her in a later performance, and she was indeed beautiful.

We played it again in the summer for three weekends. The crowd wasn't as large as before, but still every seat was filled. That isn't quite the end of "Hair." I directed it again in 1999, seventeen years after I retired. Can you see this 80 year old dude doing the nude scene rehearsal again? I remember for some reason I couldn't get my socks off and some nude girl came to help me. I said, "No dear, that's okay; I'll play the nude scene in my socks."

With another fine cast, Barney Hulse as orchestra leader again, D. Thomas Beck's excellent stage design (he had actors sliding down fire poles), lighting designer Steve Retsky, sound engineer David Rigmaiden, Patrick McAvoy as master carpenter,

Connie Gamiere as costume designer, choreographers Sherry Beck and Laura Akard, and stage manager Jim Bindi (the same man from 1974), we again had an excellent production. There are many stories about our productions of "Hair." However I do believe you have read enough about it.

CHAPTER 16

The Last Sabbatical

I TOOK MY SECOND SABBATICAL IN 1971. We waited ten years to have Maggie at a good traveling age, and Brian, having graduated from high school, received his traveling money from my sister Frances. Brian traveled with a friend and we planned to meet sometime in England. This time I took a one semester sabbatical at full salary—much smarter.

We bought a small Saab in Monterey, which we were to pick up in Slough, England. After a good flight from Oakland to Gatwick, we caught the bus to London. Our friends, Sam and Edie Karas, met us and Sam and I drove to Slough and picked up the car. It was perfect for the three of us. We stayed a few days in London then drove to Scotland, caught the Ferry to Larne, N. Ireland, and on to the farm at Kilcreen where we spent time with the Irish folks.

I left Louisa and Maggie in Ireland, for I was to start a summer session at Exeter College in Oxford. I found a small apartment and in two weeks Maggie and Louisa joined me. We remained in the apartment about two weeks and, even though we lived with the owners of the place, we found a better place on Woodstock Road. Our little apartment was on the second floor and the family lived on the ground floor. The father was a professor at Belial College.

Summer school was very interesting. There were about twenty in the class, and we met at Exeter three times a week in the morning then went to the Ashmolian Museum a couple of times a week to hear lectures on a variety of subjects. The teacher taught at a University up north and did a good job with our class. There were two other Americans in our class, one Italian lady, and several English Folk. We were honored a couple of times with an invitation to sit for dinner with the professors at the High Table.

The Italian lady told me she knew Frank Wolff, an old Stanford buddy, who was living in Rome at the time. He played the lead in "America, America," a film by Elia Kazan about Armenian immigrants trying to get to America. I saw the film when it came out in 1963, and Frank did a hell of a job acting. Now comes the amazing part, two or three years later Frank committed suicide in Rome. Makes one ask why!

I did a paper on "Oh What a Lovely War" for my work in the class. I enjoyed working in the Bodleian Library, digging through old newspapers to read the reviews when it was performed in London, and finding books dealing with theatre and other subjects as well. The opportunity to sit in that old historic building studying away made me feel great—like an intellectual. Ah no, not old Morg.

Having a car at our disposal from the moment we arrived in England was wonderful. We made trips all around the beautiful Oxford area. We enjoyed the Trout Inn and the Perch Inn. Both were on the Thames. One time we walked to the Perch from our house. We walked down the street across the commons to a bridge over the Thames, then along the river to the Perch. It was a pretty good hike. Another time as we were coming home, Louisa suggested we cross the commons at a different place and we got into a swamp over our shoe tops. After a long struggle, we finally made it out. I had visions of the Irish peat bog with just the top of my bald head sticking out.

We drove to Hastings where the Norman, King William, defeated the English, King Harold in 1066, but more importantly where Maggie celebrated her tenth birthday. The hotel staff was very kind and provided a fine cake with ten candles. That evening we walked around the town and heard a choir practicing in a small church. The door was open and we listened for a while. It was a beautiful way to end the day. The next day we drove to Rye and walked around the lovely old town.

During this period Louisa was going through menopause; I should have used a different word there. Anyway, she was a bit nauseous, so we always kept a bag just in case. Once, as we were driving along and Lou was complaining, Maggie said in a strong voice, "Oh, shut up and stick your head in the sack!" I couldn't believe my ears. Here's this ten year old speaking to her mother this way. I was so surprised that I didn't say anything; I was driving and didn't want to crash into anything. Finally, we all began to laugh, which relieved Louisa's nausea, and she became her cheerful self again.

It was now time to go to London and pick up Brian at Victoria Station. Luckily, he was there when we arrived, and the four of us stayed in London a few days and saw "Fiddler on the Roof." At intermission I came out in the lobby where I saw Layne Littlepage, my leading actress at MPC. She was with Wayne University students who were doing a USO tour for the US troops in Germany and anywhere else in Europe where the GI's were stationed—small world time again.

Louisa and I, Brian and Maggie returned to Oxford. We borrowed a small bed for Brian and were comfortable in our rental. Brian and Maggie took several trips in the car.

One final story about our time in Oxford: Our landlord's two sons took all four of us punting on the Cherwell. The oldest son, Robert, was 17 and the younger one, Charles, was 12. He was an obstreperous one, always telling Robert how to do it, jumping up and moving around in the boat. Robert was doing the work with the pole at the rear of the punt (maybe that's what one calls them) when the punt swerved quickly and Charley went overboard. We hauled him back on board. For the rest of the trip he behaved very well. One last good thing happened on that adventure; we stopped at a nice pub and ordered beer. I'm sorry I can't remember the name of it, but it was so good I ordered it from then on in England.

Two weeks later we dropped Brian off at Gatwick for his flight to the US and bid him farewell. We boarded a ferry from England to Holland and drove to Flensburg, Germany, which is 8 miles from the Danish border, to visit our friends, Ingo and Helma Eddicks. They lived across the street from us while Ingo attended The Naval Postgraduate School in Monterey. We stayed with his mother for a week. That was the first time I slept under a duvet. Maggie loved the place because she got to play bartender in the evening; no complicated drinks, just wine or beer.

Ingo's mother spoke English fairly well. In the morning she said, "Well, what kind of business should we perform today?" She made suggestions, and we piled in the car and saw interesting things and places. Ingo was still in the German Navy but was free on the weekend, so he drove us for views in that part of Germany. With all the castles, cathedrals, and old cities we saw, to mention one as my favorite seems outrageous. What Louisa, Maggie and I found to be certainly more fun than other places was the Niederegger Candy Factory in Lubeck (sounds like somewhere in Texas). The Stock group had its first taste of Marzipan there, and we gave it an A+.

Our time in Germany came to an end. We really appreciated the tours and kindness expressed by Mrs. Eddicks, Ingo's wife Helma, and Ingo. They made our German trip a great pleasure. We took the ferry back to England, flew to the US and arrived home in time for Christmas.

I came to class in the spring semester relaxed and ready to be an A #1 teacher. I taught for another eleven years, reached my 30 years in the classroom, and retired in 1982. The Karases gave me a wonderful retirement party at the Outrigger Restaurant, May 2, 1982. It was an evening of music and comedy, with students, actors, dancers and musicians.

I am so grateful I retired, for I had six more years to spend with Louisa. In April 1988 she awoke one morning and complained of a sore back. After rubbing her back and helping her with a hot bath, the pain continued—so I called 911. She was taken to the hospital where she died three hours later due to a ruptured aorta. The swift departure was fine, for I know we all wish to go like that, but her timing was off. She should have stayed on much longer. As it was, we had forty-two wonderful years together. Ah, yes: Life.

Epilogue

ONE ENDEAVOR THAT LOUISA AND I began after my retirement was delivering meals to clients for Meals on Wheels. We met all kinds of people doing this. One was an Italian lady who still had quite an accent and if Louisa were absent would ask me, "How's uh you wife?" And I would reply, "She's fine." She kept this up a number of times until I lapsed one day and answered her question, "How's uh you wife?" with "She's uh fine." My response didn't phase her, she went on talking. Another client was David Mairs who had Lou Gehrig's disease which is usually fatal within a few years—David was still going on in a wheel chair after fourteen years. I did a documentary on him and won a couple of prizes at film festivals. He is still living in El Paso, Texas. (I would strongly suggest to anyone who has a bit of time, to volunteer for Meals on Wheels.) After Louisa died, I continued on and finally retired after twenty years. It is a most rewarding for both the clients and those delivering the meals.

For several months after Louisa's passing, I didn't want to meet any ladies, but eventually a friend would introduce me to one, and you know I felt like a nervous 17 year old again. What do you say, how do you act, do I look okay? I met two or three, and they were probably very nice, but I didn't continue on with them.

A year later the Karases introduced me to a lovely lady, June Duran. At our first meeting with a party of friends I said, "How do you do, I am Morgan." She replied, "I'm glad to meet you; I'm June Duran. How is the foundation?" I was puzzled as to what foundation she was talking about. Was it one of the foundations in Monterey? Then it suddenly dawned on me, she thought I was Morgan Flagg, a very wealthy man who indeed had a foundation. I quickly said, "I am Morgan Stock." She said, "Well, how do you do, I'm glad to know you," and shook my hand. I thought that didn't start off too well.

The party left the house and headed to a hotel to watch the Super Bowl; June had to leave for a cousin's wedding. My, my, that was a quick romance!

On Valentine's Day, my friends the Weis's invited me to go with them to a party at the Monterey Beach Hotel. It was a good gathering; the Karases were there along with several other friends. I danced with a few of the ladies and then walked to the wine bar near the door. I was pouring some wine for myself when I glanced out the door and saw June coming out of the elevator with a fine looking gentleman. June said, "Hello, Morgan." Well, at least she remembered my name. I said, "Hello, would you and your friend like a glass of wine?" She answered, "I don't know about him; he just joined me in the elevator, but I would like a glass of wine." Hey, things are looking up.

I poured her a big glass of wine and we joined our friends. Later we danced together as often as we could. When the party broke up, Sam Karas suggested that a few of the close friends continue on at Doc's Lab on Cannery Row. This is the laboratory John Steinbeck wrote about in his novel, "Cannery Row," where Doc Ricketts lived and did his Marine biology work.

We enjoyed our time there; everyone sat around telling jokes and funny stories. After an hour or so, we were all ready to go home. The Weises drove off and left me. There I was, standing on Cannery Row wondering how to get home, when June drove up and asked me if I wanted a ride home. Naturally, I said yes. I was all nervous and excited again. We arrived at my house and she got out of the car and we enjoyed a big hug and agreed to meet the next day. That was the wonderful beginning.

From then on we were seldom apart; we took a trip to Europe where she met all my Irish relatives. They were very

June and Morgan's Wedding Day.

kind to June, which pleased me, for I have often heard that relatives of the first wife do not take kindly to the second wife. And the same goes for the children. But I am pleased to report that everyone gets along very well. We married December tenth, 1989. I was seventy years old. This past December we celebrated our seventeenth anniversary.

I wish to state that my love is equal between the two lovely ladies. I don't want to get in a long philosophical discussion on this. Just know that it is true.

On January 10, 1999 we had a celebration with a catered dinner on the stage at the Monterey Peninsula College, where I was honored by having the stage named for me: The Morgan Stock Stage at MPC. I am right proud of that honor.

I have had a wonderful life, and I am so grateful for my four beautiful, courageous children who have helped me in so many ways. And to my relatives and friends, a special thank you for making my time on this earth so enjoyable.